BATTLE CLASS
DESTROYERS

BATTLE CLASS DESTROYERS

Patrick Boniface

Contents

Appendices

First published in the United Kingdom in 2007 by Maritime Books, Lodge Hill, Liskeard, Cornwall, PL14 4EL

Introduction

Many valuable lessons were learnt early in the Second World War, principal amongst these were the dual dangers of submarines and large scale air attacks on naval shipping. Indeed, the Royal Navy paid an extremely high price with large numbers of warships and merchant shipping sunk to submarines and precision aerial bombing. These brutal reminders hardened the resolve of the Admiralty to devise better means of defence and new designs of anti aircraft weapons and tactics to use them were quickly evolved along with new warships designs to carry them into battle.

By 1941, with the Battle of the Atlantic still raging numerous meetings were held to discuss the latest sketch designs for new destroyers with improved defensive and offensive weaponry. This new class would mount a new HA (High Angle) 4.7-inch gun with an associated HA control system. The preferred angle was indeed high - to deal with the threat of dive-bombers such as the Stuka Ju 87's. The stated requirement was of at least 85 degrees elevation. As is the way with such meetings a large number of changes to the initial layout were made or amended to provide what was considered the best and most affordable solution. One of the earliest decisions was that the main armament would consist of two-twin 4.7-inch mountings forward of the superstructure so that a single target could receive a heavy barrage. The bridge was shifted further back than was previously accepted as experience had taught that this increased the guns' arc of fire. There was deemed to be little need for a large calibre gun turret aft as experience in the Mediterranean and elsewhere had shown that there was little operational need for it. The secondary armament comprised of 40mm Bofors and six 20mm guns which were given a stabilised mounting. For surface actions two sets of quadruple torpedo tubes would be carried.

With agreement on the basic design, a sketch layout was submitted on 22 September 1941. The new design had a standard displacement of 2,280 tons and carried 700 tons of oil fuel for a range of 4,400 nautical miles at 20 knots and 7,700 miles at an economical cruising speed of 12 knots. The 1942 Battle's were fitted with Parsons I.R single reduction turbines producing 50,000 shp, which was fed from two Admiralty 3-drum boilers with an optimum operational pressure of 400 lbs/sq in at 700°F. This combination gave the destroyers a speed of around 30.5 knots. The ships had a waterline length of 364 feet and a length overall of 379 feet. The beam at its maximum point was set at 40 feet 3 inches whilst the design had a draught of 22 feet. The displacement of 2,280 tons was broken down as 1,135 tons for the hull, 655 tons for the machinery, whilst all the armament amounted to 360 tons. All other fitted equipment, electrical gear and stabilisers added 135 tons to the total. Armour and

protection, however, only took up 30 tons of the overall displacement. The pressing need for destroyers meant that approval was given in October 1941 and orders for 16 ships were placed under the 1942 programme. Each ship was given the name of an important British Battle from across the ages.

There were some major changes made to the basic design, the first was the replacement of the 4.7-inch guns with the 4.5-inch gun. Development of this weapon had been completed in 1942 and saw extensive testing onboard the destroyer *Savage* the following year. The turret was almost a complete weapons system with the revolving trunk under the turret containing power operated ammunition hoists. Once the shells had been fired the empty cartridges were automatically collected in a special compartment. The mounting could also be automatically controlled in Remote Power Control. This system was amongst the most advanced of its kind at its introduction and incorporated a novel use of gun and radar equipment. Another change saw the siting of a single 4-inch gun abaft the funnel to fire starshells for illuminating targets at night. The 4-inch gun's position meant that it was not ideally suited for firing astern but it could add some degree to warding off a sustained aerial attack.

Twin 40mm guns were on Hazemayer stabilised mountings with Type 282 radar. These were mounted on either side of the torpedo tubes and a further pair mounted en echelon on the after deckhouse. These weapons had a rate a fire of 120 rounds per minute. The guns could elevate between -10° and +90° and could train over a full 360 degrees. Furthermore the design benefitted from the addition of four single 20mm guns distributed with one in front of the bridge, two in the bridge wings and one on the quarterdeck. Initially in the earlier ships of the class the 20mm mountings were altered to twin mountings in each position but later these were replaced by either 40mm or 2-pdr guns.

The Admiralty approved the sketch design on 9 October 1941. Whilst their Lords appreciated the need for

HMS Savage ran extensive trials of the twin 4.5-inch MkIV BD mounting that was to become the standard fit for the Battle class. (Portsmouth Royal Naval Museum)

new construction they expressed an opinion to retain the existing designs over new untried ones. They also voiced concern over having all the main armament forward, believing this would make the ships heavy forward and hard to handle in bad weather, especially in a following sea.

In total some twelve separate sketch designs were submitted, each with a number of alterations and amendments over the earlier plans. The full Staff Requirements were not received by the Admiralty Drawing Office until 2 January 1942. However, further changes continued to be forced through, the most important being the adoption in February 1942 of the 4.5-inch gun as the gun calibre for the new ships.

The Battle class ships were much delayed in their completion. This was due in large part to the late delivery of the Mk VI directors and fire control systems. These directors were crucial to the design and, with their delayed delivery, work on the ships started to slow or even halt completely on occasion. The Admiralty were determined to get as many of these directors to sea as quickly as possible but chose to refit the battleship *Anson* first and then some 'C' class destroyers before fitting the MkVI and Type 275 radar to new build Battle class destroyers

The first of the Battle class to be completed was the *Barfleur* which commissioned into service on 14 September 1944. *Barfleur* soon sailed to join the British Far East Fleet and took part in the closing stages of the Second World War.

Meanwhile, operational use of the first few Battle class ships highlighted the shortcomings of the 4-inch gun amidships. The ferocious Japanese aerial attacks meant that the crews would have preferred another pair of 40mm guns in its place as these would have been more effective. This change was duly introduced and only *Armada*, *Barfleur*, *Camperdown* and *Hogue* were completed with the 4-inch, and even on these ships it was eventually removed and replaced by two Bofors. The other ships completed before the end of 1945 were armed with a total of 14 Bofors - the heaviest light AA armament carried by any British destroyer. These weapons weighed six and a half tons and could be elevated between -15° and +90° and could be trained through a full 360°. All these ships had a lattice mast upon completion and not the tripod mast as originally planned. Radar's on the ships' comprised a Type 293, and Type 291 air warning system on a polemast aft, as well as the Type 275 and 282 gunnery radars. As designed, the Battle's also benefitted from HF/DF and various IFF transponders and receivers on the foremast.

The Hazemeyer mountings for the 40mm guns were soon found to be unwieldy and hard to maintain under operational conditions and unreliable and were replaced by the STAAG mounting. Unfortunately, the STAAG was little better, however, the newer Type 262 centrimetric aerial of the system gave better performance than the system it replaced.

The 1942 Battles were designed with the standard 'Ten Pattern' arrangement for depth charges. The practice was to drop a saturation load of weapons on or near an enemy submarine and accordingly the early Battles were equipped with four depth charge throwers on the quarterdeck. Nearby were sited the ready use lockers for the charges themselves. Depth charges were were being phased out in the early days of the Battles' careers and by the-mid 1950's depth charges were replaced by the Squid ahead throwing weapon system.

As designed, the funnel was set immediately abaft the galley and was belled out at its base to accommodate the uptakes from the forward and after boiler rooms. There were also waste steam pipes on the forward face of the funnel.

A gundeck was sited behind the funnel. It was built on the structure containing the intakes to the after boiler room. Each gundeck had a small gun crew shelter and a number of ready use lockers. These gundecks were linked by a number of catwalks, which gave access to the after superstructure in all but the very worst weather conditions.

The Emergency Steering Position was sited on the forward starboard corner of the after superstructure. It was equipped with a conventional wheel, binnacle and engine room telegraphs. Further redundancy was available

HMS Barfleur *- the first of the new generation of large destroyer designed with its main armament forward and a heavy anti-aircraft weapon fit aft.* *(Ben Warlow Collection)*

to the crew if the Emergency Steering Position was damaged by steering the ship from the Steering Compartment itself.

All the ships were equipped with a new non-slip surface called 'Semtex' which provided a less slippery surface than the bare steel deck. This substance was naturally grey in colour and was frequently painted. There were a number of colours chosen including dark blue and another shade of grey, but green was the most usual colour chosen.

The threat of mines was not overlooked throughout the design stages and a sweep system was, for a while, to be introduced onboard ships of the Battle class. Eventually, however, the destroyers were designed for, but not with, the gear necessary for dealing with mines.

The Battles were designed with a square stern, as this had proved to give a reduced resistance in tests at the Haslar experimental tank. Indeed, such was the success of the experiments that resistance, was reduced by 4-5 percent at 33 knots and 6 percent at 20 knots.

The final drawings were submitted and approved on 25 March and orders for twelve destroyers were placed on 27 April 1942 with the leading British shipyards including two to J. S. White at Cowes on the Isle of Wight. Two days after receiving the contracts the shipyard was attacked by German bombers and partially destroyed forcing the contracts to be re-allocated to Cammell Laird at Birkenhead in August.

Between March and June 1943 the Admiralty placed orders for a further 24 vessels. These would be similar to the preceding 1942 order but taking into account the lessons learnt with the design of the previous ships. There was a desire to get the latest Mk VI turret to sea and there were also calls to expand the design to accommodate another turret aft. Across the North Atlantic the Americans were manufacturing a steady supply of Mk 37 directors which were married with the British Type 275 radar once in the UK. Ultimately the approved

design retained the two Mk IV turrets, but the new Mk 37 DCT was to be fitted. These ships would, however, be fitted with an extra single 4.5-inch on the standard 55 degree MkV mounting abaft the funnel.

The 1943 Battle's were wider than the 1942's at 40 feet 6 inches and heavier with a displacement of 3,418 tons in deep condition. Other differences included a 4.5-inch QF MkIV single MkV 55 degree mounting instead of the 4-inch Mk XIV HA/LA in the earlier ships. Two sets of Pentad torpedo tubes were fitted instead of the hand worked versions and the 1943 Battles carried two more torpedoes than the eight on the 1942 ships. Another major change was the installation of the Squid Mk1 Anti-Submarine weapon in lieu of depth charges.

The MkVI 4.5-inch mounting caused a major re-design of the later ships. The new mounting was higher than the previous weapon mounted in the earlier ships and necessitated the destroyer's bridge being raised by nine inches.

The 1943 programme meanwhile, called for a number of changes to the original design. The first sketch design showed two U.D mountings, one forward and one aft, four Buster Bofor's and three twin Oerlikon's with the standard hull and machinery of the early vessels.

There were requests to improve the performance of the machinery and the Engineer in Chief reported that if certain changes were made a seven percent increase in economy could be made with only 25 tons of extra weight. Another alternative was to adopt the machinery used in the Weapon's class destroyers to achieve a 12 percent increase in performance for a penalty of an extra 655 tons. There was also a suggestion to stagger the machinery, this would have resulted in a twin funnel design, which was quickly ruled out. By the time the sketch designs had been approved 30 tons of extra topweight had been added, which was broken down to 10 tons each for the 4.5-inch BD mounting and Buster Bofors. Six tons for twin Oerlikon's in lieu of the single mounting and four tons for the American DCT and 275 radar.

When the orders were placed with the shipyards the intention was to have three flotilla's of the repeat design.

*Although sporting a different pendant number this is, once again, **HMS Barfleur** - the change of number indicates that she was, at the time, serving with the British Pacific Fleet.*
(George Pulham)

Two ships of the 1943 programme, **Waterloo** and **Ypres** were, however, to be to a new design.

Four ships were ordered in March 1943, fifteen in April and five in June 1943. Of interest was the lack of communication between the Admiralty and some of the shipyards. Fairfield's had ordered a quantity of steel for the standard design and much of it had been delivered when they were informed that the ships were to be of 41 foot beam. The order to increase the beam was cancelled and the order for the broader ships went instead to John Brown's shipyard.

Experience in the Pacific war showed the value of a heavy torpedo armament and quintuple mountings were fitted in the later vessels sacrificing their 44-inch searchlight and five depth charges due to the extra size and weight of the weapons.

On sea trials the ships were generally tested over the measured mile off Arran where practicable, otherwise testing and trials were carried out where and when it was possible to do so safely. The ships were found to be generally well designed and built, although some Captains complained about the open bridges. Another Captain wrote to the Admiralty about his ship and said:-

"As usual no provision for stowage of oil skins, sea boots or duffel coats....bread boxes of inferior design and material....attaché cases of flimsiest possible construction, after a rough day are thrown on deck more than once from the so called racks which are supposed to contain them....messes cluttered with hull and fire pumps, fans, steam pipes, shafting rod gear, handwheels, wires, far in excess of any quantity I have ever seen in a mess deck before. Ship's company bathroom accommodation can only be described as disgraceful...fitted out in a manner which would be a disgrace to a public convenience....after bathrooms are tiled. Paint of a thin, watery consistency, no covering power, etc etc....Many of the criticisms are hardy annuals, could be overcome by a little thought when ship is at the design stage....steel furniture leaves much to be desired, material is poor, design indifferent, workmanship shoddy, appearance unimpressive....Apparently no care taken in design stage to find out what requirements of stowage space are likely to be, easy course is taken of sending gear to be stowed ' as desired by ship's officers'.

Internally the ships were somewhat cramped but were generally liked by their crews. Leonard George Foot recalls in his memoirs, *"Footsteps - the Life Story of a Dorsetshire Foot"*, that the messing arrangements onboard his ship, **Cadiz** were, by today's standards, somewhat rudimentary. He remembers that the ship had a system called 'Canteen Messing'. *"This system allocated each mess a sum of money to feed itself."* He reports, *"We bought our food from the on board victualling stores (or ashore if we could find something cheaper), and prepared it ourselves. It was then taken to the galley where it was cooked for us. There were two serious drawbacks to this system. Firstly, if we did not spend all the money on food each month we could divide the 'mess savings' up between us. As we were only paid about £3 per week, of which a sum had to be remitted home, the aim was to spend as little as possible. We therefore lived on cheap beans, potatoes and meat. There was little variety and seldom a pudding."*

Another former crewmember of the **Jutland** remembered the sleeping arrangements onboard with fondness. *"There were only nine bunks on the mess deck and those were secured to the hull and reserved for the killicks (LME's) and senior ME's, the remainder of us had to 'sling hammocks'. They touched when they were slung, particularly at the head - the 'stretcher' end. Of course the stretcher could become a missile but that is another story."*

"There is no doubt that hammocks were comfortable, they moved as the ship moved, it was quite a sight to see all the hammocks slung across the mess deck, over the tables, moving as one as the ship rolled. Slinging and unslinging was quite an evolution, particularly if you had been ashore drinking. If you were lucky a friend had already slung the hammock for you prior to your return, if you were unlucky and you could not do it you slept where you could. The hammocks were of course stowed in a hammock rack in the corner of the mess deck when not in use - and tied in a very particular way."

HMS Armada - This overhead shot shows to advantage the layout of the main weapons on the Battle class destroyers. Forward are the two twin MkIV 4.5-inch turrets. Single 40mm Bofors are sited just ahead of the bridge, on each bridgewing and on the bandstand immediately aft of the funnel. Two sets of quadruple torpedo tubes are located on the centreline and can be trained to port or starboard. Two twin 40mm mountings are on the after deckhouse and the Squid A/S weapon is on the quarterdeck, offset to starboard. (Ray Lambert)

"I remember sleeping in on several occasion's and having both ends of my hammock untied and passed to me. So there I am there in my hammock half asleep holding both ends of the hammock ropes, if I were to let go of either end it would crash to the ground. The only way was to let go of the 'feet end' first and hope for the best, but whatever you did you still had to re-sling it in order to tie it up correctly prior to stowing it away."

Trevor Harman remembers that *"Conditions below decks were very cramped therefore hygiene was very important. Every day following breakfast, the morning watchmen (when at sea) would be required to scrub out the mess, in harbour this would be the duty of two mess members on a rota basis. Even the adoption of a strict hygiene regime could not, however, eradicate the dreaded cockroach, and it would not be unusual to find one or two scurrying around whenever a light was turned on. Impetigo and tropical ulcers would sometimes prove to be a problem as the prevailing conditions onboard and the humidity and heat would make their eradication difficult. There was the odd infestation of crabs and victims would be easy to spot to their strict regime of dusting down with anti flea powder."*

K. Miller joined **Sluys** around 1951 as a stoker mechanic. He reports *"I joined **Sluys** from **Wrangler** and was impressed by the standard of the newer vessel. I did think though, that the open fronted furnaces of the 3 drum Admiralty boilers were a technical step backwards from the close fronted boilers of **Wrangler**. The messdeck had a shortage of lockers and most of us had to do with, what can only be described as lidded holes under the cushions of the ships side seating."*

Towards the end of the war the Allies had some considerable success with the use of destroyers as radar picket ships in the Pacific campaign. Buoyed up by these successes the Admiralty began looking at ways in which powerful radar sets could be used at sea in the Royal Navy. The initial studies focused on destroyers but again the Admiralty were worried that such modifications would interfere with the ship's primary role as a destroyer. The postwar years did, however see a requirement for a Fast Aircraft Direction Escort (FADE) develop which would accompany the fleet and provide facilities for the detection, identification and tracking of potential targets. Such a ship would then be able to communicate all this data to friendly forces which would then attack them if necessary.

FADE would require at least four ships that were specially tailored to the task, in addition to the four members of the Type 61 frigates which served a similar function. New build options were initially explored but in the end the favoured option was the conversion of existing hulls. The Royal Navy of the 1950's had a large number of different classes of fast destroyers but the heavy weight of the proposed radar meant the choice came down to just the Battle class ships. The radar was to be the Type 965 which had two aerials, AKE-1 and AKE-2. It was this last type that was chosen and weighing in at nearly four tons was a weighty problem to fit onto a Battle class destroyer.

The decision to proceed was taken in 1955 but four years would elapse before work commenced due to technical problems with the radar sets. The four ships chosen were **Agincourt**, **Aisne**, **Barrosa** and **Corunna**. Each was refitted at different naval bases, (in order Portsmouth, Chatham, Devonport and Rosyth). The refits took nearly three years to complete and cost nearly £2.25 million each. **Corunna** returned to service in November 1962 with a substantially altered appearance. The four 4.5-inch guns were retained together with the Mk37 director carrying the Type 275 radar. However, the most striking change was a massive new lattice mast behind the bridge that carried the AKE-2 aerial of the Type 965 radar. A Type 293Q cheese aerial was positioned below this on a forward projecting platform. The destroyers traditional weapons comprising of torpedo tubes and close range armament were all removed and a series of deckhouses constructed. These housed diesel generators and radar offices and some accommodation spaces. The four ships were also equipped with a Type 277Q radar and a forest of ESM and D/F aerials.

The original after deckhouse was modified to serve as the site for the launcher for a GWS 21 Seacat guided missile system. When **Corunna** first re-commissioned this marked the first time that Seacat had gone into oper-

*HMS **Agincourt** following her extensive conversion to a Fast Aircraft Direction Escort. The massive lattice mast supporting the Type 965 aerial dominates the ship, whilst abaft the funnel, new deckhouses support a second lattice mast mounting the Type 277Q radar and a Seacat missile launcher.* (MoD/Crown Copyright)

ational service with the Royal Navy. The missile director carried a Type 262 radar and was developed from the fire control equipment incorporated into the obsolete STAAG mounting.

The refit did not completely remove all anti submarine capability in the four ships as each retained a single Squid mortar on the quarterdeck.

Aisne, *Agincourt*, *Corunna* and *Barrosa* had relatively short careers after conversion all disappearing by 1970. The reason why was due to the government's policy of withdrawing from East of Suez and the abandonment of the Royal Navy's fleet of aircraft carriers and the introduction into service of new classes of more capable warships.

Almost without fail all former crew members of the Battle class destroyers recall their ships with fondness and everyone I have spoken to have always spoken of 'The Beautiful Battles".

Previous page: **HM Ships Armada**, **Barfleur** and **St Kitts** of the 3rd Destroyer Squadron. *(Ray Lambert)*

HMS ARMADA

The "cluttered" after superstructure of the Battle class is surmounted by multiple 40mm AA mountings, as seen here on **HMS Armada**. *(Steve Bush Collection)*

29.12.42	Laid down at Hawthorn Leslie.
09.12.43	Launched.
03.45	Lieutenant Commander R. A Fell in command.
02.07.45	Completed.
Early 09.45	Malta.
12.09.45	With *Trafalgar* and *Camperdown* at Aden and onward journey to Australia to join 19th DF.
Late 45	Saigon.

Armada's planned voyage from Sydney to visit Hong Kong was cancelled and instead the destroyer was dispatched at top speed to Saigon. There the ship exchanged signals with a French destroyer. The captain soon explained to the crew that **Armada** *would make a high-speed journey up the Mekong River to pick up a civilian.* **Armada's** *speed was such that people in small boats in the river were buffeted by the ship's wake and those working on the shoreline were inundated by the wash. After tying up at a wooden wharf the ship awaited the civilian's arrival. Poor Vietnamese people soon, however, descended upon the destroyer and the crew found that in exchange for cigarettes they would barter a wide assortment of goods.*

The civilian duly arrived and as soon as his luggage was aboard the ship set a course back down the Mekong, again at high speed. The mysterious man remained in his cabin for the entire journey back to Sydney.

Christmas 45	Sydney.
01.46	In dry dock at Garden Island.
01.46	Mackay, Townsville, Cairns and Fiji via the Great Barrier Reef.
02.46	Sydney and Melbourne.
02.46	With *Hogue*, *Trafalgar*, *Finisterre* and *Camperdown* en route to Okinawa, Hong Kong and Shanghai.
16.07.46	Received a distress call from the passenger ship *SS Taiposhan*, which was under attack from pirates after beaching.

*It was as they approached Shanghai on 16 July 1946 that **Armada** received a distress call from the cargo passenger ship **SS Taiposhan** which had grounded on a sand bank about a hundred miles north of Shanghai and was under attack by pirates.*

*   **Armada** raced to the scene to find the ship under attack by large sea going Chinese junks, **Armada** fired a number of shots from her Bofor guns into the water in front of the junks. They quickly retired to a safe distance. **Armada** launched a couple of boats and managed to get a rope across to the **Taiposhan** to haul a heavy cable to attempt a tow. After struggling to pull the merchant ship from the sandbank the hawser snapped but mercifully did not hurt anyone as it flayed around the deck. One man on the destroyer did, however, suffer injury when the winch he was attending almost severed several of his fingers. A tug that was more suited to the task was on it's way but was two days away so **Armada** stayed in the area and protected the immobile ship from further attacks. The tug, eventually arrived and the merchant ship was pulled free by it and **Armada**. **Taiposhan** made for Shanghai for repairs and the British destroyer escorted her there to protect against any more pirate attacks.*

07.46	Hong Kong.
Early 47	Returned to the United Kingdom and placed in reserve at Portsmouth.
06.49	Re-activated.

***HMS Armada** in June 1950. Notice the additional 40mm gun in front of the bridge.* (John Brewer)

HMS Armada *comes alongside an aircraft carrier for a transfer of stores or personnnel by jackstay.*
(Steve Bush Collection)

04.08.49	Left Portsmouth for Mediterranean as half leader of 3rd DF.
Late 49	Cyprus and Christmas at Beirut.
02.12.49	Exercise *Swift Tactican*.
01.50	Syria and Aqaba as peacekeeper.
1950	Visited Turkey, France, Egypt, Tunisia, Crete and Malta.
01.51	Refit at Gibraltar during which an explosion of ammunition alongside killed several dock yard personnel.
08.51	Trouble in the Persian Gulf between Shah of Persia and Dictator Mossadeq of Iraq. *Armada* spent months in the heat of the region.
Late 1951	Aden and Port Sudan crisis.
10.12.51	Portsmouth.
13.12.51	Chatham.
31.12.51	Portland.
02.01.52	Portland to Gibraltar with *Saintes*.
09.01.52	Malta.
25.01.52	Tobruk.
04.04.52	Syracuse.
10.04.52	Malta.

The Squid AS weapon sited on the quarterdeck. The three barrels are each slightly offset to produce a triangular spread of charges.
(Philip Waite)

24.04.52	Phaleron Bay for unveiling of memorial to war dead.
12.06.52	Exercise *Beehive 2* before visits to Taranto, Venice and Trieste.
03.07.52	Dragomesti.
06.07.52	Malta.
11.07.52	Gibraltar for maintenance.
25.08.52	Work completed.
27.08.52	Tangiers.
01.09.52	Malta.
22.09.52	With **Saintes** at Naples for a four-day visit.
20.10.52	Anchored at entrance of Suez Canal awaiting a pilot to take her to Fayd.
12.11.52	Sailed to Cyprus and onward journey to Beirut.
11.52	Suez crisis with **Saintes**, **Vigo** and **Gravelines**.
06.12.52	No 3 dry dock at Malta for maintenance.
04.01.53	Lieutenant Commander M B Clagg took command.
08.01.53	Gibraltar.
10.01.53	Left for United Kingdom.
13.01.53	Arrived at Sheerness.
15.01.53	Chatham.
20.01.53	Paid off.

14.07.53	Sailed to Portsmouth to join Reserve Fleet.
12.55	Re-activated for 2nd time.
Early 56	Off Portland working up.
21.01.56	Spring cruise and exercises with the fleet.
04.56	Portsmouth and Portland.
Summer 56	Suez Canal Crisis started.
03.09.56	Sailed from Portsmouth to conduct exercises off Campbeltown with RAF aircraft.
23.09.56	Portsmouth.
25.09.56	Gibraltar with *St Kitts*.
06.10.56	Malta.

By mid October the prospect of war in Egypt was an odds on bet and the fleet in the Mediterranean was bolstered with extra vessels from the United Kingdom. Those in the area were subjected to intense training.

*Over the coming months **Armada** operated, along with **St Kitts**, **Alamein** and **Barfleur** with the aircraft carriers **Eagle** and **Bulwark**, but also sometimes conducted bombardments of Egyptian positions. On 1 November 1956 **Armada** kept station on **Bulwark** for intensive flying operations. She later shifted to work with **Eagle**. At 1755 action stations were secured and later she refuelled from **Olna**. By the early hours of 5 November **Armada** was on station on **Tyne**. At 0532 **Alamein** and **Urania** detached to rejoin the Carrier Task Group - **Armada**,*

The two single 40mm Bofors on the bandstand abaft the funnel. The forward quad torpedo tubes can be seen in the foreground.
(Philip Waite)

*HMS **Armada** passes through the Kiel Canal in June 1958*   (Ray Lambert)

Barfleur and *St Kitts* *forming a forward bent line screen.*

*With the Army ashore the local opposition was overpowered and as such it was decided that **Armada** could, on 6 November, proceed down the swept channel to Port Said. At noon **Armada** anchored in 7 fathoms with immediate notice for steam and at a very high state of alert. Four hours later she weighed anchor and set course and speed, necessary to form astern of the cruiser **Jamaica**.*

09.11.56	Discovered body of Egyptian sailor in the area.
10.11.56	With *Albion* and *Bulwark*.
14.11.56	Bombarded positions ashore for twenty minutes.
23.11.56	Sailed from Port Said to refuel from *RFA Tidereach*.
09.12.56	Sailed from Port Said for Malta.
15.12.56	Gibraltar.
18.12.56	Portsmouth.
28.01.57	Sailed to visit Brixham.
31.01.57	Plymouth.
02.57	Visited Dartmouth, Cardiff, Greenock and Rothesay.
18.02.57	Portsmouth.
23.02.57	No 15 dock for refit.
19.03.57	Maintenance completed.
28.03.57	Sailed for Mediterranean.
17.04.57	Gibraltar and onwards to Malta after 2-days alongside.
05.57	Cyprus patrol looking for terrorists.

07.08.57	Visited Messina, Sicily, Dubrovnik and Trieste.
06.09.57	Malta.
10.09.57	Barcelona.
18.09.57	Gibraltar.
31.10.57	Malta.
29.11.57	Portsmouth for refit.
Spring 1958	Re-commissioned at Portsmouth.
23.05.58	With *Camperdown* at Dornoch.
Summer 58	Exercise *Cover Point* and visits to Kiel, Newcastle and the Clyde for Perisher submariner course.
30.07.58	Portsmouth.
05.09.58	Commander M. W. B. Kerr took command.
09.58	Worked up at Portland.
20.09.58	Sailed for Gibraltar with *Saintes* and *Camperdown*.
10.58	Sailed for World Fair. Later took part in MEDASWEX 26 and 27 off Toulon.
10.58	Collided with a dockyard tug at Malta. Six weeks in dockyard hands to fit a new bow.

HMS Armada *taking on fuel from the cruiser HMS Bermuda in November 1958*   *(Jim Ashby)*

Early 1959	Exercise *Dawn Breeze 4* off Gibraltar then Cyprus patrol.
05.59	Malta.
06.59	Visited Barcelona and Palmas Bay with **Saintes** and **Delight**.
06.07.59	Left Malta for Piraeus and Istanbul.
20.07.59	Malta.
26.07.59	Transferred to Home Fleet at Gibraltar.
28.07.59	Corunna, Spain.
04.08.59	Sailed back to Portsmouth.
09.59	Weapons training.
11.9.59	With cruiser **Bermuda** in Scottish waters.
09.59	Exercise *Barefoot* and *Blue Frost* with aircraft carrier **Victorious** in Norwegian Sea.
10.59	Rosyth, Londonderry and Clyde areas.
7-28.11.59	Icelandic fishery patrol duties.
30.11.59	Rosyth.
12.59	Bremen.
11.12.59	Portsmouth to pay off.
Early 1960	Re-commissioned.
15.01.60	Sailed from Portsmouth for Rosyth.

*This 1958 shot of **Armada** shows her after a partial modernisation. Two STAAG 40mm mountings have replaced the after Hazemeyers, while the midships mountings have been removed and the 4-inch starshell gun has been replaced by single 40mm Bofors. Although not quite visible the depth charge arrangement on the quarterdeck has been replaced by the Squid A/S mortar.* *(MoD/Crown Copyright)*

21.01.60	Rosyth to Cod War off Iceland and *Operation Whippet*.
15.02.60	Portsmouth.
22.02.60	Sailed to Portland for trials.
03.03.60	Portsmouth.
14.03.60	Clyde for COQEX.
18.03.60	Greenock.
21.03.60	Sailed for Red Bay.
25.03.60	Exercised with submarine *Trump* off Londonderry.
28.03.60	Portsmouth.
Early 04.60	*Armada* was prepared for the reserve fleet.
20.05.60	Arrived at Chatham.
18.12.65	Arrived Inverkeithing to be broken up by Ward Brothers.

Armada Memories

Douglas Macaulay first joined *Armada* in June 1949, where she was undergoing a refit, having been brought forward from reserve. *"I served in her from June 1949 to December 1951 as a Leading Writer and latterly as a Petty Officer Writer. During the whole of this period, she was by far the happiest ship I had the privilege of serving on."*

"Armada sailed from Portsmouth on 4 August 1949 to join the Mediterranean Fleet and was 'A half leader' of the 3rd Destroyer Flotilla. On arrival at Malta we underwent a six week work up exercise before proceeding to various Italian ports. One I remember was Genoa where we represented the Navy at a memorial service to a minesweeper that was lost sweeping the harbour of mines."

"Exercise Swift Tactician started on 2 December. Our calls in the latter part of 1949 were to Cyprus with the ship spending Christmas in Beirut before moving on to Syria in the New Year. In 1950 we had a variety of tasks, one of which was being anchored at Aquaba for some six weeks at a time as peacekeeper. Numerous other calls were made in 1950, mainly to Turkey, France, Egypt, Tunisia and Crete but at all other times we were based at Malta."

"1951 was a more eventful year. In January we were at Gibraltar for a refit and unfortunately the ammunition unloaded from the ship into a Dockyard Lighter exploded the following day. We had moved along the jetty prior to going to Dock. Regrettably several Dockyard personnel were killed and injured. Until August of 1951 we exercised with many fleets and visited many ports. Our one tragedy onboard was the passing of our commissioned Gunner who was found dead in his bunk".

He recalls that in August 1951 trouble was brewing in the Persian Gulf between the Shah of Persia and the Dictator Mossadeq who he believed wanted to nationalise the oil fields and dispense with the UK's commitments. *"This was a most unpleasant time onboard as temperatures were in excess of 100 degrees and being anchored in the middle of the 'Shat-el-Arab' river opposite the refinery at Abadan was somewhat tetchy. We used to spend between 4 and 6 weeks at a time in this situation, briefly going to Basrah for a break. We were very relieved and thankful to eventually leave this area but unfortunately it was out of the frying pan and into the fire. On leaving we called into Aden and thence to Port Sudan where it appears the Navy were required to quell some violence and give support to the local 'Brits'. By this time we had been away from home well over two years with no sign as to when we may return. We were the longest serving ship in the Flotilla, both Saintes (The Leader of the 3rd DF), Vigo and Gravelines were all on their way back to Malta and onward homecoming. Eventually in December 1951 we arrived back from whence we came and entered Portsmouth Dockyard on 10 December. Having been married for only three months before we sailed my wife and I, quite naturally, both appeared to be strangers."*

Ivor Parker, an Engine Room Artificer, recalls that during his time onboard, the ship experienced some difficulties with her engines. He reports *"We were programmed to escort the carrier **Albion** to Singapore while she was on passage to Korea. On the Sunday before we were due to sail I was on duty on board. Most of the ships company were ashore enjoying the last hours of leave especially the married ones who had their families with them. After Sunday morning divisions I was called by the duty stoker below in the engine room that we had a leak which required my urgent inspection. So, still in my full white uniform, I went into one of the main Condenser inlets which subsequently turned out to be leaking due to corrosion. This needed the attention of the Engineer Officer and the Captain in view of our impending departure the following day - so I had them recalled from shore leave. The end result was that on Monday morning we were towed by tug to the dockyard where over the next six weeks a new condenser inlet was made and fitted and the ships company enjoyed some regular runs ashore and we were headline news in the 'Times of Malta'. We were not very popular with the ships company of the destroyer that was recalled to take our place as **Albion**'s escort to Singapore. This, however, was not the end of the story as on completion of the repair, the dock was flooded, testing completed and we duly left the dockyard to return to Sliema Creek. Before clearing the harbour we collided bows on with a dockyard tug and guess who came off worse? So we returned to the dockyard for what turned out to be another six weeks for a new bow to be fitted and more headlines in the 'Times of Malta' and more smiles from the ships company with more time ashore in Malta."*

HMS BARFLEUR

HMS Barfleur *in March 1945 prior to sailing to join the 19th Destroyer Flotilla in the Far East. (Ben Warlow Collection)*

28.10.42	Laid down at Swan Hunters.
01.11.43	Launched.
14.09.44	Completed.

Barfleur *on completion had been 80 percent readied for Arctic conditions, but with the end of the European conflict the final work necessary to complete her never occurred. In this state she sailed for the Far East. Perhaps these design changes caused the slippage in her construction.* ***Barfleur*** *had been due to complete in March 1944, with RDF 272 Mk V and HF/DF on the foremast. By August the depth charge throwers had yet to be fitted but the Admiralty decided that the destroyer should commission as soon as possible. She ran trials and achieved a speed of 31.65 knots on 2958 tons and returned to Wallsend to await the arrival of the missing equipment. During gunnery trials some Triplex glass in the bridge was cracked when B gun was firing aft.*

07.45	Commander M.S Townsend DSO, OBE, DSC took command and took her to the Far East to join the 19th DF.

16.07.45	Joined the USN TG.38 for combined attacks on Tokyo and Yokohama.
17.07.45	Escorted British aircraft carrier *Indefatigable*.
12.08.45	Returned to Manus due to shortages of fuel. Later force was re-designated as TG-38.5.
03.09.45	Tokyo Bay to witness Japanese surrender onboard *USS Missouri*.
Late 1945	Visited Colombo, Singapore, Hong Kong, Yokohama and Darwin.
Christmas 1945	Sydney.
Early 1946	Hong Kong and Singapore.
06.46	Visited Singapore, Colombo, Trincomalee, Penang, Kure, Yokohama, Tokyo, Kobe and Nagoya.
10.46	Siled for the United Kingdom.
1947	Paid off into reserve.
1951	Work started to re-activate the ship.
17.03.53	Commander K C Currie took command.
22.05.53	A Handley Page Hastings transport aircraft of the Royal Air Force crashed into the Mediterranean while en route to Castel Benito (Idris) in Libya.

On board the aircraft were Air Commodore Moreshead and other high ranking officials from Transport Command Headquarters. The aircraft lost all power from its four engines and ditched soon after the propellers had been feathered. Everyone onboard the Hastings survived the crash and took to the life rafts and awaited rescue. Two twin-engined Albratross amphibious aircraft were dispatched to look for the aircrew who were

HMS Barfleur *leaving Portsmouth in a dark grey colour scheme with white pennant numbers.*
(Portsmouth Royal Naval Museum)

*HMS **Barfleur** (left) with sisterships of the 3rd Destroyer Squadron, **St. Kitts** and **Saintes**, attract quite a crowd whilst open to visitors during a 1954 visit to Marseilles.* (Alan Duke)

*quickly found. However, sea conditions were too rough for a safe landing by the Albatross and they instead dropped a powerful VHF radio to contact **Barfleur** which was in the vicinity. The survivors were advised that if the destroyer had not arrived by sundown, another Albatross would be dispatched to retrieve them. The weather conditions, however, prevented this and after further air drops of life rafts from an RAF Lancaster an Albatross eventually, after some hours, succeeded in landing nearby the crew. The original crew transferred into the warmth of the Albatross as they awaited the arrival of **Barfleur**, which was guided to the scene by a Lancaster that dropped flares. When **Barfleur** arrived the crew were transferred to the destroyer and were checked over by a medical officer. However, the swell had built up again and meant that the Albatross itself was unable to take off. **Barfleur** stayed nearby in case the crew of the rescue plane needed to be rescued themselves. As it turned out the Albatross eventually took to flight and returned to base.*

15.06.53	Coronation Review at Spithead.
Late 1953	Returned to Mediterranean as Captain (D) 3rd DF.
01.01.54	At Malta.
16.01.54	Port Said during Suez crisis with ***Cheviot***.
20.02.54	Left Port Said.
24.02.54	Arrived back at Malta.
01.03.54	Alongside ***Ranpura*** for maintenance.
15.03.54	Sailed for Gibraltar with ***Indefatigable***, ***Glasgow***, ***Aisne***, ***St Kitts*** and ***Saintes*** before taking part in *Exercise Touchline*.
28.03.54	One of sixteen ships that left Gibraltar to rendezvous with the aircraft carrier ***Eagle***.

30.03.54	En route to St Raphael for Exercise *Medflexable*.
04.54	Naples as escort for HM Queen Elizabeth for tour of Italy in **Britannia**.
Spring 1954	Operated out of Malta.
10.05.54	Gibraltar.
13.05.54	St Austell Bay.
14.05.54	Devonport to de-commission.
24.05.54	Commander E L Locke took command.
26.05.54	Sailed to Portland.
30.05.54	Sailed to Gibraltar, where she arrived 3-days later.
07.06.54	Malta.
02.07.54	Tripoli with **St Kitts** for 3-day visit.
19.07.54	*Operation Turnip*.
27.07.54	Palermo.
02.08.54	Sorrento.
10.08.54	Back to Malta for removal of her director.
15.08.54	STAAG mounting removed whilst at Gibraltar.
13.09.54	Small fire in No-2 boiler room.
28.10.54	Completed her refit and sailed from Gibraltar.
11.54	Visited Catania, Sicily.
01.12.54	Leghorn.
07.12.54	Malta.
13.12.54	Gibraltar.
18.12.54	Plymouth Sound.
20.12.54	Devonport No.1 wharf.

After a hard days work **Barfleur's** *Chief Mouser takes a cat nap.*
(Alan Duke)

*A fine shot of **Barfleur** as she enters port. Her secondary armament is clearly showing.* (Maritime Photo Library)

17.01.55	Left Devonport for Portland for exercises and trials until 29 January at start of the Home Fleet Cruise to Mediterranean.
04.02.55	Gibraltar.
25.02.55	Marseilles. Ship open to visitors.

At the end of the day the record showed that no less than 2991 people had toured the destroyer. On 2 March she slipped and headed for St Raphael where again the destroyer was open to visitors throughout her five day stay.

03.55	St Raphael.
15.03.55	Malta with **Saintes** and **St Kitts**.
26.03.55	Arrived Gibraltar after exercises with **Ocean** and **Theseus**.
01.04.55	Devonport.
25.04.55	Sailed for Bremen with **St Kitts**.
05.55	Londonderry training areas.
29.05.55	Invergordon.
06.06.55	Plymouth and secured on cruiser **Belfast** at No.8 berth.
15.07.55	Commander E L Cook DSC was relieved by Commander J Pearson.
16.08.55	New ships company embarked destroyer following refit.
16.09.55	Dockyard crane damaged STAAG mounting.
27.09.55	Re-commissioned.
06.10.55	Damaged one of her screws on the corner of No.1 jetty in Devonport's South Yard.

10.10.55	Anchored in Plymouth Sound.
20.10.55	Entered No 9 dock in Devonport to repair screw damage.
14.11.55	Left dock.
29.11.55	Moved by tugs to alongside the battleship *Vanguard*.
Early 1956	Returned to the Mediterranean.
Summer 1956	Usual round of exercises and port visits.
05.11.56	Operation Musketeer against Suez Canal.

Following the closure of the vital waterway, British and French forces were assembled in and around Malta and Cyprus. Amongst these were four Battle class destroyers, including **Barfleur**. *Whilst the politicians tried to solve the problem the French and British fleets spent late summer and autumn 1956 conducting intensive battle practice in the Mediterranean to hone their skills for the expected use of military force.*

On 5 November 1956 **Barfleur**, **Armada** *and* **St Kitts** *were formed into a screen as a defence for the depot ship* **Tyne**. *Thursday 8 November saw a jackstay transfer with* **Armada** *when a doctor was hauled between the two ships. The next day whilst* **Armada** *sailed to investigate the discovery of an Egyptian sailor's body in the sea,* **Barfleur** *assumed her position in the patrol line.*

With the imminent danger of strikes reduced **Armada**, **St Kitts** *and* **Barfleur** *anchored in Port Said at a high state of alert.*

08.12.56	Sailed from Port Said.

HMS Barfleur *transfers a casualty to the Royal Yacht* **Britannia** *in 1955.* (Alan Duke)

Every inch a classic Royal Navy destroyer. **Barfleur** *at sea.*   *(Steve Bush Collection)*

12.56	Malta and Gibraltar.
17.12.56	Detached from **Armada** and made her way independently to Plymouth.
12.04.57	Portland.
17.04.57	Arrived at Gibraltar.
04.57	Operated with the aircraft carrier **Albion** around Malta.
05.57	Exercises continued along with Cyprus Patrol.
07.57	Visited Sardinia, Sicily, Augusta and Messina.
13.08.57	Augusta to take part in Group 1 regatta.
19.08.57	Dubrovnik.
27.08.57	Trieste.
04.09.57	Plotting exercise with **Kenya** and **Hogue** before returning to Malta.
27.09.57	Sailed from Malta.
10.10.57	Barcelona.
20.10.57	Gibraltar.
28.10.57	Sailed for Malta to take part in MEDASWEX 20.
21.11.57	Final farewell to Malta.
24.11.57	Gibraltar with **Armada**.
27.11.57	Plymouth.
1958	It was announced that **Barfleur** would de-commission.
01.58	Final cruise to the Caribbean that included visits to Kingstown, Beguia Bay, Jamaica and

	Bermuda. Then Halifax in Canada for Exercise *Maple Royal 1* and *2* and *Dawn Breeze 3*.
02.04.58	Devonport.
1959	Target ship for new 21-inch Mk20 homing torpedo in non-destructive tests.
1960	Placed on the disposal list.
29.09.66	Arrived Clyde for breaking up at Dalmuir.

Barfleur Memories

1946 saw the destroyer visiting numerous ports around the region notably Hong Kong and in April was along-side at Shanghai when according to T. Westlake the amenities ship **Menestheus** arrived which was *"a Matelot's dream."* He recalls that *"It proved a great success because they had waited so long for such a ship. The attraction was 'Davy Jones brewery providing 1000 gallons of near English beer each day and 'big eats' were to be had in its 400 seat dining rooms."*

In 1947 **Barfleur** was placed into reserve where she would remain until 1951 when she was taken in hand by dockyard workers at Portsmouth and prepared for further service. W. A. Cable remembers working in Portsmouth Dockyard as a M.E.D between 1951 and 1953 and recalls work that was carried out on **Barfleur**. *"Both the A and B turrets were removed from the ship and stood in a frame on the 240 ton crane. Pipe systems and various units were removed for refitting and modifications, this was during the winter so you can imagine the working conditions. The turret deck rings were strengthened as the deck structures were being weakened in sea service."*

HMS CADIZ

HMS Cadiz in August 1946 minus her AA armament of STAAG and 40mm mountings.   (Portsmouth Royal Naval Museum)

12.08.42	Fairfield Govan awarded contract.
10.05.43	Laid down.
16.09.44	Launched.
12.04.46	Completed.

*The first steel plates were laid down on 10 May 1943. Progress was swift and the ship was, by 16 September 1944, ready for her launch into the waters of the Clyde. On 12 September 1945 Lieutenant Commander (E) F C Burge was appointed to the **Cadiz** to supervise the construction work on the ship. Shipyard workers completed the destroyer on 12 April 1946 as they handed her over to the Royal Navy. The shipyard carried out their own trials of the ship and recorded her speed during trials as 33.75 knots on 2806 tons.*

*Many former crewmembers recall that the destroyer upon her entry into service had a partially completed appearance this was due to the fact that not all of her armament had been delivered to the shipyard in time. Amongst items missing were **Cadiz's** STAAG mountings for the after shelter deck. She was also without two twin 40mm mountings on the midship gundeck. These omissions were soon corrected, however, when the supply of such items became more regular after the problems created by the war were overcome.*

Early 1946	Joined 5th Destroyer Flotilla.
03.06.47	Operated with ***Sluys*** and ***Vengeance*** before visit to Norway.
05.06.47	Arrived at Oslo before visiting Kristiansand, Bergen, Trondheim, Mosjoen, Mo, Budo and Tromso.

25.06.47	Returned to Rosyth.
22.07.47	Clyde Fleet Review at Greenock.
Late 1947	Home waters and Gibraltar.
Early 1948	Visited Pool of London.
Summer 1948	Training at Invergordon, Pentland Firth and Londonderry.
01.09.48	Arrived at Portsmouth.
07.09.48	Left for Portland to join Home Fleet Autumn Cruise to the Caribbean.
23.09.48	Sailed.
09.10.48	Arrived at San Fernando before visiting Pointe a Pierre, Port of Spain, Great Courland Bay and Bridgetown.
11.48	Visited Barbudo, Antigua, Virgin Islands and Hamilton, Bermuda.
28.11.48	Portsmouth
01.49	At Portland before sailing to Gibraltar and Lisbon.
25.03.49	Portsmouth.
31.05.49	Flight exercises off Lizard Point with *Vengeance*.

A Firefly from ***Vengeance*** *crashed into the sea off Lizard Point and close to the ship on the night of 31 May.* ***Cadiz*** *searched for the two man crew and quite quickly located the Observer, however, the pilot was lost.*

27.06.49	At Portland with *Solebay*, *St Kitts*, *St James*, *Battleaxe*, *Scorpion* and *Crossbow*.
17.08.49	After a month at Portsmouth, sails for Gibraltar.

Wearing pennant number R09, ***Cadiz*** *is seen here in 1947. Although she has two single 40mm Bofors aft of the funnel, the remaining deckhouses still lack her main AA armament.* *(Maritime Photo Library)*

HMS Cadiz *seen operating in warmer climes. The metal struts around the bows and B turret were for the deck awnings which would be rigged when the ship is at anchor or in port.* *(John Brewer)*

20.08.49	Gibraltar.
21.08.49	Sailed to join Mediterranean Fleet and visited Malta, Cyprus, Beirut and Port Said. After transiting the Suez Canal visited Port Suez where she became Red Sea guardship at Aqaba.
04.11.49	Malta.
08.11.49	Sailed for Gibraltar and onward to Portsmouth.
08.12.49	Arrived at Portsmouth.
26.01.50	Left for Portland to join Spring Cruise to the Mediterranean with **St James**. Visited Palmas Bay, Leghorn, Calgari, St Rapheal and Oran.
23.03.50	Gibraltar.
31.03.50	Portsmouth.
12.07.50	Left for Portland.
19.09.50	Exercise *Easy Prey* in Bay of Biscay
30.09.50	Visited Tangiers (with **Sluys***)* and Casablanca.
04.11.50	Gibraltar. After a visit to L'Orient in France, arrived back at Plymouth on 7 December.
17.01.51	Sailed for Gibraltar.
09.02.51	Sailed to Leghorn and Golfe Juan.
05.03.51	At Gibraltar before continuing to Portsmouth.
Early June 51	*Exercise Unite* in Irish Sea. Later *Exercise Progress* with **Indomitable** in Bay of Biscay. After exercise both ships visited Stockholm on 14 June 1951.
29.06.51	Arrived Invergordon.
Summer 51	In the Mediterrean.

HMS Cadiz *shows a clean pair of heels as she turns at speed.* (MoD/Crown Copyright)

November 51	Ordered home to Portsmouth and crew paid off.
February 52	Lieutenant Commander P J Bayne DSC in command.
31.07.52	Commander D G Clutterbuck took command
31.07.52	Crew exchanged ship with **Sluys** at Devonport.
Sept 52	Exercise *Mainbrace*.
25.09.52	Stavanger.
01.10.52	Rosyth.
08.10.52	Training at Invergordon and Londonderry.
30.11.52	Devonport.
23.01.53	Portland before sailing to Gibraltar.
March 53	Returned to Portsmouth and placed in reserve.
15.06.53	Coronation Review at Spithead.
01.02.57	Re-commissioned under Pakistani flag as **Khaibar** after being refitted at Alex Stephens and Sons Ltd.

*In Pakistani service the ship was not altered substantially and retained her original armament and sensors. In 1963 the ships pennant number was changed from D79 to 163. It was, however, during the Indo-Pakistani war of 1965 that the ship came into her own and took part in the celebrated Operation Dwarka. The Pakistani plan had benn to try to draw the main units of the Indian navy out of Bombay to be attacked by the submarine **Ghazi**. A second objective was to try to destroy radar installations at Dwarka.*

*On 7 September 1965 Pakistani Naval Headquarters issued the command, "Task Group comprising **PNS Babur**, **PNS Khaibar**, **PNS Badr**, **PNS Jahangir**, **PNS Alamgir**, **PNS Shahjahan** and **PNS Tipu Sultan** is to be in position 239 degrees - 120 miles from Dwarka light house by 071800 E Sep with maximum power available. Task Group thereafter to carry out bombardment of Dwarka about midnight using 50 rounds per ship. Force is to retire from bombardment area by 080030 E Sep and return to present patrol area at full speed. One or two enemy frigates may be expected to be encountered in the area in addition to enemy air threat."*

Under radio silence the Commodore in command of the Pakistani task force started his attack on the radar installations and targets of opportunity. Upon their arrival off the city of Dwarka they found it to be completely blacked out. Radar, was the only way of identifying the targets but, was used sparingly so as to avoid being detected themselves. At 0024 the bombardment started with the Pakistani ships positioned some 5.5 to 6.3 miles from Dwarka. In under four minutes over 350 rounds of ammunition were fired into the city. After the last shot had been fired the Pakistani ships sped away without suffering any damage and resumed their normal patrol duties by 0635 on 8 September.

04.12.71   During some of the worst fighting of the Indo Pakistan war *Khaibar* was operating twenty miles off Karachi. The Indian Navy had successfully sunk *Shah Jakar* (ex *HMS Charity*) and two minesweepers, and were attacking *Khaibar*. The fighting lasted over an hour but in the end it was the Indian's who scored the final blow. An Indian Osa 5 class fast attack boat got close enough to fire a missile. The missile slammed into the side of the ship and caused a great deal of damage and a large number of casualties amongst the crew. Fires broke out and the ship quickly started to sink. From when the captain ordered the crew to abandon the crippled destroyer it was only a matter of time before she slipped beneath the water and became the only member of the Battle class to have been sunk in action.

*Now flying the flag of Pakistan **PNS Khaibar** was sunk by an anti-ship missile in December 1971 during the Indo-Pakistan war.*
(Portsmouth Royal Naval Museum)

Cadiz Memories

Leonard Foot recalls his time on board in the Red Sea. *"I was watch keeping in the W/T office. Long periods of watch keeping are most debilitating and the Captain noticed that I and two other Telegraphists in particular were looking pale and less healthy than the rest of the ship's company and he ordered us to be issued with camp beds and to sleep on the upper deck to get more fresh air."* This was nothing compared with his next recollection. *"An incident at Aqaba, which I will always remember, was that one night whilst I was on watch in the W/T office, the Signalman called down the voice pipe to tell me we were being fired on. I, like a foolish young 18 year old, left the office and went down the passage and on to the iron deck to 'see what was happening'. I crouched under the Captain's motor boat just as some machine gun fire hit the boat and a splinter flicked on to my forehead and caused it to bleed. The reason for the firing was that the Signalman who had been told to illuminate any vessel which came near had, in illuminating an Arab fishing boat, shone the searchlight on the Jewish encampment near to the modern day Israeli resort of Eilat. The Jews responded in a manner that we now know as being most characteristic, by immediately firing at us in retaliation."*

Another less dramatic incident occurred whilst the ship was at Aqaba. Leonard remembers how *"the mackerel used to teem around the gangway lights in their millions. It was easy to catch them with an un-baited hook or even just scoop them out of the water."* Anything for a fresh change of diet!

HMS CAMPERDOWN

HMS Camperdown *at anchor showing the arrangement of the after AA batteries.*   *(Steve Bush Collection)*

30.10.42	Laid down at Fairfield, Govan.
08.02.44	Launched.
13.02.45	Lieutenant Commander J. J. S. Yorke DSC took command.
18.06.45	Completed.
06.08.45	Left Greenock for Gibraltar.
09.08.45	Gibraltar before onward journey to Malta, Alexandria and Suez en route to Far East and 19th Destroyer Flotilla.
12.09.45	Aden.
19.09.45	Colombo before sailing onto Singapore.
30.09.45	Hong Kong.
14.10.45	Yokohama and Japanese waters until 7 November.
11.45	Mostly spent at Hong Kong.
15.11.45	Sailed for Darwin.
22.11.45	Crossed the Equator before arriving at Darwin.
23.11.45	Sailed for Sydney.
30.11.45	Sydney.
17.12.45	Left Sydney to visit Darwin and Dilli.
02.02.46	Hong Kong as escort to merchant ship *E-Sang*.
13.02.46	Shanghai.

01.03.46	Sailed to escort merchant ship *Tsinan* to *Tsingtao* before returning to Shanghai.
29.03.46	Sailed for Hong Kong where she spent the whole of April.
06.05.46	Sailed for Singapore, Colombo and Trincomalee.
June/July 46	Visited Penang, Singapore, Hong Kong, Chingwangtao, Pei Tai Hoi, Kure, Yokohama and Tokyo.
06.08.46	Sailed from Tokyo for Yokohama, Kobe and Nugoya.
29.09.46	Exercise *Homeward Bound*.
01.10.46	First leg of return journey to UK, via Hong Kong, Singapore, Trincomalee and Aden.
03.11.46	Port Suez.
10.11.46	Gibraltar.
15.11.46	Arrived Plymouth and placed in reserve.
1953	Rammed whilst in reserve during filming of the classic British film *The Cruel Sea*, by the flower class corvette *Coreopsis* causing £10,000 worth of damage. Later in June towed to the Solent for the Coronation Review.
24.09.53	A fire caused some damage onboard.
1953	Towed to Liverpool for refit.
19.10.57	At Trafalgar Dock, Liverpool where she re-commissioned.
31.10.57	Sailed for sea trials, which lasted until 21.11.57.
21.11.57	Arrived at Devonport.
11.12.57	Sailed for Portland.
16.12.57	Returned to Plymouth.

HMS Camperdown at Malta with other NATO warships.   (MoD/Crown Copyright)

*A gleaming **HMS Camperdown** preparing to enter Portsmouth.*　　　　　*(Portsmouth Royal Naval Museum)*

September 58	**Camperdown**, **Saintes** and **Armada** re-commissioned for General Service Commission in Mediterranean and Home Fleet.
20.09.58	Sailed Portland, but a serious fire in her boiler room postponed her departure.
01.10.58	Arrived at Malta.
Winter 58	Visited World Fair at Tunis followed by MEDASWEX 26 and 27 and a visit to Toulon. Later she took part in the ongoing Cyprus Patrol.
January 59	Maltese waters
Mid April 59	MEDFLEXGUARD and ongoing Cyprus Patrol.
01.06.59	Sailed from Malta to Barcelona and Palmas Bay.
15.06.59	Malta
22.06.59	Commander P. R. Wood DSC took command. Operation *Whitebait*.
06.07.59	With **Saintes**, **Armada**, **Birmingham** and **Delight** en route to Istanbul.
16.07.59	Piraeus
18.07.59	Sailed for Malta.
24.07.59	Gibraltar.
28.07.59	Corunna.
05.08.59	Plymouth.
11.09.59	Sailed for Invergordon and night bombardment exercises.
22.09.59	Exercise *Barefrost* at Trondheim with **Victorious**.
01.10.59	Rosyth.

Early 10.59	Operation *Lightning Strike* around Isle of Man, Londonderry and Lisahally.
05.11.59	Icelandic Fishery Patrol.
30.11.59	Rosyth.
05.12.59	Bremen with *Armada*.
11.12.59	Devonport.
15.12.59	Commander D. K. Hawkinson took command.
29.02.60	Commander G. T. Risdon took command.
26.04.60	Re-commissioned for last commission.
23.05.60	Following a day at Brixham visited Portland for work-up.
Early 07.60	Devonport, Londonderry, Rothesay and Faslane.
28.07.60	Devonport and back to Londonderry.
11.09.60	Rosyth.
15.09.60	Exercise *Fallex*
18.09.60	With *Ark Royal* and *Hermes* for Exercise *Swordthrust* in Arctic Circle.
02.10.60	Devonport.
02.10.60	Left for Gibraltar with *Victorious*.
November 60	Visited Malaga, Toulon and MEDASWEX in the Gulf of Lions.

In the immediate post-war period, Battle class destroyers made up a large proportion of the Royal Navy escort fleet. Here **Camperdown** *exercises with another destroyer.* *(Edward*

*A delightful photograph of **Camperdown** at speed.*

(Edward Booker)

26.11.60	Arrived Lazaretto Creek, Malta.
December 60	Visited Palermo with Christmas at Malta.
26.01.61	Repairs at Gibraltar.
Late 02.61	SAR duties for Queen's flight from Pakistan. ***Camperdown*** took up a position between Greece and Italy. Also a three-day visit to Corfu.
14-20.04.61	MEDFLEX INVICTA
8.05.61	With ***Centaur*** and weekend break at Messina.
29.05.61	Barcelona for International Samples Fair
June 61	Visited Marseilles, Naples and Capri.
Summer 61	Diverted to Persian Gulf following threatened invasion of Kuwait by Iraq.
21.08.61	Left Aden.
25.08.61	Northbound passage of Suez Canal.
27.08.61	Malta.
14.09.61	Devonport.
14.10.61	Exercise *Sharpsquall* 5 with ***Finisterre*** and ***Saintes***.
21.10.61	Anchored at Scapa Flow.
15.11.61	After time at Londonderry arrived at Devonport.

24.11.61	Wallasey.
06.12.61	SAR duties for Queen's flight from West Africa, positioned off the Canary Islands.
09.12.61	Gibraltar.
15.12.60	Devonport.
Early 1962	Visited Le Havre, Bordeaux, Greenock and Bilbao.
09.04.62	Paid off at Devonport. Later towed to Portsmouth and reserve.
24.09.70	Arrived Faslane for scrapping.

Hi Mom!! A traditional group photograph for squadron personnel. The small numbers would indicate a departmental gathering.
(Ben Warlow Collection)

HMS FINISTERRE

*A very smart looking **HMS Finisterre** under a stormy sky in September 1945.*   (Steve Bush Collection)

27.04.42	Ordered from Fairfield, Govan.
08.12.42	Laid down.
22.06.44	Launched.
06.07.45	Lieutenant Commander V. A. Wight-Boycott, OBE, DSC took command.
11.09.45	Completed.

*She was one of only two Battle class destroyers to be completed with Denny Bros designed stabilisers at the time of her construction - the other being **Camperdown**.*

24.09.45	Portland.
10.10.45	Portsmouth.
13.10.45	Gibraltar.
17.10.45	Work-up at Malta.
12.45	Visits to Alexandria, Port Said, Aden, Singapore and Hong Kong to join 19th Destroyer Flotilla.
01.46	Visits to Japan, China and Indo China.
06.46	Sydney.
22.06.46	Sailed with *Glory* to Adelaide.
27.06.46	Adelaide.

03.07.46	Trincomalee.
Summer 46	Visits to Hong Kong, Singapore and Japan.
Christmas 46	Spent at Hong Kong.
31.01.47	Left Hong Kong for Amoy (China) before returning to Hong Kong.
22.02.47	Singapore.
27.02.47	Port Sweetenham (Malaya) before calling at Dimdings River, Penang and Bass Harbour.
03.47	16 days at Trincomalee.
30.03.47	Colombo.
08.04.47	Aden.
14.04.47	Port Said.
18.04.47	Malta.
29.04.47	Chatham Dockyard.
02.06.47	Sailed from Chatham to Portsmouth to be converted into a gunnery training ship running out of Portsmouth Harbour.
22.07.47	Clyde Fleet Review at Greenock.
06.09.48	Exercise *Chicken Serial 1* with the aircraft carriers ***Illustrious*** and destroyers ***Crossbow*** and ***Battleaxe*** around the Azores.
16.09.48	Devonport before sailing to Portsmouth.
1949	Training in and around the Solent, but occasional trips further afield such as Worthing and the Isle of Arran.
07.03.50	At Dover to welcome French President Vincent Auriol who was on an official visit to Britain. ***Finisterre*** escorted the steamer ***Arromanches*** as she passed the battleship ***Vanguard*** and escorts ***Zephyr***, ***Wizard***, ***Wrangler*** and ***Roebuck***.
04.51	On the scene of the loss of the submarine ***Affray***.

*During the tragedy that surrounded the loss of the submarine **Affray** in April 1951 T. M. Reeves remembers seeing the **Finisterre** speeding out of Portsmouth Dockyard. "I was duty quartermaster in the radar training ship **Boxer** during the dog watches on a sunny evening. We were berthed alongside the small ships canteen in Portsmouth dockyard. Across the water from us was **Finisterre**, the duty 'guard ship'. There came a sudden burst of activity onboard her. **Finisterre** literally shot astern from her berth, turned on her axis and went down harbour at a very high speed. She passed the Gosport ferry and gave the two ferries a very rough ride with her wash. I had never seen a ship leave harbour at such a speed before or since, a splendid sight indeed."*

25.08.51	Lieutenant Commander F. C. Boys took command.
1952	***Finisterre*** lost her twin 40mm Bofors Mk2 STAAG mountings from the shelter deck during refit.
06.53	At Coronation Review at Spithead.
15.09.53	Lieutenant Commander E. R. S. Clouston DSC took command.
1953	More classrooms were built amidships.
1954	The STAAG mountings were refitted to the ship as were five single 40mm Bofors Mk1 guns mounted (one abaft B turret, two in the bridge wings and two abaft the funnel). Following an inspection of the main armament it was declared unsafe by engineers from Vickers and ***Finisterre*** was placed in reserve and replaced as the gunnery training ship by sister-ship ***Vigo***.

Roger Strofton recalls the incident. "On one of these full calibre shots the alarm bells rang in "B" turret; a crack had appeared in the turret wall. We returned immediately to Portsmouth where a team from Vickers came down and condemned the turret and said, 'a few more salvos and the turret would have gone over the side, complete with gun team."

08.59	Following the damage to the ***Hogue***, ***Finisterre*** was refitted at Portsmouth to replace her in the fleet.
15.09.59	Steaming crew onboard.
19.09.59	Sea trials.
21.09.59	Sailed to Portland to load weapons.
22.09.59	Portsmouth.
09.10.59	Gibraltar.
10.59	Visited Malta, Port Said, Malta, Aden and Colombo.
22.10.59	All electrical power failed, whilst at sea. 20 minutes later full power was restored.
30.10.59	Alongside the crippled ***Hogue*** at Singapore.
31.10.59	Commander J. R. Pardoe assumed command.
20.11.59	Left Singapore with ***Hogue***'s former crew.
27.11.59	Crossed the equator.
29.11.59	Manus.

The Battle class were reported to be quite wet ships in a swell. **HMS Finisterre** *appears to be shipping water along the waists in a relatively light swell.*
(Cliff Pantrey)

06.12.59	Cairns.
11.12.59	Bowen.
16.12.59	Sailed for Sydney.
19.12.59	Sydney for Christmas.
1960	On first leg of journey home, *Finisterre* visited Aden, Suez, Malta and at Gibraltar took part in Exercise *Dawn Breeze*.
01.04.60	Devonport.
06.04.60	Chatham.
07.06.60	Commander G. J. Balfour took command of the ship, which was then in No 7 dry dock.
01.09.60	Sailed for Plymouth.
09.60	Working up at Portland.
11.60	Malta.
16.11.60	With 7th Destroyer Flotilla and the cruiser *Bermuda* off Malta.
19.11.60	Toulon.

All smile!...the ship's company gather for a photograph at Gibraltar in 1961 (Cliff Pantrey)

*With deck awnings rigged **HMS Finisterre** operates in the Persian Gulf in the summer of 1961 during the Kuwaiti crisis. A torpedo can just be seen being fired over the portside from the after set of torpedo tubes.* (Cliff Pantrey)

01.61	Malta.
18.01.61	Sailed to visit Cagliari and Toulon for MEDASWEX 42.
02.61	Visited La Spezia for Exercise *Inner Circle* before visiting Suda Bay and Piraeus.
24.02.61	Malta.
03.61	Palma followed by Gibraltar for Exercise *Dawn Breeze*.
18.03.61	Brest and then to UK.
22.06.61	Off Malta and collided with the cruiser **Lion** during a towing exercise.
Summer 61	Dispatched to Persian Gulf for Kuwaiti crisis.
14.09.61	Returned to the UK.
14.10.61	Exercise *Sharpsqual 5* off East Coast of Scotland.
21.10.61	Arrived at Scapa Flow then *Exercise Smallex.*
17.11.61	Greenock for NATO Exercise with **USS Essex**, **Robinson**, **Stribling**, **Noa**, **Jonas Ingram**, **Miller** and **Waccamaw**.
30.11.61	Exercise ended at Belfast.
06.12.60	Royal SAR duties for Queen's flight before returning to Gibraltar.
15.12.61	Devonport.
Early 62	A series of exercises in UK waters.
03.02.62	Devonport
24.02.62	Avonmouth for opening of the new port facilities.
07.03.62	Bordeaux.
29.03.62	Bilbao.
08.04.62	Returned to the UK to decommission.
12.06.67	Arrived Dalmuir for breaking up.

HMS Finisterre *at speed*

(Cliff Pantrey)

HMS GABBARD

HMS Gabbard *entered service without her two STAAG mountings due to supply shortages.* *(Steve Bush Collection)*

18.08.42	Order placed with Swan Hunter.
02.44	First plates laid down.
16.03.45	Launched.
21.05.46	Commissioned into service.
08.46	The incomplete destroyer was moved to Newcastle on Tyne for Victory Celebrations.
10.12.46	Completed.
16.12.46	Arrived at Chatham.
20.12.46	Captain J. A. Micklethwait assumed command.
03.01.47	Left port for trials to continue.

During her speed trials held on 8 January 1947 **Gabbard** *achieved a speed of 31.663 knots on a displacement of 3,105 tons. Due to delays in the supply of STAAG mountings* **Gabbard** *entered service without the two mountings on the after shelter deck, she also lacked the two twin 40mm mountings on the midships gundeck.* **Gabbard** *had her armament brought up to standard after four months in service.*

02.47	Portland. Then on to the Mediterranean with visits to Tangiers, Oran and Lagos before returning to Chatham.
30.04.47	Sailed north to Scandinavia, where she visited Oslo, Aarhus, Copenhagen, Gothenburg and Malmo. At Malmo collided with a local ferry.
22.07.47	Clyde Fleet Review at Greenock.

03-04.48	At Chatham for refit and basin trials.
02.09.48	Sailed from Chatham for Solent.
23.09.48	Sailed from Portland with Home Fleet on Atlantic Cruise taking in port visits to Trinidad, Tobago, Bridgetown, Barbuda, Charlestown on Nevis and the Virgin Islands.
15.12.48	Arrived Chatham.
01.02.49	Sailed from Chatham at start of Arctic Cruise codenamed *Operation Rusty*, with **Vengeance**, **Loch Arkaig**, **Artful** and **RFA Wave Premier**.
09.03.49	Arrived Chatham.
27.06.49	At Portland for start of Operation *Verity* before returning to Chatham on 21.07.49.
18.10.49	Assisted recovery of the aircraft carrier **Albion**, which had collided with the small collier **Maystone** off Berwick-on-Tweed. Towed the carrier back to Rosyth.

*Roy Emmington recalls the above incident. "The PO's mess were playing the Caledonia Tiffy's at cricket. We had played a couple of overs and we were recalled back to the ship. All we were told was that some ship was in trouble in the North Sea. It turned out to be the aircraft carrier **Albion**, she had been in collision with a collier in the North Sea on 18 October. She was being built in Newcastle for a few years so her bottom was foul with seaweed, so she was being towed up to Rosyth for dry docking and bottom scraping. She was off Berwick on Tweed at midnight and a small collier, the **Maystone** ran into her and put a hole in her port side aft. It pierced the propeller shaft tunnel that hadn't got a propeller shaft fitted so the Engine room and other compartments were flooded." The **Maystone** soon sank off Farne Island with all but four members of her crew. The **Albion***

HMS Gabbard *in the Arctic during Operation Rusty, a series of cold weather trials.*   *(Brian Davies)*

Gabbard shows off her classic destroyer lines to good effect. The design of the Battles, however, was a compromise between affordablility and effectiveness. *(Steve Bush Collection)*

had a large list on and we were told why we were there. The Dockyard Mateys would not go out to take her into the Dockyard. There were a few Ex Ganges Boys on **Gabbard** *to help them out. We had to climb up ropes to fix towing wires. I was on the forecastle with a dozen hands so I was the first Captain of the Forecastle of* **Albion**! *That was the only time I was on an aircraft carrier. We got her into Rosyth and into dry dock before she could roll over."*

14.11.49	Arrived Chatham.
19.01.50	Left Chatham to escort *Vanguard*, *Victorious*, *Implacable* and *Vengeance* on a cruise to Gibraltar.
02.50	Training in the Mediterranean, with visits to Palmas, St Tropez and Mers-el-Kebir.
07.50	Training plus visits to Rosyth, Rotterdam and Flushing. Five days were also spent anchored off Eastbourne.
09.50	Home Fleet's Autumn Cruise with *Vanguard*, *Vengeance*, *Cleopatra*, *Swiftsure* and other destroyers. Ports visited included Porto Grande, Funchal and Gibraltar.
18.11.50	At Chatham for short refit.
17.01.51	Refit completed.
02.51	Visited Bastia, St Raphael and Gibraltar.
15.03.51	Arrived back at Chatham in company with *Corunna* and *Broadsword*. Exercised with *Eagle* at Invergordon before sailing to Gibraltar to escort the Yugoslav training ship *Galeb* with Marshall Tito onboard from the Bay of Biscay to the River Thames.

10.51	Training at Londonderry.
09.10.51	Sailed from Belfast for Falmouth and Gibraltar.
07.12.51	Chatham.
16.01.52	Sailed from Chatham to take part in Exercise *Grand Slam* off Gibraltar.
02-03/52	Training.
31.03.52	At Sheerness to unload ammunition.
01.04.52	Arrived Chatham Dockyard.
22.09.52	Sailed from Chatham for training at Portland and Invergordon.
11.12.52	At Chatham for Christmas Leave.
19.01.53	Sailed to take part in Exercise *Able* and Exercise *Baker* off Gibraltar.
26.03.53	At Chatham.
12.12.53	Farewell cruise of British ports.
03.02.54	Arrived at Chatham for Category II reserve. Then mothballed in Basin 2.
1954	Purchased by Pakistan.

*Behind the scenes the, British government had been approached by the Pakistani government with a view to buying second hand surplus warships for their fledgling navy. Eventually **Gabbard** and sister ship **Cadiz** were purchased and modernised with money provided from the US Marshall Defence Aid Plan (MDAP).*

10.03.55	Towed to Palmer's Yard at Hebburn to be modernised.
27.01.57	Refit complete and ship headed for Portsmouth as the *Badr*.
Late 03.57	Sailed for Karachi.
1963	Pennant number was changed from D47 to 161.
1979	Lost two single 40mm Bofors Mk7 and quadruple torpedo tubes in a refit.
1985	Became HQ ship of the new Maritime Safety Agency.
01.87	Renamed *Indus*.
1990	Used as target for guided missiles and gunfire before wreck broken up in Pakistan.

Gabbard Memories

Maurice Wragg recalls his time onboard **Gabbard**. *"On completion of my training at **HMS Mercury** as a wireless telegraphist, I was drafted to **Gabbard**, 5th Destroyer flotilla Home Fleet, she was then in dry dock at Chatham nearing the end of a complete refit."*

*"We completed sea trials and then took part in various exercises. We went up to Invergordon with the aircraft carrier **Eagle** and the rest of the fleet for exercises."*

*"One of our most important trips was to Gibraltar to escort the Yugoslav training ship **Galeb** with Marshall Tito on board across the Bay of Biscay and into the Thames arriving in thick fog. That night was spent fending off all the press boats - which was great fun".*

*"Our commanding officer was Commander Dickens the great grandson of Charles Dickens and the youngest commander of a naval vessel at that time, he was also one of the finest seamen and took the **Gabbard** out of the Thames to Folley Point in thick fog, the only ship to rendevous on time, we then escorted the Battleship **Vanguard** over to Brest on a goodwill visit. Tied up alongside we seemed very small."*

"We also did a goodwill visit to Londonderry and again arrived in thick fog, the pilot would not come down the river so Commander Dickens took us up into Londonderry charting every buoy, I was on the bridge during these trips as my station for entering and leaving harbour was manning the radio position there."

HMS GRAVELINES

HMS Gravelines *had the shortest career of any of the Battle class, serving from 1949 until just 1956. A refit was carried out at a cost of £1,750,000 but was cancelled causing a public outcry at the waste of money.* *(Steve Bush Collection)*

12.08.42	Ordered from Cammell Laird.
10.08.43	Laid down on slipway.
30.11.44	Launched. Lieutenant Commander H. R. Rycroft DSC took command.
14.06.46	Completed and immediately placed in reserve at Plymouth on the River Tamar.

Bill Campbell remembers his first impression of **Gravelines**. *"I first spotted her when I was serving on the destroyer* **Onslaught**. *We had arrived in Devonport for a boiler clean and were alongside the wall in the South Yard. The* **Gravelines** *suddenly appeared on the scene, being manhandled by a couple of tugs to a spot just down away from where we were lying. She looked a mess, really down and out, a real ugly duckling, compared to which we seemed almost pristine - even with a boiler clean taking place."*

"After leaving **Onslaught** *in Scotland I was drafted to barracks in Devonport at the latter end of July 1949. Next thing I was being detailed as part of a working party to the* **Gravelines** *in the nearby yard. The next couple of months were spent getting the old ship back to a semblance of normality, this involving much hard and dirty work which had us knackered at the end of each working day when we'd return to our billets in Guzz barracks. But it didn't quite deter us from going ashore after tea or dinner each night. With us working on the* **Gravelines** *we were excused duty watch in Drake and could go ashore as often as we liked."*

08.07.49	Lieutenant Commander D. Shaw assumed command.
09.49	Commissioned.

15.09.49	In Number 4 Basin at Devonport.
20.09.49	Ammunitioning at No 1 wharf Devonport.
27.10.49	Left for the Mediterranean.

"When we did leave for the Mediterranean," Bill continues, *"it was without notice and a lot of girls ashore were left wondering why their beaus failed to turn up at the designated spot the following day. It seems we were waiting to tow something across to the Mediterranean but the weather kept deteriorating until we had no option but to sail without it. The first any of the lads knew about it was when they came back off shore leave late on the night of October 26. The next morning saw us setting off on the great adventure without as much as a wave of a handkerchief from shore."*

30.10.49	Arrived Gibraltar.
04.11.49	Arrived Malta.
02.12.49	Exercise *Swift* with **Tactician**, **Forth**, **Armada** and **Childers**.
05.12.49	Princess Elizabeth welcomed onboard.
13.12.49	Exercised with Dutch destroyers **Drente** and **Rotterdam**.
01.50	Visited Philippeville in Algeria.
03.50	Visited Toulon to exercise with French Navy.
11.03.50	Visited Mers-el-Kebir before sailing onto Oran.
03.50	Exercises before visiting Aranci Bay on the Cote d'Azur.
01.04.50	Cannes.

*A port side view of **HMS Gravelines**.* (Steve Bush Collection)

HMS Gravelines *leaving harbour in Malta.* *(Dave Scoble Collection)*

05.04.50	Villefranche.
10.04.50	Monaco for the Coronation of Prince Rainier.
17.04.50	Malta.
14.05.50	Port Said before sailing through the Suez Canal.
16.05.50	At Aqaba for two weeks.
04.06.50	Back at Malta.
14.06.50	Arrived at Corfu for five days.
07.50	Visits to Istanbul and Piraeus with *Glory* and *Gambia*.
06.07.50	Sailed for Marmaris in Turkey for Fleet Regatta.
16.07.50	Transited Suez Canal and returned to Mediterranean.
30.07.50	At Malta.
28.08.50	Sailed from Tripoli before going onto Malta and Taormina in Sicily.
31.08.50	Visited Italian Navy at Taranto.
13.09.50	Entered dockyard at Malta for refit.
11.50	SAR duties for Princess Elizabeth's flight to Malta.
14.12.50	Diverted to ship in distress off Sicily.
15.12.50	SAR duties for Princess Margaret.
02.01.51	Sailed for Greek Islands.
05.01.51	Arrived at Dragomesti then back to Malta with future Prime Minister Jim Callaghan onboard as a passenger.
02.51	Visited Trieste, Taranto, Volos, Marmarice, Aqaba, Beirut and Cyprus.

18.3.51	Escorted *Glory* to Port Said.
22.03.51	Sailed through Suez Canal to operate in Persian Gulf. Visited Aden, Colombo, Bahrain, Kuwait, Abadan and Basra.
07.51	Back in the Mediterranean where, together with *Saintes*, *Vigo* and *Armada,* she relieved the 1st Destroyer Squadron of *Chevron*, *Chequers*, *Chivalrous* and *Chieftain*.
12.51	Returned to the UK.
11.52	Off Malta before returning to Devonport in December.
05.03.53	Exercises off Gibraltar with *Barfluer* and *Cadiz*.
10.03.53	Commander E. N. Sinclair took command. The entire ship's company exchanged ships with the crew of *St Kitt's* at Gibraltar.
16.03.53	Arrived at Chatham.
05.11.53	Left Chatham for training in UK waters. Upon return briefly entered reserve fleet.
1955	Returned to operational status with 3rd DS in the Mediterranean.
Sum/Aut 1956	Operation *Musketeer*.

Gravelines and other members of the 3rd Destroyer Squadron were already in the Mediterranean and were immediately assigned to the Operation Musketeer during the Suez crisis. July, August and September were a hectic period of preparations where ships and crews practised battle manoeuvres, night and day until in October and November the shooting started for real.

   Gravelines stayed with the aircraft carriers far out to sea as escort and also assumed plane guard duties. After what was a military success came the crushing political defeat and the ensuing withdrawal of British, French and Israeli forces. *Gravelines* again patrolled the seas off Egypt in support of British interests. The fleet eventually sailed for Malta and resumed normal operations in the area.

End of 1956	Returned to the United Kingdom for refit at Devonport.
1958	Refit abandoned after £1,750,000 spent - causing a public outcry.
17.03.61	Towed from Devonport to Rosyth to be broken up.

HMS HOGUE

HMS Hogue returned to the UK in 1947 to pay off into reserve following her initial Far East commission.

(Steve Bush Collection)

06.01.43	Laid down at Cammell Laird.
21.04.44	Launched.
12.04.45	Commander A. St. Clair-Ford DSO took command.
24.07.45	Completed.
08.45	Sea trials then sailed for the Far East calling at Gibraltar, Malta, Port Said and Singapore to join the 19th Destroyer Flotilla. In Far East *Hogue* visited Hong Kong, Shanghai, Trincomalee, Darwin and many Japanese ports.
01.46	Lieutenant Commander F. M. Graves took command.
Spring 47	*Hogue* sailed back to the United Kingdom and was placed in reserve.
1957	Work started to re-activate her.
06.05.57	Commander V. A. D. Turner DSC took command.
21.05.57	Re-commissioned.
05.57	Sailed to the Mediterranean. Took part in Exercise *Combine* off Sardinia and Exercise *MEDASWEX* off Malta. Visits were made to Venice, Trieste and Cyprus.
09.57	Cod War with Iceland code-named Operation *Whippet*. *Hogue* became flagship of the Fishery Protection Squadron.
28.09.57	Collided with the trawler *Northern Foam*.
03.10.57	Arrived at Devonport having been relieved by *Ulster*.
Early 1958	Visited Gothenburg and Frederikshaven.
1958	Mediterranean with visits to Venice, Tobruk, Tarragona and Gibraltar. At Gibraltar, No 2

boiler room was flooded to a depth of ten feet whilst in dock. The damage caused a delay to her departure.

18.11.58	End of commission.
20.11.58	Commander J. R. Pardoe took command for a General Service Commission Home/Med fleet with 1st DS.
Christmas 58	Off Iceland on fishery patrol.
06.01.59	At Rosyth.
10.01.59	At Devonport.
09.02.59	At sea exercising with *Llandaff* before sailing to the Mediterranean and Gibraltar.
25.02.59	Sailed for Lisbon with *Lagos*, *Apollo* and *Tyne*.
15.03.59	Operation *Onion One* and *Cabbage Two* with *Eagle* and *Victorious*.
23.03.59	Arrived at Devonport for a short refit.
13.05.59	Sailed to Rosyth for Navy Days.
15.05.59	Exercised in Moray Firth with *Gambia*.
25.05.59	Short visit to Plymouth before sailing to Brest.
06.59	Visits to Pinto Bay, Palmas Bay and Malta before operating with the US carrier *USS Intrepid* and British carrier *Centaur*.
26.06.59	Arrived at Port Said with *Llandaff*, *Solebay*, *Lagos* and *Centaur*.
29.06.59	Completed transit of Suez Canal.
02.07.59	Aden for Exercise *Shop Window* with *Centaur*.
31.07.59	Karachi at start of Exercise *JET*.

HMS Hogue *in September 1958.*   *(John Brewer)*

*The impact of the collision with **INS Mysore** is clearly evident in this picture of the resultant damage, **Hogue**'s bow being crushed up to the foot of "A" turret.*   *(Bungy Williams)*

17.08.59	Arrived at Cochin and met up with the Indian cruiser **Mysore**.
18.08.59	Night-time mock attack on a number of ships simulating the Blue Convoy of the exercise.
21.08.59	Arrived Trincomalee for four days rest.
25.08.59	**Hogue** and **Mysore** collided at sea at high speed.. One rating RO(3)(S) Revill was killed and another seriously injured. The destroyer was towed back to Trincomalee by the tug **Aliya**.

*A stoker recalls that the **Hogue** was exercising in the Indian Ocean with ships from India, Australia and New Zealand. "I doubt that I ever knew the purpose of the exercise but our ship was lost. As I went on watch in No 1 boiler Room, I believe it was the first watch, I noticed that the night was very dark with little or no moon. Not a night for dashing round the ocean with no lights!"*

"The watch proceeded with frequent changes of speed and course when suddenly the Engine Room telegraph rang Full Astern. I signalled to my Stoker to switch on more sprayers and as I controlled the forced air fan and fuel pump, we were in collision. The young Stoker seemed to float a foot in the air before crumpling to the plates. As he picked himself up, both water sight glasses burst, going off like a rifle shot. The Engine Room telegraph now rang to Stop. I telephoned the Engine Room requesting urgent repairs to my sight glasses as I only had an unreliable distant reading gauge by which to maintain the correct water level in the boiler."

"It was only after coming off watch that I learned more of the earlier happenings. We had been struck fine on the starboard bow by an Indian cruiser at a combined speed in excess of 50 knots. The communications mess deck, the most forward, had been wrecked killing one rating, RO(3) (S) Revill, and seriously injuring another. All other communication ratings were involved with the exercise and were away from their mess."

*"The tug **Aliya** was despatched from Trincomalee and we were towed stern first to harbour. A team of specialist underwater welders arrived from the UK and cut off that part of the bow that was folded back on the port side. Plates were then welded over the gap. Watertight bulkheads were shored and the newly created forepeak was filled with concrete for strength and ballast."*

"While all this work was progressing, the crew were given the opportunity to sample life at an RAF R&R centre up in the hills near Kandy. All very pleasant and the only time I have ever played golf. The local chef produced some excellent curries. Meanwhile, a steaming crew had flown to the UK to steam out a relief ship hurriedly brought out of the reserve fleet."

*"After our patched bow had been given several coats of grey paint, complete with black boot topping, we sailed for Singapore at a sedate 10 knots accompanied by **HMNZS Pukaki**, a New Zealand frigate which had sailed with us to Trincomalee."*

29.08.59	Arrived at Singapore escorted by **HMNZS Pukaki**.
30.10.59	*Finisterre* arrived from the UK with a steaming crew onboard.
02.11.59	Crew of **Hogue** transferred to **Finisterre**.
07.03.62	What remained of the **Hogue**, after being stripped of useful equipment, was scrapped at Singapore.

HMS Hogue *never returned to service following her collision in 1959. She was taken to Singapore where she was stripped of all useful spares and scrapped in March 1962.*
(Maritime Photo Library)

HMS LAGOS

HMS Lagos in the Mediterranean, off Malta, in January 1946.   *(A. Irlam)*

08.04.43	Laid down at Cammell Laird.
04.08.44	Launched.
04.45	Commander H. Unwin DSC took command.
21.11.45	Completed.

*During her trials **Lagos** achieved a speed of 30.46 knots on 3,060 tons displacement. With the pressure of a speedy delivery for war service removed the destroyer's trials were conducted at a more sedate pace and were completed by the end of the summer. Another kind of pressure, however, materialised when it was realised that the warships in the Far East needed to be relieved on station. **Lagos** was amongst the newest destroyers in the fleet and she started her voyage east in January 1946.*

01.46	Sailed for Far East to join 19th Destroyer Flotilla.
Spr/Sum 46	Singapore, Hong Kong, Japan and Australia.
13.11.46	Sailed with *Glory* for Singapore.
25.12.46	Christmas at Hong Kong.
01.01.47	Left Hong Kong to visit China, Malaya and Singapore.
27.02.47	At Port Sweetenham in Malaya.

04.03.47	Penang.
14.03.47	Trincomalee.
04.47	Visited Colombo, Aden and passage through Suez Canal into Mediterranean.
29.04.47	Returned to UK and placed in reserve at Chatham.

*Many of her crew could have been forgiven for believing that the ship would soon return to sea, but this was not to be. Soon after her arrival it was decided that many of the Royal Navy's warships were to be either decommissioned, scrapped or placed in long term reserve. **Lagos** was amongst the latter and she was to remain in reserve for the next ten years, receiving periodic inspections and overhauls to ensure that the ships' structure was in a satisfactory state.*

Early 57	Re-activated for General Service Commission in Mediterranean.
21.05.57	Re-commissioned.
30.05.57	Left Chatham to ammunition at Sheerness.
04.06.57	Arrived at Portland.
12.06.57	Gibraltar.

HMS Lagos *takes fuel from a light fleet carrier during exercises. Note the staggered position of the two AA mounts on the after deckhouse.*
(MoD/Crown Copyright)

HMS Lagos *dressed overall.*   *(Steve Bush Collection)*

17.06.57	Malta.
21.06.57	Exercised with submarines **Sanquine** and **Sentinel**. Later **Lagos** suffered a main machinery breakdown.
25.06.57	Entered No 4 dry-dock at Malta for maintenance and repairs.
16.07.57	Sailed from Malta with **Armada**, **Solebay** and **Hogue**. **Lagos** returned to Chatham Dockyard
06.09.57	Arrived off Iceland for Operation *Whippet*.
11.11.57	Visited Lagos Bay en route to Malta.
12.57	Christmas and New Year spent at Gibraltar.
01.58	Visits to Gibraltar and Malta before joining **Alamein**, **Agincourt** and **Diamond** for joint exercises.
12.02.58	Visited Nice and welcomed onboard 1742 visitors. Similar numbers visited the ship at Naples.
25.02.58	Having left Naples, the destroyer operated with **Ark Royal** en route to Malta.
09.03.58	With **Solebay**, **Agincourt** and **Barossa** arrived at Gibraltar.
10.03.58	Sailed for Cadiz.
20.03.58	Arrived Lisbon.
25.03.58	Sailed for Chatham and exercised with **Eagle**.
31.03.58	Arrived at Chatham and later entered dry dock for short refit.
13.04.58	Sailed for Rosyth.
05.58	Exercises in areas from Scapa Flow to Loch Eriboll and Cape Wrath to Invergordon.
06.06.58	Arrived Dover.
06.58	Visits to Harwich, Gotenburg, Aarhus and Den Helder.
07.58	Loch Foyle, Molville, Lisahally, Londonderry, Portsmouth and Bangor.
27.07.58	Anchored for the night at Short Reach in the River Medway before entering Chatham Dockyard the next morning to take part in Navy Days.
03.09.58	Sailed from Sheerness for Icelandic fish patrol.
28.09.58	Patrol completed returned to Chatham.

10.58	Visited Portland, Rouen and a blustery passage to Rosyth and the start of another Icelandic fish patrol.
Mid 11.58	Returned to Chatham.
24.11.58	Commander R. P. Dannreuther assumed command.
03.02.59	Left Chatham for Mediterranean with *Solebay* and *Hogue*.
11.05.59	Visited Lisbon with *Solebay*, *Llandaff* and the carrier *Centaur* whilst enroute to the Far East.
13.06.59	Malta and Exercise *Whitebait*.
27.06.59	Port Said.
07.59	Visited Umm Said, Dubai, Bahrain and Karachi.
12.08.59	Rescued crew of helicopter from *Centaur*.
22.08.59	Two days rest at Trincomalee during JET exercises.
04.09.59	Singapore.
21.10.59	Yokosuka (Japan) for ten days.
11.59	Australia with visits to Portland and Sydney.
12.59	Melbourne and Fremantle.
11.01.60	Sailed from Fremantle for Singapore.
02.60	Visited Cochin and Gan.
12.03.60	Mombasa with *Centaur*.
17.04.60	Northbound transit of Suez Canal.
24.04.60	Arrived Chatham and declared surplus to requirements.
06.67	Towed from Chatham to be broken up by McLellan in Bo'Ness.

The Battle class destroyers were a familiar sight in the Mediterranean and in Malta in particlular.

(Portsmouth Royal Naval Museum)

HMS SAINTES

*An early image of **Saintes** still displaying her "R" pennant number.* (Steve Bush Collection)

27.04.42	Award of contract to Hawthorn Leslie.
08.06.43	Laid down.
19.07.44	Launched.
02.10.45	Lieutenant K. Alan Williams assumed command.
27.09.46	Completed.
09.46	Trials.
1947	Due to fuel shortages spent most of 1947 in port.
04.47	Refitted at Portsmouth to act as trials ship for the new Mk VI 4.5-in gun. One turret fitted in B position (*see page 68*).
Late 1947	Home Waters.
1948	Mediterranean with 3rd Destroyer Flotilla for almost two years.
08.08.49	Sailed from Portsmouth for Gibraltar.
15.08.49	Malta.
10.49	Visited Amalfi, Capri and Cyprus for Cyprus Patrol and to Beirut.
04.11.49	Malta.
Early 1950	Mediterranean with 3rd DF.
Summer 1950	Training in Maltese waters.
9-12.12.50	Malta dockyard for maintenance.
Summer 1951	On standby for Suez Crisis. She was held at Cyprus for a possible military action that never materialised.

Early 12.51	Portsmouth.
01.01.52	Sailed for Portland en route to the Mediterranean.
05.01.52	Gibraltar.
01.52	Maltese waters.
25.01.52	Tobruk.
04.04.52	Syacruse and Athens.
06.52	Exercise *Beehive II* and visited Taranto and Trieste.
01.07.52	Dragomesti.
09.52	Naples with *Armada*.
10.52	Visits to Port Suez, Famgusta and Beirut.
25.12.52	Christmas and New Year at Malta.
03.53	Returned to UK and used as Gunnery Training ship at Portsmouth. Parts of her armament were cocooned to protect them from the elements while not rquired.
11.09.53	With *Theseus* and *Daring*, rendered aid to Cyprus following a massive earthquake including the port of Paphos, which had been almost destroyed.
16.03.54	Off Malta with *St Kitts* and *Barfleur*.
19.03.54	Gibraltar.
28.03.54	Rendered aid to the troopship *Empire Windrush*, which was on fire with 1,500 servicemen and families onboard. The destroyer took the ship in tow but it sank before reaching port.
11.04.54	With the Royal Yacht *Britannia* at Naples. For three days she escorted the yacht.
05.54	Again Royal duties with *Glasgow* and *Barfleur* as *Britannia* was escorted from Gibraltar

*At anchor, **Sainte's** forward 40mm are quite evident clustered around the bridge superstructure.*   *(MoD/Crown Copyright)*

back to the UK. *Saintes* reversed course and arrived at Malta via Palermo and Sorrento on 7 August.

08.54	Gibraltar for maintenance and modernisation.
26.11.54	Returned to service.
12.54	Portsmouth.
01.55	Portland training.
29.01.55	Sailed for Gibraltar.
02-03.55	Visited Marseilles, St Raphael, Malta and Gibraltar before returning to Portsmouth.
Spring 1955	Training at Londonderry and Invergordon that also included visits to Bremen, Oslo and Tromso.
11.06.55	Rosyth.
14.06.55	Sailed for Icelandic waters and official visit to Reykjavik.
25.06.55	Great Yarmouth and later anchored off Hastings.
06.07.55	Mock attackby aircraft from *Bulwark*, staged for TV crews onboard the carrier.
07.07.55	Sailed from Hastings for Portsmouth to start a refit. On completion returned to the Mediterranean and the Cyprus Patrol.
10.55	Visits to Sicily and later Minorca, Cannes, Nice and Barcelona.
25.12.55	Alongside *Ranpura* at Malta.
01.56	Cyprus Patrol that included the capture of an ex-American corvette running guns to the island. Another trip to Beirut was organised before sailing through the Suez Canal to the Red Sea port of Aquaba.
06.56	At Malta, before sailing home to Portsmouth where she was de-commissioned.
01.08.56	Administration handed over to Senior Officer, Reserve Fleet at Portsmouth. Later towed to Rosyth for extensive two-year refit.
24.03.58	Commander L. Pearson took command.
09.58	Commissioned with *Camperdown* and *Armada* for General Service Commission in the Mediterranean and Home Waters. *Saintes* became leader of the squadron.
20.09.58	Left Portland.
24.09.58	Gibraltar.
01.10.58	Malta before visits to Tunis and Toulon.
14.03.59	Exercise *Dawn Breeze 4* for eleven days.
04.59	Exercise *MEDFLEXGUARD*.
19.04.59	Cyprus Patrol.
01.06.59	Sailed for Barcelona.
09.06.59	Sailed for Palmas Bay.
06.59	Gibraltar and transfer to Home Fleet on 26 July.
05.08.59	Portsmouth.
11.09.59	Off Invergordon for training.
Mid 9.59	Exercise *Swordthrust*.
22.09.59	Trondheim.
29.09.59	Rosyth.
10.59	Exercise *Barefoot*.
12.10.59	Operation *Lightning Strike* in Irish Sea.
2.12.59	Left Rosyth for Bremen.
11.12.59	Devonport.

1960	Returned to Mediterranean.
01.05.60	Escorted Royal Yacht off Lipari Islands whilst off Italy.
02.05.60	Naples.
06.05.60	Commander M. J. Porter assumed command.
Late Spring 60	Returned to UK.
07.60	After refit at Portsmouth *Saintes* returned to duty.
08.60	Northern British waters for training.
09.60	Exercise *Fallex*.
04.10.60	Devonport for maintenance.
21.10.60	Work up in English Channel.
24.10.60	Gibraltar.
10-11.60	Visited Malaga, Toulon, Monte Carlo and Malta, for Christmas and New Year.
01.61	Visited Almeria.
Summer 61	Dispatched to the Persian Gulf to deter Iraqi invasion of neighbouring Kuwait.
05.07.61	Off Kuwait with *Victorious*, *Centaur*, *Bulwark* and twenty other warships.
Autumn 61	Returned to the Mediterranean.
15.10.61	Off UK East Coast in bad weather with *Solebay*, *Finisterre* and *Camperdown*. Later off Welsh coast for Exercise *Smallex*.
Mid 11.61	Devonport before sailing to West Africa for Royal escort duties.
11-12.61	Visited Monrovia, Freetown and Bathurst.
5.12.61	Dakar.
16.12.61	Gibraltar.

*By April 1947 **Saintes** had been chosen to test the new 4.5-inch Mk VI mounting in the B position. This weapon was fitted at Portsmouth Dockyard. Apart from her conventional MK IV in A position she had no other gun armament.*
(Portsmouth Royal Naval Museum)

HMS Saintes is seen here wearing the broad funnel band of a Squadron Leader. Note also the associated lack of pennant numbers.
(Maritime Photo Library)

15.12.61	Devonport.
01.62	Exercises in UK waters.
21.02.62	Chatham Dockyard followed by visit to Newport (Wales).
01.03.62	Portsmouth.
03-04.62	Visited Bilbao and Cherbourg.
10.04.62	Plymouth to de-commission after collecting family and friends of the ship's company at Portsmouth earlier in the day. Selected to be a static training ship at *HMS Caledonia* at Rosyth.
18.06.62	Arrived at Rosyth under tow and replaced *Cheviot* and *Concord* in the role. For ten years *Saintes* served at *HMS Caledonia* until *Duncan* replaced her in 1972.
26.06.72	Sold.
01.09.72	Arrived at Cairn Ryan for breaking up.

Saintes Memories

Don Foxell, a Stoker Mechanic, recalls his time onboard *Saintes*, "*I joined **Saintes** in August 1955 from **HMS Vernon** after doing my auxiliary steam watchkeeping certificate on the minesweeper **Marvel**. We marched as a complete ship's company from Portsmouth Naval Barracks to the Dockyard and onto the ship, which was in dry dock and what a grubby looking thing at that! After settling in, we all had our duties outlined and cleared lower deck to meet our new skipper and staff. He was A.A. Fitzroy Talbot RN. He turned out to be the son of the famous motor car giant 'Sunbeam Talbot.' In fact he carried his own personal Sunbeam Talbot car on board, strapped*

*A dramatic overhead view of **Saintes** at speed.*   *(Edward Booker)*

on the forward torpedo tubes and hoisted on and off at various ports. The Captain had just come back from Russia, after being British naval attaché in Moscow for several years and he was a real life swash buckling Errol Flynn type character. We also carried a Commander Engineering, because we were the leader. We found later that being Captain D, we always got the inside berth whenever we docked and we didn't have to trudge across two other boats to get ashore, a bit of a privileged ship really."

"Shortly after leaving dry dock and generally cleaning the ship, we sailed for the Mediterranean and across the Bay of Biscay in a Force 9 gale. We soon acclimatised to the ship and her movements. We eventually entered the Med and berthed at Gibraltar for a week. The time at Gibraltar was spent with all hands cleaning and painting the ship (inside and out) as it was pretty dirty after being in dockyard hands. By the time we sailed for Malta the Squadron looked immaculate."

"On arrival in Malta, our ships all had their special buoys in Sliema Creek."

"We had a 'Dghiasa', a rowing boat like a gondola attached to our ship and the two brothers who ran it worked so hard and were so talented. They used to cut hair far better than a barber; their dhiasua was painted to match the ship completely. The oars, were great long ones. The craft was propelled by standing on the back end and pushing the oars in front of them and very effective it was too. They had painted these oars to match the jacket of the Captain - four and a half gold rings on a sleeve was quite artistic."

It wasn't long before the **Saintes** would become involved in the Cyprus Patrol, as Don Foxell explains, *"The object was the Archbishop Mickarios was waging a terrorist war and creating all sorts of problems with the British troops and families there."* He recalls that the patrols were usually very boring and placed great strain on the crew. *"All of us were desperately tired, being in three watches, which meant you were on watch every third watch, one full nights sleep out of three. For the nights you were on watch from midnight to four in the morning (called the middle) and next the morning (which was from four in the morning until eight) and then a full night's sleep. You came off at Midnight, washed or showered, got turned in then, up at 0700 to be on watch again at eight in the morning, week in week out. Tempers were very frayed and many arguments broke out, but rarely ended up in fighting".*

"While all these night watches were taking place the radar would be tracking anything that moved on the sea. One night our ship had a report that something was moving towards the beach, I think it was Limmasol, from the Army radar on shore. So we stopped and dropped the sea boat to investigate the mystery thing approaching the shore. It turned out to be a large rock which wasn't on the charts, so as always the lower deck was cleared, all off watch crew, to hoist the sea boat again on board. This routine happened three to four times every night, so you didn't get your full night's sleep even then."

After Cyprus patrol **Saintes** returned to Malta and dropped off a dozen, Royal Marine's from Cyprus who had been given a lift for some leave on the island. Don continues, *"We then sailed to Catania in Sicily for a run ashore. A bus trip was organised to take us as far up Mount Etna as possible, probably a thousand or so feet from the summit. Even though this was the end of October the summer was still very warm in the Mediterranean, but on Etna there was a foot of snow all around for the last three quarters of a mile climb to the top and a look into the volcano, which was always smoking."*

"From Sicily we sailed to Minorca for yet another shore run. The ship's football team took on the locals. After leaving Minorca we did more exercises that included the use of torpedoes. One day, our skipper decided to try to manoeuvre the ship alongside a fired torpedo to retrieve it. Unfortunately, he misjudged the astern manoeuvre and promptly ran this torpedo down with a hell of a thump. It split the torpedo's floating warhead which was filled with compressed air, so it would float, and it sort of exploded and sank. Many thousands of pounds of equipment were lost and the skipper looking rather sheepish."

"We sailed for the South of France, Cannes and Nice played lots of football with the locals but the run's ashore were well out of our league, money being so low and us on the millionaires' playground, we were glad

to get back to sea again. We then went to Barcelona. I and my mates always were the first to have our names down for free bus trips put on my locals and pre arranged prior to our arrival. Our trip in Barcelona was to a James Bond type of place called Monseratt very high up in the mountains and the most terrifying bus trip ever. The road or rather track wound back and forth. When we got to Monseratt all that was open was a few shops for souvenirs and a bar and the temperature was down to freezing. So all the way back, the poor driver had to stop for us to have a wee, as we'd topped ourselves up with Gold lagers which went straight through the system. We probably stopped a dozen times or more before getting back to Barcelona."

"While at sea on Remembrance Sunday 1955 we'd all changed into our No.1's for the service on the Forecastle upper deck. About an hour before, we were due to refuel from a supply ship, I think it was the **RFA Wave Emperor**, a massive ship by most standards. So we had to lift the fuel tank covers down in our deck. Some of the fuel tanks were situated under our mess deck so we had, by orders, left these two inspection lids clipped wide open. We went on deck for the service and two minutes silence and an address from the skipper. The sea was absolutely dead calm and a gorgeous sunny day. There were about eighteen ships all told cruising as a fleet when suddenly the whole fleet made a ninety degree turn to starboard. The consequence of this manoeuvre when we got back to the ladder down to the mess deck was all we could see and smell was thick black oil fuel reaching half way up the ladder into our mess, which went from one side of the ship to the other, the full width of the ship, had spilled out over 3 tons of oil fuel. Now this was a place where at least 60 stokers lived and slept, had their meals and recreation. Two or three lads took off their shoes, socks and bell bottomed trousers and gently climbed down the steps to the mess, 'mess being appropriate word'. The seating in a mess was long leather cushions on top of little lockers where all sorts of mess gear was stored and secured, the oil had flooded into these lockers so everything in these was ruined. There were lots of personal items, bits of uniforms, matelots' raincoats all dripping in this oil which was over eight inches deep right across the boat."

"Bearing in mind, most of us were in our best suits, we had to change on the upper deck into overalls, which were urgently issued to us, and some sea boots and equipped with dust pans and scoops, proceeded down to the mess to try and scoop the oil into buckets and tipped back into the open fuel tanks in the deck."

"It took most of the rest of the day to clear the surface oil, it was so slippery, especially with rubber boots on, several lads slipped up and were in a right mess, don't forget this crude fuel oil is not far short of being tar which in cold temperatures has to be pre heated to burn and run otherwise it thickens like lumps of tar."

"The oil had penetrated under the thick lino-like floor covering, so we had to rip most of that up also and this had only been renewed while we were at Portsmouth. Everything was pure chaos, most of the lads had arranged themselves in the corridors and made themselves as comfortable as possible and most still had to go down on watch. Our rum ration that day went down well and we had our meals where we could."

"We spent Christmas 1955 tied up alongside **Ranpura** as we had to renew the brickwork in our boiler furnaces and conduct a bit of a general overhaul. I'm glad we were, because the weather was foul, a Force 9 blowing and rain. In fact on Boxing Day the fleet left for sea because the ships moored in the main stream were pulling on the buoys and threatening to break loose."

"We had to go for our second spell of six weeks back to Cyprus and we picked up some more marines, who'd had leave and were going back for another spell of duty. On the first night out of Malta, in a moderate sea we showed the film, 'The Cruel Sea' with Jack Hawkins and it was on our messdeck, as we had the full width of the ship for our mess. Shortly into the film, which showed a destroyer ploughing through mountainous seas we heard the familiar sound of someone wishing to be seasick and the cry went up from us unsympathetic matelots 'Get up top Royal and let a real sailor spew'. To a roar of laughter, all but two of these unfortunate marines showed they were not quite as tough as they thought they were."

"We had a very successful tour of duty which resulted in us capturing an ex-American corvette running guns to the island's terrorists. It started with our darkened ship about 10 o'clock one night, there was no moon and

it was pitch black and no noise apart from the sea lapping our bow's. Dead calm. When all of a sudden our bright searchlight on the bridge was switched on and two hundred yards ahead of us was this corvette. Apparently we had this located on our radar for over two hours before it came into the International waters limit and had entered local waters. The whole scene was illuminated."

"The runner tried to run for it and sped up but no way could it outrun a destroyer capable of 35 knots, although she would not stop. Our skipper put a series of Bofors shots across her bows, which made us all who were on deck watching this jump out of our shoes. This action immediately halted the raider and our sea boat was dropped into the water with an armed boarding party on board and proceeded across to the other ship. We could see a lot of cargo being jettisoned over the side of this boat before our boys reached it. After a couple of hours searching that ship we escorted it to Limasol for the marines ashore to have a more detailed search."

"We sailed after this tour of duty to Beirut for a run ashore. So my mate and I both us only 5'6" tall, went ashore. What an eye opener it was, all the taxi's there and there were thousands. Most were the great big Yankee gas guzzlers, Buicks, Oldsmobiles, Chevys and Cadillacs all almost new. I can understand how easily trouble breaks out in Beirut because my mate and I had just had a meal and a drink at one of the many cafes and were walking up a road just looking for souvenirs when this big open topped lorry blocked our path and in it were about thirty Arab types all armed with sticks and knives and sword like weapons - we thought we had had it at that moment, frightened to death. However, our lives were saved and a Beirut policeman who was even shorter than us and armed only with a large staff. He got between them and us and the lorry roared away with its crew. We shook the hand of this little man and made with haste our way back to the ship as we'd found out the attitude the Arab's had for the British was hate."

*A stunning, but undated, study of **Saintes**. With the ship dressed overall and the crew at Procedure Alpha and cheering ship, it is probable that this was taken during one of her periods as escort to the Royal Yacht. (MoD/Crown Copyright)*

"A few days later we sailed for the Suez Canal, and arrived at Port Said to form up a convoy of about twenty ships of all types from oilers to liners and passenger carrying cargo boats. The canal rules were an armed warship would always lead a convoy through. It took about two days very slowly to reach Port Suez at the other end of the Red Sea. During our trip through we passed many British army camps at which the army directly they saw the white ensign they'd run like hell to the water's edge to give us a wave and exchange banter with us. We felt very sad and sorry for these poor fellows stuck in the middle of the desert with almost unbearable temperatures. We proceeded through the Red Sea for a couple of days, towing a baited shark hook and line, but no takers, the weather and sea beautiful."

"We arrived at our destination shortly after dinner time on the third day out of Suez, it was a place called Aquaba an absolute hell hole where five Middle East borders all meet and to cap it all 10,000 British troops were stationed there to keep order. One regiment was the renowned tough Scottish Black Watch, the kilt wearing boys and tough as old boots."

"Our orders were to try and brighten their dowdy boring existence up a bit by taking them out to sea around the bay and making them welcome onboard. We could only take a few hundred at a time, so we took them on at every conceivable sport and entertainment we could, football, cricket, boxing, swimming, wrestling, shooting, all sorts and they beat us soundly at all of them."

Whilst at Aqaba **Saintes** experienced a number of sandstorms. "We had four sandstorms in the ten days we were there and these deposited over three inches of sand all over the ship. It was everywhere - down on the messdecks and machinery spaces due to the giant fans sucking it into these spaces. The Army also took us to the hidden temples, a short distance into the hillsides; these were actually dug out of the solid sandstone rocks and are ancient works of art."

"The morning we sailed from Aqaba it seemed the whole ten thousand troops were at the jetty to wave farewell. About two days later **Saintes** anchored off Port Suez before the trip north which took the destroyer to Malta."

"We set sail for Portsmouth from Malta and in early June 1956 and arrived about a fortnight later after stopping off at Gibraltar. We berthed at Middle Slip jetty and four weeks leave was granted to the crew. **Saintes** was to be put into dry dock and decommissioned with the crew transferring to sister ship **Armada**. The reason given for **Saintes** docking was to repair her propeller which had been damaged during the collision with the torpedo months earlier and to repair the damage caused by the oil leak in the messdeck."

HMS SLUYS

*A pleasing study of **HMS Sluys** making very little way as she enters harbour.*   (Steve Bush Collection)

12.08.42	Ordered from Cammell Laird at Birkenhead.
24.11.43	Laid down.
28.02.45	Launched.
30.09.46	Completed.

*Sluys had two twin Bofors STAAG mountings on the after deck house, six single Bofors Mk VIII mountings posi-
tioned one on B deck abaft the gun mounting, two sited on the signal deck, two port and starboard on the midships deck house and one on the quarter deck. During her trials the ship achieved a top speed of 30.29 knots
on a displacement of 3,080 tons.*

1946	With the 1st Destroyer Flotilla.
Early 1947	Inactive for a number of months.
03.06.47	With *Cadiz* and *Vengeance* on visit to Norway.
05.06.47	Oslo.
06.47	Visited Kristiansand, Bergen, Trondheim, Mosjoen, Mo, Bodo and Tromso.
25.06.47	Rosyth.
22.07.47	Clyde Fleet Review at Greenock.
01.09.48	Devonport.
03.09.48	Mevagissy.
23.09.48	Sailed on autumn cruise to the Caribbean.

09.10.48	Port of Spain, Trinidad.
15.10.48	San Fernando and Tobago.
25.10.48	Barbados.
04.11.48	Barbuda.
09.11.48	Charleston Nevis.
21.11.48	Hamilton, Bermuda.
11.12.48	Plymouth and secured alongside *Vanguard*.
02.01.49	Commander A. J. F. Milne-Holme assumed Command.
28.01.49	Sailed to Portland.
02.49	Sailed with *Solebay* for Gibraltar.
03.02.49	Arrived at Gibraltar.
24.02.49	Algiers with *Solebay*.
14.03.49	Left Gibraltar area to visit Lisbon.
21.03.49	Sailed for Plymouth.
25.03.49	Arrived Plymouth.
01.05.49	Refit at Plymouth.
21.05.49	Small fire onboard - no damage to company Galley spaces.
16.06.49	Refit completed.
17.06.49	Sailed for Portland.
24.06.49	Mevagissy Bay with *Jutland*.
27.06.49	Portland before returning to Mevagissy Bay for more AA practice.
06.49	Penzance with French, Belgian and British ships.
07.07.49	Weymouth Bay.
08.07.49	Devonport.
07.49	Plymouth Navy Days.
17.08.49	Sailed to Gibraltar.

HMS Sluys *is pictured leaving Devonport Naval Base.* *(Steve Bush Collection)*

HMS Sluys *in the confines of Portsmouth Harbour.*   *(Steve Bush Collection)*

20.08.49	Gibraltar.
22.08.49	Malta.
08.49	Tobruk with Rear Admiral H. G. Norman, GB, CBE onboard.
29.08.49	Suez Canal.
01.09.49	Port Suez to Aquaba for Operation *Sandstorm*.
14.09.49	Lith.
16.09.49	Port Sudan.
18.09.49	Sherm Weth.
20.09.49	Northerly passage of Suez Canal.
24.09.49	Famgusta.
29.09.49	Off Rhodes.
04.10.49	His Excellency the Governor-General of Crete onboard the ship.
05.10.49	Navolion.
11.10.49	Salonika.
12.10.49	Visited Skyros and Phaleron Bay.
22.10.49	Malta where she picked up Army personnel for passage to Gibraltar.
15.11.49	Left Gibraltar.
18.11.49	Plymouth and secured on *Anson* before entering refit.
20.01.50	Refit completed.
23.01.50	Portland.
27.01.50	Sailed to Gibraltar en route exercised with *Victorious*.

02.02.50	Gibraltar.
03.50	Palmas Bay.
03.50	St Raphael with *Cadiz*. Welcomed onboard 62 French Railway workers and local school children.
14.03.50	Left St Raphael for night time encounter exercise.
16.03.50	Oran with *Gabbard* and *St Kitts*.
23.03.50	Gibraltar with aircraft carrier *Implacable*.
27.03.50	Sailed for Plymouth arriving after three days.
04.50	In dockyard hands.
22.04.50	Commander J. F. D. Bush took command.
08.05.50	Sailed from Devonport for exercises in Weymouth Bay.
09.05.50	Small fire in lifebelts, quickly put out.
15.05.50	Londonderry and Lisahally.
06.50	FOSM's Summer War in Irish Sea with *Vengeance*, *Implacable*, *Crispin*, *Creole* and other ships.
18.06.50	Rosyth.
07.50	Rosyth Navy Days.
07.50	Dornoch Firth, Scapa Flow and Orkney Islands.
10.07.50	Aalesund in Norway. 1185 people toured the ship.
17.07.50	Bergen.
24.07.50	Left Bergen for Plymouth.
27.07.50	Secured on battleship *Howe* at Devonport.
05.08.50	Plymouth Navy Days.
06.09.50	Sailed to Portland before sailing onto Gibraltar with fleet.

Any First Lieutenant would be proud if his ship looked as good as this one.   *(Maritime Photo Library)*

19.09.50	Exercise *Easy Prey*.
20.09.50	Gibraltar.
30.09.50	Tangiers.
10.50	Casablanca.

Keith Miller recalls an incident when the ship came across a sinking vessel. "It was a broken down smugglers boat going from North Africa to the south of France. She was in a waterlogged condition when we found her and cartons of cigarettes and packets of nylon stockings were floating around. In our attempts to "rescue" the goods, a guardrail gave way and several sailors went for a swim." Less appealing was the ships collection of rodents. "The ship had a population of rats and to encourage the ships company to eliminate them the first lieutenant awarded one shilling for each rat caught, but he was a bit squeamish and wanted only the rat's tails as proof. In the boiler room the rats lived in wooden shavings in the spare gear boxes and would venture around the auxiliary fuel pumps for fresh water where we dispatched them with pokers and sawed off their tails with hacksaws. They also lived in the wooden shores and planks stored just forward of the funnel. So one day the ships company were ordered to clear the racks of timber and kill the rats. You can imagine a still sunny day in the Med, the ship stopped and the upper deck amok with the crew chasing rats with brooms!"

04.11.49	Gibraltar.
27.11.49	Left Gibraltar for Lorient.
1.12.49	Secured on **Solebay** at the Petroleum Jetty.
04.12.49	Sailed for Devonport.
07.12.49	Devonport.
1951	Festival of Britain tour which included visits to Ifracombe and Liverpool.
10.12.51	Commander David Granville Clutterbuck took command.
31.07.52	Exchanged ship's company with **Cadiz** whilst at Devonport.
1952	Visited Gibraltar, Malta and Londonderry.
23.07.53	Ceremonial marchpast of crew to Royal Naval Barracks following decommissioning. **Sluys** remained in reserve for 13 years.
07.66	General Rezvani of the Imperial Iranian Naval delegation agreed to pay £37,500 for **Sluys**, which was renamed **IIS Artemiz**.

In a memo dated 21 November 1966 it states that "there is easily ten years of economical life left in it To install new machinery would take up to two years to design and at least two years to manufacture and fit." Amongst the many design modifications discussed was the installation of Type 164 sonar to replace the elderly Type 144. Another was the installation of Type 170 sonar with an Anti submarine Limbo mortar Mk10. In fact five pages of detailed recommendations were submitted to the Iranians by the MoD to the Imperial Navy which General Toufanian agreed to on 28 October 1966.

   The scale of the design changes and their cost implications raised some concerns with Vosper Thornycroft who had won the contract to recondition the ship. Mr A. A. C. Griffith, OBE wrote to D. G. Seymour at the MOD (Naval) Sales department. "As I am sure you appreciate, it would be madness, and in fact quite impossible, to quote a fixed price for the refit in advance of thoroughly surveying the ship, opening up machinery and checking and testing the various components of the weapons systems. The arrangements outlined in this draft letter of intent would allow us to carry out all this survey work and prepare a detailed specification with a fixed price quotation and at the same time, be progressing the basic hull work and the ordering of long lead items.

   Our own experience, and I believe that of the Royal Dockyards as well, suggests that a fair number of water-

Stripped of her lattice mast the former **HMS Sluys** is seen under conversion at Vosper Thornycroft to become the Iranian **Artemiz**. *(Maritime Photo Library)*

line plates may require renewal and this in turn, could lead to the re-running of main run cables all of which is very fundamental stuff and must be carried out before we can make any worthwhile progress on the fitting of accommodation."

The cost of the accommodation changes to the **Artimez** amounted to £85,000, a not insubstantial amount of money back in 1966.

Ray Freeman joined Vosper Thornycroft in the summer of 1968 as a Weapons Engineer to support the shipyard's work on Mk 5 Destroyers being built for the Iranian Navy at the time. *"On joining I was immediately dispatched to the company's ship repair division based at Southampton docks where the conversion of **Sluys** was underway. My brief was to become familiar with the new equipment being fitted. This included the new Contraves Sea-Hunter digital fire control system, a Plessey AWS1 surveillance radar and the Short Bros, lightweight Sea Cat system. In the event I spent most of the time along with a colleague, testing and tuning the two 4.5-inch gun mountings and re-commissioning the Squid anti submarine mortar system."*

Ray Freeman remembers that the project was an enjoyable experience. *"A large set up was in place to support the refit and the whole team integrated well with the Iranian crew members being very easy to work with and they all seemed to be greatly enjoying their time spent in the UK."*

"The weapons programme went well. The new equipment fitted into the space vacated by that removed and quite frankly you would have thought that the ship had been designed with that in mind. The Swiss engineers, who were extremely professional, were also good to get on with although I would say that it took them a little time to relax and to take life a bit less seriously. I do remember that we spent an extremely long time carrying out the combined machinery and weapon sea trials."

The ships' bridge was fully enclosed and the new trunk-foremast carried the main fire control radar tracking head. The boat davits were re-arranged and those for the motor cutter were of the power operated 'gravity' pattern. Although the torpedo tubes were replaced by a continuous superstructure, their davits were retained for

general purposes. The single Bofors gun abaft the funnel and abaft the mainmast was covered, as was the special triple Seacat missile launcher on the after end of the superstructure.

Ray Freeman, (now Chief Combat Systems Engineer at Vosper Thornycroft) remembers some of the changes that were demanded by Sluys new owners. "Apart from my own specialisation, there was a major improvement in the area of the Commanding Officers accommodation. A bath with gold fittings was installed and it was said that the standard of that area had to be suitable for the Shah should he ever come on board."

Once the ship had been refitted and prepared to sail she welcomed aboard her Iranian crew. They took the Artemiz to sea and on her journey to Iran called into Portland to exercise with the Royal Navy. It was on 12 February 1970 that the destroyer grounded within the very well marked harbour. However, only weeks later, she arrived in Iran having sailed through the Mediterranean and the Suez Canal.

12.02.70	*Artemiz* grounded in Portland harbour whilst on trials.
	Soon afterwards sailed to Iran via Mediterranean and Suez Canal.
1975-76	Refitted at Cape Town given Standard surface to air missiles.

Between 1975 and 1976 Artemiz was refitted in Capetown, South Africa where she was refitted with four GMC Standard surface to air missile boxed missile launchers for SM-1MR anti-aircraft missiles. These were sited amidships behind the funnel.

1979	Following the fall of the Shah, *Artemiz* became part of the New Iranian Navy and took part in the Iran/Iraq War.
1985	Renamed *Damavand* and lost the Sea Cat missiles.
1996	Reportedly broken up in Iran.

The new enclosed bridge and two new plated in masts are apparent in this undated mid-conversion photograph.
(T. Ferrers Walker Collection)

Sluys Memories

Dick McBurney joined **Sluys** on 14 December 1950. He remembers that he joined "*the after messdeck inhabited by Quartermasters and Boatswains Mates. My job was to assist the QM in his duties attending the gangway in harbour. When at sea, whilst the QM steered the ship, I was on the bridge broadcasting orders over the ships internal broadcast system, running messages for the officer of the watch or making his Kai, a very thick cocoa.*"

"*I remember in Gibraltar when all the ships of the flotilla were in port we were ordered to "clear lower deck" and send ship's companies to the sports fields, adjacent to the Fleet Canteen. Once there we were addressed by a very important personage, either Lord Louis Mountbatten or Sir Phillip Vian. The squadron split up after a combined exercise in the area. There would be two rows of ships facing each other a mile or two apart. They then headed towards each other at an incredible rate of knots and race each other, passing between the two rows of opposing ships at just a few cables apart. Thereafter the squadron split up again and visited various places in the Mediterranean. **Sluys** went to Cannes. I remember someone pointing out a large steam yacht which belonged to Erroyl Flynn. We had onboard at this time a man called Lionel Gamlin. He was well known in the UK for his radio programmes and for narrating the Movietone News films in the cinema. He came with us on sight seeing trips in coaches around Grasse, Nice, Menton and other places. I do remember the girls in the perfumeries sprinkling perfume over our navy collars.*"

G.B. Cowley recollects a dramatic situation whilst onboard the ship. "*I was the buoy jumper for about two and half years and had quite a few near misses. On 19 January 1951 it was snowing and blowing a gale. I was on the buoy for about four hours. The picking up wire parted and I fell in the sea. I somehow managed to swim back to the buoy and I finally managed to shackle the ship to the buoy after four hours. I was told later, that four others had fallen into the sea (from the other ships) and I was the only one to survive.*"

Dick McBurney remembers that in 1951 **Sluys** was given the task of meeting the navy to co-incide with the Festival of Britain. "***Sluys** went off on a "meet the public" trip. We were fortunate enough to draw a visit to Ifracombe where we anchored off shore. Then we went on to Liverpool. They did us proud. We received free passes to the overhead railway, and some of us went on a coach trip to Wales where we visited the John Summers steel factory.*"

G.B. Cowley remembers that 1951 saw the ship visiting Norway with visits to Stavanger and Bergen. "*We then went to the Island of Arran. But Captain D gave each ship a task and we had to build a pier there.*"

Dick McBurney witnessed **Sluys** exercising her main armament against Cape Wraith on numerous occasions. "*At some point **St James** went with us to an island, possibly Inchmarnock. One ship went to each side of the island early in the morning and landed their ship's company with instructions to climb to the top of the mountain and do battle with the "clan" we would find at the top. This was supposed to be a re-enactment of some past Scottish battle. It was my task to provide bag meals for the members of my mess going on this expedition. I remember constructing very large Cornish pasties, moulded round a large dinner and filled with a secret ingredient - corned beef. I never discovered whether or not these were eaten by the men or used as missiles against the enemy!*"

HMS SOLEBAY

*An early photograph of **HMS Solebay** showing depth charge racks and throwers on the quarterdeck.*

(Maritime Photo Library)

03.02.43	Laid down.
22.02.44	Launched at Hawthorn Leslie.
11.10.45	Completed.
27.03.46	Chatham Dockyard.
29.03.46	Sailed for trials and work up at Portland.
04.46	Got as far as Malta before being recalled to Home Fleet as Captain (D) 5th Destroyer Flotilla.
07.46	Anchored off Southwold in Suffolk, scene of the Battle of Solebay.
02.09.46	Chatham Dockyard.
1946	*Operation Deadlight*. The sinking of captured German U-boats 150 miles North East of Ireland. **Solebay** sank one submarine using 11 rounds of 4.5-inch ammunition.
1946	**Solebay** became German Waters Guard ship and visited Wilhelmshaven, Cuxhaven, Kiel, Flensburg and Hamburg.
22.11.46	Returned to Chatham Dockyard for extensive refit.
22.07.47	Clyde Fleet Review at Greenock.

22.07.47	King George VI, Queen Elizabeth and Princesses Elizabeth and Margaret welcomed onboard.
Late 1947	While at sea off Tyne was damaged by depth charges during display for shipyard workers from Hawthorn Leslie.
13.08.47	Chatham Dockyard.
17.09.47	Sailed to join flotilla on cruise to West Indies. Also spent time in Scottish waters.
Late 1947	Operating from Chatham Dockyard.
16.02.48	In Home waters.
26.07.48	In Dockyard hands at Chatham.
09.09.48	Weymouth Bay at start of summer cruise to Caribbean with the battleship **Duke of York**.
10.48	Visited San Fortin, San Fernando, Trinidad, Tobago, Kingston and St Vincent.
11.48	Islands visited in November included Castrias, St Lucia, Monserratt, Beef Island and Bermuda.
06.12.48	Azores.
13.12.48	Chatham Dockyard.
28.01.49	Portland.
04.02.49	Sailed with **Aisne** and **Jutland** for Gibraltar and onward journey to Malta.
24.02.49	Tangiers.

HMS Solebay *on a Mediterranean port visit. The tower in the background must be a recognisable landmark, but the author was unable to identify this port.*
(Steve Bush Collection)

This aerial view of **HMS Solebay** *gives a good idea of the layout of the Battle class destroyer.* (MoD/Crown Copyright)

Mid 03.49	Lisbon with **Duke of York**, **Alamein** and **Barrosa**.
21.03.49	Chatham Dockyard for self-maintenance period.
02.05.49	Sailed to join 5th DF at Portland.
05.49	Operation *Vestry* off Penzance.
27.06.49	Sailed with **Theseus** for Guernsey
08.08.49	Captain T V Briggs OBE took command at Chatham.
06.10.49	Sailed to join Home and Mediterranean Fleets.
24.11.49	Chatham Dockyard.
24.01.50	Portland.
02.02.50	Gibraltar.
02.50	Visited Palmas, St Raphael and Oran.
31.02.50	Chatham Dockyard.
08.05.50	Sailed for Londonderry and Portland with **Gabbard**, **St Kitts** and **Sluys**.
06.50	FOSM's Summer War in Irish Sea and Loch Ewe.
18.06.50	Rosyth for Navy Days.
04.07.50	Sailed to operate with **Sluys** in Orkney areas.

10.07.50	Aalesund in Norway for a 10-day visit followed by further visit to Bergen.
27.07.50	Chatham Dockyard.
05.09.50	Sailed to join *Vanguard* on cruise to Gibraltar.
12.10.50	Operated with Canadian destroyers and *HMCS Magnificent* before visiting St Vincent in the Cape Verde Islands.
11.50	Visited Casablanca and Lorient.
07.12.50	Sailed Portsmouth.
08.12.50	Arrived Chatham Dockyard.
15.01.51	Sailed to Portland.
17.01.51	From Portland to Gibraltar with *Swiftsure* and *Cadiz*.
15.02.51	Leghorn for 5-days before visiting Golfe Juan and Gibraltar on 5 March.
10.03.51	Exercise *Foxhunt* with *Vanguard*.
15.03.51	Sheerness and later same day Chatham Dockyard.
06.51	Portland areas.
14.07.51	4-day visit to Southampton before calling at Great Yarmouth and Southwold in Suffolk.
26.07.51	Chatham Dockyard.
10.51	In Scottish and Northern Irish waters.
15.10.51	Sailed from Falmouth for Gibraltar.
07.12.51	Chatham Dockyard.
15.01.52	Sailed for Portland and onward journey to Gibraltar for Exercise *Grand Slam*.
06.03.52	St Maxime.
31.03.52	Sheerness to off load ammunition before going onto Chatham Dockyard.
04.04.52	Captain J. G. Hamilton took command.
04.52	Gibraltar and Malta.
23.04.52	Phaleron Bay for unveiling of memorial to war dead by King Paul of the Hellenes.
08.05.52	Chatham Dockyard.
08.52	Exercise *Mainbrace*.
01.10.52	Rosyth.
10.52	Invergordon, Irish Sea and Londonderry areas.
11.12.52	Chatham Dockyard.
20.01.53	Sailed for duties in Home Waters and Mediterranean.
02.53	Off Gibraltar.
19.03.53	Visited Vigo for 4-days.
28.03.53	Malta.
14.04.53	Naples and secured on Molo Anginino alongside *St James*.
08.05.53	After visits to Malta and Gibraltar arrived at Chatham Dockyard
28.05.53	Sailed to take part in Coronation Review at Spithead.
24.06.53	Refit at Chatham, Squid launcher replaced original depth charges, STAAG mounting fitted along with improved radar. At the end of refit *Solebay* was reduced to reserve.
04.56	Work started to re-activate *Solebay*.
17.07.56	Post restoration refit trials commenced within Chatham Dockyard.
08.56	Sea trials.
16-17.09.56	*Solebay* was experimental test ship for Exercise *Sleeping Beauty*. This was a trial to see how quickly a mothballed ship could be re-activated. *Solebay* took a month to become fully operational once again.

HMS Solebay, *a workhorse of the immediate post-war Royal Navy, looking impressive in a swell.* *(John Brewer)*

16.05.57	Sailed for Portsmouth.
28.05.57	Re-commissioned as leader of 1st Destroyer Squadron. After work up at Portland, she sailed with the squadron for Malta.
16.07.57	Sailed from Malta with **Lagos**, **Armada** and **Hogue**. Next nine months spent in Mediterranean with frequent exercises with French, Italian and American forces.
09.03.58	Gibraltar.
10.03.58	Cadiz for 5-day visit
20.03.58	Lisbon and secured on Cais de Roche in the city.
30.03.58	Arrived at Chatham Dockyard.
05.58	Sailed to Forth Exercise Areas and Dornoch Firth, Cape Wrath and Scapa Flow.
05.58	Visited Loch Eriboll, Invergordon, Rosyth and Harwich.

*The ships company cheer ship as **HMS Solebay** steams past the Royal Yacht in May 1960.*   *(MoD/Crown Copyright)*

10.06.58	Gothenburg and onward journey to Aarhus.
25.06.58	Overnight passage of Kiel Canal.
25.06.58	Arrived at Den Helder to exercise with Dutch warships.
30.06.58	Sheerness.
06.07.58	Loch Foyle for exercises.
07.58	Visited Londonderry, Lisahally, Portrush and Bangor and operated with **Albion**. At the end of the exercise **Solebay** sailed for Portsmouth.
08.58	Portsmouth Navy Days.
16.09.58	At Rosyth before Exercise *Ship Shape*.
09.58	Portsmouth.
13.10.58	Sailed for Portland.
16.10.58	Was due to sail to Londonderry, but instead sailed for the Mediterranean.
11.58	Off Malta.
12.12.58	Portland to Portsmouth.
12.58	Remained at sea over the festive period.
10.01.59	Portsmouth.
01.59	Plymouth to join **Llandaff** and **Hogue** on journey to Gibraltar.
02.59	Exercise *Dawn Breeze*.
23.02.59	Left Gibraltar for Lisbon with **Apollo** and **Tyne**.
04.03.59	Led **Lagos** and **Hogue** out of Lisbon in line ahead.
03.59	Plane guard duties to **Eagle** and **Victorious**.

24.03.59	Chatham Dockyard.
14.05.59	Off Rosyth with **Hogue** and later Rosyth Navy Days.
19.05.59	Exercised with **Gambia** in Moray Firth.
05.59	Visited Plymouth, Brest and Lisbon.
04.06.59	Rendezvoused with **Hogue**, **Llandaff** and **Centaur** off Portugal en route to Gibraltar.
11.06.59	Anchored in Pinto Bay with **Delight** and **Birmingham**.
17.06.59	Malta.
06.59	Operated with **USS Intrepid** and Exercise *Whitebait*.
26.06.59	Tobruk before sailing for Port Said and Suez Canal.
07.59	Aden and Exercise *Shop Window* in Persian Gulf.
16.07.59	Umm Said for 4 days before going onto Dubai.
31.07.59	Karachi for exercises including Exercise *Jet* around Cochin and Trincomalee.
25.08.59	**Hogue** rammed by **INS Mysore**. **Solebay** and **Lagos** assist **Hogue** to Trincomalee.
28.08.59	At Trincomalee before sailing onto Singapore.
10.59	Started journey home to United Kingdom which included visits to Malta and Gibraltar before arriving home for Christmas.
Early 1960	Home waters.
26.03.60	Left Gibraltar for Exercise *Dawn Breeze V*.
01.04.60	Portsmouth for refit.
Spring 1960	Home waters.
04.60	Chatham Dockyard.
04.60	Leader of 1st DS, following amalgamation of 1st and 3rd DSs.
04.60	Worked up around Portland before deploying to Mediterranean to relieve 7th DS at Malta.
01.05.60	Met Royal Yacht **Britannia** off Lipari Island with the cruiser **Lion** to escort the Queen to Naples.
Summer 1960	Returned to United Kingdom for leave.
21.10.60	Dummy torpedo attack on Eddystone lighthouse with **Saintes** and **Camperdown**.
22.10.60	Sailed for Gibraltar in bad weather conditions.
04.11.60	Malaga.
11.60	Visited Toulon for Exercise *MEDASWEX* in Gulf of Lions.
26.11.60	Malta.
12.60	Palermo.
13.12.60	**Solebay** collided with **Trafalgar** in Malta's Sliema Creek. **Solebay** remained at Malta over Christmas for repairs.
Early 1961	Royal visits to Italy and red carpet for the King and Queen of Greece. Queen Elizabeth visited Venice and **Solebay** was escort for the occasion. **Solebay** went on to escort **Britannia** on a visit to the battlefields of Gallipoli.
04.09.61	Sailed from Malta to Gibraltar.
14.09.61	Sheerness to de-store.
15.10.61	Having arrived at Portland was joined by **Camperdown**, **Finisterre** and **Saintes** to sail to Scottish waters in heavy weather.
21.10.61	Scapa Flow with **Centaur** for Exercise *Smallex*.
15.11.61	Portsmouth.
11.61	Again became Royal escort to **Britannia** on tour of West Africa. Visited Takoradi, Dakar, the Gambia and Sierra Leone. **Solebay** stole the show at Freetown when illuminated at night.

HMS Solebay *at Venice in company with the Royal Yacht* **Britannia**. *(Ben Warlow Collection)*

15.12.61	Portsmouth.
12.01.62	Sailed for exercises.
02.02.62	Returned to Portsmouth for radio trials.
26.02.62	Final visit to Southwold in Suffolk.
03.03.62	Portsmouth.
Spring 62	Visited La Havre, Greenock and Bilboa.
07.03.62	Bordeaux with *Saintes*, *Camperdown* and *Finisterre*.
08.04.62	Arrived Portsmouth to decommission.
01.62	Became harbour training ship at Portsmouth.
11.08.67	Arrived at Troon to be broken up.

HMS ST JAMES

HMS St James *early on in her career, still awaiting the fitting of her AA armament aft.* (Steve Bush Collection)

12.08.42	Ordered from Fairfield Shipbuilders at Govan.
20.05.43	Laid down.
07.06.45	Launched.
12.07.46	Completed.
Late 1946	Joined 5th DF.
25.08.46	Accidentally sank the tug *Buccaneer* off Portland with a 4.5-inch shell.

During calibration trials off Portland St James fired a 4.5-inch shell at a target being towed by the tug Buccaneer. The tug, however, was struck by the shell under the rubbing strake at the after end of the engine room, while another shell plunged close to the counter. Lieutenant Commander S. E. Veal MBE RN (Rtd) in command of the Buccaneer, ordered that a collision mat be placed over the hole but this failed to check the inrush of water. At the same time the loss of steam prevented the effective use of the ship's salvage pump. The St James, under the command of Commander J. Lee Barker DSO RN, whose "B" turret had fired the fatal shot, closed the tug and went alongside to take off the crew. This was achieved successfully but twenty-five minutes after being hit the Buccaneer started to settle. The craft became vertical, heeled over while vertical and sank in under a minute, catching St James while doing so. This damaged the destroyer's starboard propeller over a length of 2 foot six inches and gouged eight inches into the metal of the blades.

All concerned with the loss of the Buccaneer were ordered to assemble onboard the cruiser Superb at 0900 on Wednesday 28 August 1946 at a board of inquiry. Those in attendance were Captain W. G. A. Robson, DSO, DSC RN of Superb, President of the inquiry. Also in attendance were Commander H. F. Bone, DSO, DSC RN from the battleship Howe and Lt Commander T. K. Jones RN from the battleship Nelson. Commander J. Lee

*Barber from **St James** attended the inquiry along with Lt J. Lind Holmes and Lt F. C. B. Cotland Griffiths and other members of the ship's company. The board of inquiry decided that no action would be taken against Commander Barber in regard to the incident.*

30.08.46	Chatham.
01.47	With **Vanguard** on start of Royal Tour of Africa before visiting Lisbon.
05.47	Damaged when the keelplate was buckled. Repairs were undertaken at Devonport.
22.07.47	Clyde Fleet Review at Greenock.
03.10.47	At Scarborough for seven days.
03.09.48	Visited St Austell before returning to Portland at start of Home Fleet Autumn Cruise to the Caribbean, which started on 23 September 1948.
10.48	Visited Antigua, Tobago and Barbados.
03.11.48	Kingston, Jamaica.
11.11.48	Sailed to visit Norfolk Virginia with the battleship **Duke of York**.
16.11.48	Washington D.C.
25.11.48	At Bermuda before returning to UK via the Azores.
12.12.48	Devonport.
28.01.49	Sailed to Portland to undertake Exercise *Eurostep*, an ASW exercise involving the submarine **Astute**.
01.02.49	Sailed to Gibraltar.
17.02.49	Visited Tangier Bay before returning to Gibraltar, where she remained until 16 March, when she sailed for the UK.
24.03.49	Devonport.
02.05.49	Commander C. W. Malins DSO, DSC took command.
24.06.49	After a refit **St James** carried out a lengthy series of trials at Devonport and Portland.
06.49	Operation *Verity* off the Lizard with French and Dutch warships.
04.07.49	With **Theseus** in the English Channel.
15.07.49	Bournemouth and opened to the public.
14.07.49	St Peter Port on Guernsey. Opened to the public.
20.07.49	Plymouth.
26.07.49	Type 262 radar installed.
07.09.49	Penzance.
09.09.49	With the cruiser **Cleopatra** and destroyers **Barrosa** and **Agincourt** and the aircraft carrier **Implacable**.
Autumn 49	In Scottish waters for training exercises.
21.11.49	Devonport.
23.01.50	Sailed for Portland.
27.01.50	Sailed with Home Fleet on cruise to the Mediterranean with **Victorious**, **Implacable**, **Vanguard** and **Superb**.
02.50	Visited Palmas Bay, St Raphael and Oran.
27.03.50	Sailed from Gibraltar for the UK.
15.04.50	Londonderry.
08.05.50	Loch Ewe and Exercises in Western Approaches.
Spring 50	Scottish waters for training exercises.
Summer 50	FOSM's Summer War with **Vengeance**, **Implacable** and seven destroyers.

20.06.50	Rosyth for flotilla regatta.
01.07.50	Rosyth Navy Days.
04.07.50	Sailed for Scapa Flow.
10.07.50	Uddevalla in Sweden.
17.07.50	Frederickshaven.
27.07.50	Devonport including Navy Days.
02.11.50	Sailed for Gibraltar.
29.11.50	Visited Lisbon enroute UK.
29.12.50	Commander D. F. Townsend took command.
21.01.51	Gibraltar for training.
10.03.51	Returned to UK.
11.03.51	Exercise *Foxhunt* with **Vanguard.**
14.03.51	Devonport.
05.51	Scottish waters including visits to Invergordon and Rosyth on 26 May.
01.06.51	Anchored in Dovarnenez Bay south of Brest to take part in Exercise *Progress* in Bay of Biscay.
08.06.51	Cherbourg.
15.06.51	Lamlash with **Swiftsure**, **Agincourt** and **Gabbard.**
18.06.51	Glasgow where she was open to the public and afterwards sailed for Invergordon.
04.07.51	Tynemouth's Albert Edward Dock.
10.07.51	Filey Bay. Spent six-days at anchor.
17.07.51	Southend-on-Sea with **Vengeance** for another six-day visit.
30.07.51	Devonport.
10.51	Visits to Invergordon, Belfast and Loch Eriboll.

HMS St James *was among a number of Battle class present at the 1953 Coronation Fleet Review.*

(Maritime Photo Library)

15.10.51	Brief stop at Falmouth before continuing onto Gibraltar.
Christmas 51	At Devonport.
01.52	Sailed to the Mediterranean to be based at Malta.
27.05.52	Commander H. A. Stuart Menteth took command.
26.01.53	Cruises to Gibraltar with *Theseus*, *Swiftsure* and *Barrosa*.
19.03.53	Escorted *Eagle* on visit to the Spanish port of Vigo before returning to Malta.
11.04.53	Admiral Earl Louis Mountbatten visited the ship for 30 minutes.
14.04.53	Visited Naples and secured alongside Molo Anginino.
27.04.53	Sailed for the UK.
06.05.53	Devonport.
09.06.53	Sailed to Portland for start of Coronation Review in the Solent.
12.06.53	On Line D between *Finisterre* and *Cadiz* at the Review.
19.06.53	Plymouth and later put into Reserve Fleet.
Late 1957	Refit commenced to re-activate the destroyer.
1958	Work abandoned and *St James* placed on the disposal list. She was used for trials for a time within Devonport Dockyard.
19.03.61	Arrived at Cashmore's in Newport, Wales to be broken up.

HMS St James *ended her Royal Navy career in 1957 and went to the breakers in 1961.*   (Maritime Photo Library)

HMS ST KITTS

Bathed in sunlight, **HMS St Kitts** *at anchor.*   *(Steve Bush Collection)*

27.04.42	Ordered from Swan Hunters.
08.09.43	Laid down.
04.10.44	Launched.
31.07.45	Lieutenant Commander J. T. B. Birch DSO, DSC took command.
21.01.46	Completed.
Summer 46	With 5th DF in the Home Fleet.
10.01.47	Sailed from Chatham for Royal Tour of South Africa with *Vanguard*.
07.02.47	King George VI and Queen Elizabeth toured the destroyer.
27.03.47	Chatham Dockyard.
30.04.47	Sailed for duties in Home and Mediterranean waters.
22.07.47	Clyde Fleet Review at Greenock.
04.08.47	Lieutenant C. H. R. Wynn took command.
14.08.47	Chatham for refit.
16.02.48	Sailed for sea trials.
03.09.48	St Austell and Portland in preparation for autumn cruise to the Caribbean.
15.12.48	Chatham for maintenance.
02.49	Operation *Rusty*, with *Gabbard* in the Arctic to determine the effects of ice and cold on ships, equipment and men before returning to Chatham at the beginning of March.
18.06.49	Mevagissy.
07.49	Operation *Verity*.

21.07.49	Chatham for another refit.
09.49	Scottish waters for training including visits to Invergordon, Lamlash and Lossiemouth.
11.11.49	Portland.
27.01.50	Lieutenant Commander G. A. G. Ormsby, DSO, took command at Chatham.
03.50	Sailed for the Mediterranean.
17.03.50	Oran.
05.50	Portland and Londonderry for training.
06.50	Exercise *Unite* with **Corunna**, **Contest**, **Fleetwood** and **Redpole** in the Irish Sea and SouthWestern Approaches.
04.07.50	Sailed for Moray Firth.
07.50	Visited Egesund, Amsterdam and spent four days at Lowestoft.
26.07.50	Arrived Chatham.
Autumn 50	Home Fleet Cruise to the Mediterranean.
20.09.50	Gibraltar.
12.10.50	Leixos and onwards to Casablanca.
11.50	Off Gibraltar.
27.11.50	Nantes.
16.01.51	Sailed from Chatham for Portland.
21.01.51	Gibraltar with **Swiftsure** and remained at Gibraltar until March.
Summer 51	Visits to Portrush, Southampton, Spithead and Folkestone.
31.07.51	Commander E. N. Sinclair DSC took command and sailed to Scottish waters for training.
Summer 51	Chatham for maintenance period.

HMS St Kitts *at anchor for the 1953 Coronation Review of the Fleet.* *(Portsmouth Royal Naval Museum)*

HMS St Kitts *coming alongside a much larger vessel to take on some fuel.* (MoD/Crown Copyright)

08.51	Sailed to Clyde for NATO exercise. Later escorted the aircraft carrier **Ocean** through the Suez Canal and into the Red Sea.
Autumn 51	Visited Massawa, Port Sudan and struck a jetty at Port Suez during a sandstorm damaging the bow. Repairs were carried out at Malta.
Winter 51	Visited Nice, Cannes and Monte Carlo.
11.12.51	Chatham.
23.01.52	Sailed for Portland and thence to the Mediterranean.
26.01.52	Gibraltar.
03.52	Exercise *Grand Slam* before visiting St Raphael.
08.05.52	Chatham.
06.51	Exercise *Castinets*.
26.06.52	Filey.

07.51	Amsterdam.
10.07.52	Sheerness to de-store ammunition. Once completed **St Kitts** proceeded up the River Medway to Chatham and commenced a refit.
17.02.53	Sailed from Chatham to Portland and onwards to Gibraltar.
10.03.53	Commander F. B. P. Brayne-Nicholls, DSC took command. On the same day exchanged ship's companies with **Gravelines** whilst alongside at Gibraltar.
Spring 53	Combined exercises and visits to Vigo, Malta and Naples.
19.05.53	Plymouth.
16.06.53	Coronation Review at Spithead, anchored between **Barfleur** and **Camperdown**.
06.53	Visited Milford Haven and exercised with **Theseus.**
21.06.53	Gibraltar.
27.06.53	Malta.
07.53	Exercises in Maltese waters and a visit to Athens.
27.07.53	Istanbul for four-days.
10.53	Exercise *Weldfest* off Malta.
24.10.53	Suez Canal while tension existed in region, with **Saintes** and **Wrangler**.
04.12.53	Fire in 'A' gunhouse off Ismaila. No damage nor injuries.
10.12.53	Malta.
11.01.54	At sea for exercises with **Barfleur**, **Glasgow** and **Bermuda**.
01.54	A Comet airliner crashed near Elba, **St Kitts** searched the seabed for wreckage.
03.54	Rescued servicemen from troopship **Empire Windrush** before taking survivors of the

*This time a light jackstay transfer with the cruiser **HMS Glasgow** in a late evening sun.* (MoD/Crown Copyright)

HMS St Kitts *leaving Portsmouth Harbour.*

(Portsmouth Royal Naval Museum)

	fire to Malta.
03.54	Exercise *Toughline* off Gibraltar with **Indefatigable**.
07.54	In Maltese waters and a visit to Tripoli.
Summer 54	Visited Palermo and Sorrento and Malta.
04.11.54	Malta.
24.11.54	Catonia in Sicily before visiting Leghorn four days later.
25.11.54	Gibraltar.
14.01.55	Devonport.
16.01.55	Portland.
02.55	Visited Marseilles, St Raphael followed by Malta in March.
01.04.55	Devonport.
25.04.55	Bremen.
04.55	Training off Londonderry and Invergordon.
01.06.55	Plymouth for refit.
30.10.55	Gibraltar.
01.11.55	Sailed for Malta.
04.11.55	At Malta.
13.12.55	Cyprus Patrol.
01.56	Malta.

23.01.56	Sailed to visit Beirut with *Armada*, *Ulysses*, *Undine*, *Chieftain* and *Retainer*.
20.02.56	Sailed through Suez Canal to Aqaba.
02.56	Commander A. D. Bulman took command.
Spring 56	Visited Cannes, Barcelona and Malta before returning to UK in late summer.
21.09.56	Invergordon for CASEX 6 with submarine *Sea Devil*.
Autumn 56	Mediterranean for Operation *Musketeer*, Suez Canal operation.
Winter 56	*St Kitts* escorted *Bulwark* and tanker *Tiderace*.
08.12.56	Anchored in Port Said.
10.12.56	Ordered to return to UK and refit at Portsmouth.
19.03.57	Refit completed.
03.57	Worked up off Portland.
21.04.57	Operated with *Albion* and *Barfleur*.
29.04.57	St Paul's Bay, Malta.
Summer 57	Cyprus Patrol.
07.57	Exercised with cruisers *Birmingham*, *Kenya*, *USS Newport News* and *USS Salem*. Followed by visits to Sardinia and Augusta.
08.57	At Malta.
13.08.57	3rd DS regatta at Augusta.
19.09.57	Malta.
10.10.57	Devonport and crew transferred to *Camperdown*. *St Kitts* taken to lay up berth off Wilcove in the Hamoaze to await disposal.
19.02.62	Arrived at Young shipyard in Sunderland to be scrapped.

HMS TRAFALGAR

HMS Trafalgar was completed too late to see wartime service, but sailed for the Far East after the war had ended.
(Steve Bush Collection)

15.02.43	Laid down at Swan Hunters Wallsend shipyard.
12.01.44	Launched.
08.44	Laid up awaiting the delivery of a director tower.
09.07.45	Captain A F Pugsley CBE, DSO took command.
23.07.45	Completed.
Autumn 45	Sea trials over the Skelmorlie course.
Autumn 45	Off Malta - a premature firing of one of the 4.5-inch guns destroyed one of the two barrels in "B" turret. Repairs undertaken at Malta.

Francis John Bate joined the ship at Greenock as a Boy Telegraphist on July 31 1945 and recalls the incident: The gun was fired but essentially destroyed one of the two barrels. The barrel was peeled back to the sleeve. Large bits of the weapon showered down onto the deck and into the canteen flat. Thankfully, no one was injured in the incident. So with fifty percent of our main armament out of action the ship was obviously useless as an addition to the anti kamikaze situation. Therefore, it seemed, Captain D would transfer to another ship and **Trafalgar** *would have to return to the United Kingdom for best repairs. The reality, however, was very different. We raced back to Malta. With the European war over it was possible to dock the ship under floodlights and the work was carried out at night. The work involved ripping out the damaged barrel and then it was replaced with a wooden*

log which had been sanded and painted to look like a proper barrel - from a distance you couldn't tell the difference from the real thing!

Late 45	Joined the 19th DF with ***Barfleur*** and ***Armada*** and went onto visit Singapore, Hong Kong and Yokohama and Sydney with ***HMAS Shropshire***. At Sydney she landed ex-POW's for medical care.
1945-1947	Frequent visits to Hong Kong, Singapore and Japan and carried out security patrols as part of Allied occupation of Japan.
Mid 1947	Ordered home to United Kingdom to enter reserve.
1952	Became Mobile HQ ship for the Admiral Commanding Reserve fleet.
15.06.52	Spithead Coronation Review.
1953	Returned to Reserve Fleet at Portsmouth.
20.05.58	Re-commissioned at Portsmouth with ***Dunkirk*** and ***Jutland*** to form 7th DS
28.05.58	Left for Weymouth Bay to work up.
09.06.58	Gibraltar.
12.06.58	Malta for remainder of June.

*In yet another colour scheme and flying ahe flag of a Rear Admiral **HMS Trafalgar** is seen underway with her secondary armament covered. (Photograph courtesy of the Imperial War Museum Neg No: MH27482)*

*A fine post war aerial view of **HMS Trafalgar** as she steamed in the English Channel.* (Douglas Busby)

01.07.58	Sailed to Cyprus.
04.07.58	Famgusta for anti-terrorist patrol.
15.07.58	Sailed to meet aircraft carrier *Eagle* and proceeded to the Lebanon at start of the Lebanon crisis.
03.08.58	Entered dry dock at Malta.
24.08.58	Sailed for Messina and Cyprus Patrol.
02.09.58	Relieved the frigate *Torquay* at Limassol.
05.09.58	Gently rammed by the minesweeper *Dufton* during jack stay transfer.
19.09.58	At Dhekelia before returning to Malta.
05.10.58	Sailed for exercises.
10.58	Visited Civitavecchia and passed through the Dardanelles enroute to a visit to Istanbul.

Christmas 1958 is celebrated in No1 Mess (Electrical Department) whilst the ship was at Malta.   *(Douglas Busby)*

23.10.58	Sailed for Akrotiri and exercises with *Eagle.*
26.11.58	Sailed for Haifa with *Dunkirk* and cruiser *Sheffield*
12.58	After Malta sailed for exercises and visits to Palma and Gibraltar.
25.12.58	Christmas at Malta.
28.01.59	Monaco.
29.01.59	Their Serene Highnesses Princess Grace and Prince Rainier toured the ship.
13.02.59	Tripoli.
17.02.59	Malta
19.02.59	Exercised with *Centaur* around Cyprus.
13.03.59	Sailed for Trieste
23.03.59	Malta.
08.04.59	NATO's Grand 10th anniversary parade at Malta
11.04.59	Gibraltar
16.04.59	*Trafalgar* towed broken down vessel to port.
21.04.59	At Portsmouth, where she stayed until 29 May.
01.06.59	Exercise *Fairwind* in Scottish waters.
11.06.59	One of 17 ships reviewed by Prince Bernhardt embarked in the Dutch aircraft carrier *Karel Doorman.*
13.06.59	Off Iceland during Cod War on fishery patrol.

08.07.59	Visited Morecambe.
14.07.59	Bournemouth.
19.07.59	Ryde.
20.08.59	Searched for missing RAF Victor bomber off Portland.
08.59	Cod War patrol off Iceland.
11.09.59	Bombardment exercise near to Invergordon.
22.09.59	Off Norway for Exercises *Bare Foot* and *Bare Frost* with the aircraft carrier ***Victorious.***
22.09.59	Searched for missing Skyraider aircraft without success.
01.10.59	Rosyth.
24.11.59	Commissioned for General Service Commission based in Home and Mediterranean waters.
05.02.60	Sailed from Portsmouth to Portland.
10.03.60	Left Portsmouth for Gibraltar.
14.03.60	Lagos.
01.04.60	Palma with the cruiser ***Tiger*** and destroyer ***Broadsword.***
04.04.60	At Malta before going onto Crete for Cyprus Patrol.
02.05.60	Malta.
17.05.60	Naples.
24.05.60	Malta.
07.06.60	With ***Jutland*** and ***Dunkirk*** and visited Tripoli for four-days.
25.11.60	Barcelona for five-day visit.
01.12.60	Exercise *Royal Flush IV*.
13.12.60	***Solebay*** collided with ***Trafalgar*** in Sliema Creek; damage minimal but took remainder of December to repair.
23.01.61	Toulon for Exercise *MEDASWEX 42*.
02.02.61	La Spezia.
02.61	Visited Olympia, Navarino and Patras.
15.02.61	Passed through Corinth Canal and witnessed an eclipse of the sun.
16.02.61	Visited Athens with the cruiser ***Bermuda***.
24.02.61	Malta.
08.03.61	Alicante.
15.03.61	Gibraltar.
18.03.61	Brest for Exercise *Dawn Patrol VI*.
24.03.61	Portsmouth.
27.04.60	Sailed for work up following refit.
01.05.60	Collided with ***Jutland*** off Portland, ***Trafalgar*** returned to Portsmouth for repairs.
11.05.60	Halsingborg with ***Jutland*** and ***Dunkirk.***
23.05.61	Captain R. R. B. Mackenzie, MVO, MBE took command.
24.05.61	***Trafalgar*** re-commissioned.
06.06.61	Portland to conduct exercises with ***Broadsword***, ***Jutland*** and ***Dunkirk.***
21.06.61	Embarked men of company of Duke of Wellington Regiment for Exercise *Dorset Lad*.
18.07.61	Plymouth.
21.07.61	Visited St Helier.
24.07.61	Tarbaret and Largs.
04.08.61	Portsmouth for Navy Days.

09.08.61	Sailed for Bantry Bay.
16.08.61	Berthed on North Queens Jetty at Falmouth.
21.08.61	Falmouth.
23.08.61	Portsmouth.
27.09.61	Sailed to visit Amsterdam and Ijmviden.
04.10.61	At Antwerp before returning to Invergordon for exercises that were interrupted by bad weather.
10.61	Exercised with US Navy including aircraft carrier **USS Essex.**
30.11.61	Visited Belfast at end of exercises.
04.12.61	Sailed to Portsmouth, where she arrived the next day.
15.01.61	Sailed to Portland before going onto Londonderry.
17.02.62	Portsmouth.
09.03.62	Gibraltar.
05.04.62	Malaga.

Steam Power! **HMS Trafalgar** *working up to full speed.*
(Photograph courtesy of the Imperial War Museum Neg No: MH20792A)

09.04.62	Sailed for Malta.
07.05.62	Sailed to Corfu and returned to Malta after five days.
08.06.62	Admiral Sir Deric Holland-Martin transferred his flag to *Trafalgar* from *Surprise.*
01.06.62	Barcelona.
08.06.62	Sailed to Palma.
15.06.62	Malta.
19.06.62	Sorrento for a six-day visit.
06.62	Docked at Malta for maintenance.
03.07.62	Sailed for Gibraltar.
08.62	Visited Leghorn, San Remo, Theoule and Malta.
09.62	Visited Lemnos and Zonguldak.
10.62	Visited Larnaca, Haifa and Split before returning to Malta.
31.10.62	Sailed to Izmir where she operated with other ships until 12 November.
23.11.62	In Cartagena area until end of November.
12.62	Malta.
17.01.62	Sailed to Taranto with *Dunkirk*, *Scorpion* and *Aisne* for a three-day visit.
30.11.62	Struck on starboard bow by *Aisne.*

*On 30 January whilst preparing to leave port at 0610 **Trafalgar** was struck on starboard bow by her sister ship **Aisne** whose stern rope had parted. Thirty minutes later **Aisne** was pulled clear by local tugs. The damage to **Trafalgar** was minor but was sufficient to keep the destroyer alongside in Malta whilst it was repaired.*

04.02.62	Sailed for Naples and stayed in area until 17 February.
18.02.62	Sailed to Cyprus with *Aisne* for Cyprus patrol.
21.02.62	Bombarded Khrysokhov Bay.
23.02.62	Beirut.
28.02.62	Suda Bay.
03.03.62	Malta.
10.03.61	*Trafalgar* left port flying her paying off pennant.
13.03.62	At Gibraltar.
19.03.62	Anchored at Spithead.
20.03.62	Entered Portsmouth Harbour.
05.04.62	Secured on *Rame Head* at Fountain Lake Jetty West to de-store.
23.05.62	Reserve Fleet.
08.06.70	Sold to Arnott Young and subsequently broken up at Dalmuir.

Trafalgar Memories

After having made the journey to the Far East in late 1945 *Trafalgar* joined the 19th Destroyer flotilla together with *Barfleur* and *Armada*. Having left Singapore, Francis Bate recalls how the destroyer sailed through a typhoon. *"I remember vaguely spending several days strapped into the seat of a Bofor gun (covered by storm covers) with a packet of broken ships biscuits in my oilskin pocket all courtesy of the leading hand of my mess. We arrived at Hong Kong and saw the chaos that still remained ashore. We didn't stay at Hong Kong for long as we were almost immediately ordered to Japan to represent Britain in the Occupation because we were the latest in British ship design. There was no economical steaming in those days, we sped to Yokohama and seem-*

ingly passing through an ocean full of US liberty ships all pouring things into Japan. If I remember correctly, the food shortage started on this leg. At Yokohama we were alongside and thought that we'd be replenished from the 10 thousand Liberty ships, though this was not to be case. The war was over and lend lease had finished, like a guillotine drop, an instant finish. No food, repairs, fuel, spares, but we could have free films on a floating 'film display barge' and ice cream."

"The Aussie navy saved us from starvation. They gave us some baked beans and what seemed to be a mass of cases of tinned asparagus. There may have also been some corned beef as well; as I remember being able to stow a small corned beef sandwich with my water bottle as I was inspected for shore leave. If you couldn't show food and water you couldn't go ashore. The theory being there was nothing to eat ashore and if there were any water it would be polluted. So the Royal Navy solution was to go ashore with a butty in one hand and a water bottle in the other."

*"I can't remember visiting Hong Kong, but we must surely have. the next memory was of arriving off Sydney very early in the morning to allow the cruiser **HMAS Shropshire** and escorts, packed with ex Prisoners of War, to enter harbour. We secured around 0800 and took in a culture shock immediately upon stepping off the gangplank. Firstly the dock area bore no relation to the usual sleazy dirty HM Dockyards - it was clean, uncluttered, without dangerous cables, cranes or rails. The buzz had gone around that this naval base had a canteen. There were a huge variety of fruits and plenty of food available and the sailors used the canteen well. So well in fact that within 24 hours the squadron's medical officer had cleared the lower decks and read the riot act of the 'Stupidity of grown men going from virtually a starvation diet to a deluge of milk, fruit, green salads and beer.' The diet also had its affect on the ship's heads as they quickly became blocked and overflowing from the excesses of the men."*

HMS VIGO

HMS Vigo as originally built - minus her AA armament and with a standard two digit pennant number.

(Steve Bush Collection)

12.08.42	Ordered from Fairfield, Govan.
11.09.43	Laid down.
27.09.45	Launched.
31.10.46	Accepted into service.
09.12.46	Completed.

During her trials Vigo stopped in 90 seconds from full speed ahead and achieved a speed of 33.54 knots on a displacement of 2757 tons. Vigo had the distinction of being the only member of the Battle class in Royal Navy service to have three digits in its post 1948 pennant number, in Vigo's case D231.

19.12.46	Arrived at Chatham Dockyard and placed into reserve.
Early 49	Re-commissioned.
03.08.49	Sailed from Chatham Dockyard under command of Captain Robert Franks.
21.08.49	Arrived at Gibraltar at start of Mediterranean cruise.
August 49	Visits paid to Malta and Amalfi.

A crew member onboard Vigo had a remarkable escape after suffering a series of misfortunes. During depth charge operations a valve broke off a drum of acid used to make smoke. The decks were shaking because the depth charges sent shudders through the ship and the acid sprayed out over the depth charge crew. The man called Hobson, in agony from the acid, decided to jump into the sea to stop the pain. Unfortunately, two depth charges rolled over the side at the same time. The man was drawn down towards the ship's propellers and every-one thought that he would surely be killed. They hadn't however, counted on the depth charges. They blew up

and threw the unfortunate man free and was subsequently recovered by his shocked crewmates. The salt water had also eased the painful acid burns on his skin. Hobson was one of 10 sailors who were burnt in the incident.

10-12.49	Visited Famgusta and Beirut before returning to Malta.
07.01.50	After spending Christmas at Malta Vigo left to visit Philippeville.
23.01.50	Escorted **Glory** on rough crossing from Malta to Naples.
19.02.50	With **Chequers**, **Gravelines**, **Toredo**, **Implacable**, **Liverpool** and **Vengeance** on visits to Palmas Bay and Golfe Juan and Algiers.
04.50	Visited Cannes, Villefranche whilst in June and July the destroyer visited Corfu. She then visited Marmaris, where she took part in the annual fleet regatta.
15.02.51	Visited Marseilles, where she secured alongside the Quorn de Port and was open to the public during the visit.
1951	Became the first winner of the annual Bulawayo Cup.
1951	Continued a series of visits including Marmarice and Cyprus. Suez, however, occupied a great deal of time in 1951. The Egyptian government demanded a complete withdrawal of all British forces from the Canal Zone and direct action against British nationals followed. Eventually, all British forces were withdrawn from Suez.
12.51	3rd DS returned to the UK for leave and maintenance.
1952	Returned to the Mediterranean for anti-terrorism patrols around Cyprus.
21.04.52	With **Solebay**, **Theseus** and **Glasgow** visited Piraeus for the unveiling of a new war memorial by King Paul of the Hellenes.
03.53	Returned to the UK and planned to enter reserve.
16.07.53	Suffered a fire.

HMS Vigo with a reduced AA armament. Compare the uncluttered after decks with some of the earlier photographs. (MoD/Crown Copyright)

110

A lovely shot of a destroyer that was home to many a sea cadet when first gaining experience of the Royal Navy. **HMS Vigo** *operated as part of* **HMS Excellent** *along with her sister ship* **HMS Finisterre**. *(Portsmouth Royal Naval Museum)*

01.07.54	Suffered a second fire onboard whilst being refitted to act as gunnery training ship.
13.10.54	Re-commissioned for service at **HMS Excellent** replacing sister ship **Finisterre** in the role of Gunnery Training Ship.
Autumn 54	Gales in the English Channel. Went to the assistance of the merchant ship **Viga**. Later she also went to the assistance of the South Goodwin Light ship, which was in difficulties. She stood by whilst an American birdwatcher was plucked to safety by helicopter before the light ship turned turtle with the loss of the crew.

The autumn of 1954 saw a series of gales in the English Channel and some were very severe. **Vigo** *went to the assistance of the merchant vessel* **Viga***, which was in difficulties in the Channel. Roger Strofton recalls the event. "Whilst doing my National Service I was serving on* **Vigo***. We were Portsmouth Guard ship and at about 1600 the pipe went "Clear lower deck - ship sails in half an hour."*

"It transpired that the South Goodwin Light Ship was in serious difficulties and we were to go down to give what aid we could. The weather was appalling, gale force winds in the Channel gusting Force 8. We arrived there to witness a scene reminiscent of a Naval Review. Ships of all shapes and sizes were milling about. The light ship was rolling beam ends over. A helicopter from Manston in Kent managed to pluck an American birdwatcher who was on the light ship off to safety just before the lightship turned turtle with the sad loss of her crew. **Vigo** *could not turn round because of the weather but eventually managed to turn in the lee of one of the first super tankers by using main engines. We stayed around for I think twelve hours and then returned to Portsmouth."*

Over time the importance of her main guns reduced and they were subsequently cocooned. A new classroom was also constructed on the midship's gundeck.

08.59	De-commissioned at Portsmouth.
06.12.64	Arrived at Faslane to be scrapped.

Previous Page: *Ships of the 7th Destroyer Squadron in the Mediterranean in June 1958 - **Jutland** (nearest), **Dunkirk** and **Trafalgar**.*
(MoD/Crown Copyright)

HMS AGINCOURT

HMS Agincourt *1946.*   *(Maritime Photo Library)*

March 43	Ordered from Hawthorn Leslie.
12.12.43	Laid down.
29.01.45	Launched.
16.02.47	Captain R. G. Swallow took command.
25.06.47	Completed.
Early 1948	Trials including visit to Londonderry.
Autumn 1948	At Portland.
23.09.48	Slipped from Portland bound for Freetown along with the aircraft carriers **Illustrious** and **Vengeance**.
04.10.48	Alongside Kiss Jetty at Freetown with **Alamein.**
06.10.48	Sailed for Takoradi.
08.10.48	Arrived Takoradi before sailing on to Simonstown.
18.10.48	Arrived at Simonstown.
28.10.48	Port Elizabeth before continuing onto Durban.
08.11.48	Left Durban for Cape Town.
16.11.48	Left Cape Town for return trip to UK via Freetown.
12.12.48	Arrived at Portsmouth.
29.12.48	Sailed for Portland.
31.12.48	Sailed for Gibraltar and onward journey to Malta.
Early March 49	Returned to Gibraltar and home via Lisbon.

04.04.49	Gibraltar for exercises.
04.07.49	Arrived Portland.
12.07.49	Ostende and Anvers.
21.07.49	Portsmouth.
29.08.49	Captain D. E. Holland-Martin DSO, DSC, took command.
04.09.49	Lizard area then passage to North Sea and Invergordon.
October 49	Off Londonderry for Exercise *Tangible* and Exercise *Healthy*.
November 49	Exercise *Porcupine*.
22.11.49	Portsmouth.
28.01.50	After a period in dockyard returned to sea areas off Portland.
02.02.50	Gibraltar.
March 50	Visits to Palmas Bay, Nice and Philipeville.
22.03.50	Gibraltar.
01.04.50	Portsmouth.
Summer 50	Exercises off Londonderry and Scottish waters.
10.07.50	Kristiansund Sound in Norway.

The main distinguishing features of the 1943 Battles were the US pattern Mk37 director sited behind the bridge and a single 4.5-inch gun amidships.
(John Brewer)

Destroyers in their natural element - at speed in the turn. **HMS Agincourt** *leads her squadron into a high speed turn to* *port.*
                                                                                                    (MoD/Crown Copyright)

17.07.50	Larvik.
28.07.50	Portsmouth.
September 50	Home Fleet Autumn Cruise to the Mediterranean with **Vanguard**, **Swiftsure** and **Vengeance** together with Canadian warships.
December 50	Portsmouth for refit.
28.02.51	Refit completed.
15.03.51	Captain M. J. Evans CBE, DSC, took command.
Summer 51	Festival of Britain cruise including visits to Southend on Sea, South Shields and Glasgow. Later sailed to the Mediterranean and Persian Gulf.

HMS Agincourt *conducting a ceremonial sailpast (either that or she is late for her allotted harbour entry time!)*
(Alan Ashworth)

March 52	Portsmouth for a short refit.
11.08.52	Captain J. Lee Barber DSO took command.
Autumn 52	Training off Invergordon also Exercise *Mainbrace* in the Arctic.
September 52	Put into Trondheim to repair storm damage.
03.10.52	With **Eagle** as plane guard.
Oct/Nov 52	Exercise *Autumn Bear* in the Arctic.
01.12.52	Portsmouth.
23.01.52	Sailed Portland at start of Mediterranean cruise.
30.01.53	Participated in Exercise *Able* and Exercise *Baker*.
26.03.53	Portsmouth.
June 1953	Spithead Coronation Review on Line D next to **Decoy** and **Barrosa**.
05.01.54	Sailed from Portland to Gibraltar.
Feb/Mar 54	Visited Casablanca and took part in Exercise *Ginblast*.
19.03.54	Exercise *Toughline*.
02.04.54	Portsmouth.
June 54	Invergordon, Cromarty Firth and Scapa Flow areas.
22.07.54	Portsmouth.
September 54	Exercise *Morning Mist* followed by visits to Liverpool, Cardiff, Falmouth and Gibraltar.
22.11.54	Portsmouth.

Early 12.54	Gibraltar and Malta.
Early 1955	Training around Malta plus refit until July.
July 1955	Visited Split to operate with Yugoslav Navy.
Summer 1955	Visited La Rochelle-Pallice, Trondheim and Londonderry for Exercise *Sea Enterprise*.
03.10.55	Portsmouth.
26.10.55	Left for Rosyth.
November 55	Visits paid to Liverpool, Londonderry and Rothesay.
08.12.55	Portsmouth.
January 1956	Exercises at Portland.
02.02.56	Ceuta.
10-24.02.56	Maintenance at Gibraltar.
Early March 56	Valencia before Exercise *Dawn Breeze*.
26.03.56	Portsmouth.
May 1956	Lorient and South Shields.
29.05.56	Re-commissioned for General Service Commission in the Mediterranean.
01.07.56	Malta.
21.07.56	Port Augusta and later Naples.
23.07.56	Exercise *MEDASWEX 12*.
31.07.56	Cyprus Patrol.
11.08.56	Beirut.
28.08.56	Malta.
Late 8-56	Visited Corunna before returning to Portsmouth for refit.
January 1957	At Malta with 4th Destroyer Squadron.
05.04.57	Portsmouth.
September 1957	Exercise *Standfirm* with **USS Forrestal** along with **Albion**, **Eagle**, **USS Northampton** and **Decoy**, **Diana** and **Barrosa**.
November 1957	Returned to the Mediterranean.
Christmas 1957	At Malta.
09.02.58	Nice before onward journey to Naples to operate with Italian Navy.
28.02.58	Malta.
09.03.58	Gibraltar.
Summer 1958	At Malta.
October 1958	Returned to Portsmouth for refit.
19.11.58	Refit completed.
November 1958	Training off Londonderry.
10.12.58	Portsmouth.
Late October 58	Returned to Portsmouth for maintenance.
19.11.58	Sailed for exercises off Londonderry.
12.12.58	Portsmouth.
16.02.59	On completion of a maintenance period sailed for Vigo.
March 1959	Exercise *Dawn Breeze 4*.
26.03.59	Portsmouth.
18.04.59	Visited Le Havre and Pool of London before visiting Antwerp and Amsterdam.
04.05.59	Portsmouth.
May 1959	Icelandic Fishery Patrol until 29 May.

02.06.59	Portsmouth.
01.12.59	Lieutenant Commander D. Fisher took command at start of major conversion to radar picket at Portsmouth.
30.01.62	Lieutenant Commander G. J. R. Elgar took command.
01.05.62	Re-commissioned at Portsmouth.
16.05.62	Collided with the aircraft carrier *Centaur* as she approached South Slip Jetty. *Agincourt* sustained the bulk of the damage.
November 62	Exercises in the Southern Irish Sea.
16.11.62	Gales in rea caused helicopter from *Hermes* to crash and *Agincourt*, *Duchess*, *Berwick*, *Lowestoft* and *Scarborough* sent on search. Later went to the aid of *RFA Green Ranger* which became stranded near Hartland Point.
08.12.62	Portsmouth.
Early 1963	Returned to Mediterranean with 4th DS.
05.08.63	Visited Haifa.
04.03.63	Malta before returning to Devonport.
29.03.64	Entered refit at Portsmouth.
23.03.64	Lieutenant Commander C. Grant took command.
11.04.64	Commander D. J. Halifax took command.
01.07.64	Refit completed.

*Once refitted as Radar Picket Ships, **HMS Agincourt** and her three sisters took on an altogether different appearance. Most prominent was the large AKE 1 radar on a lattice mainmast.* (MoD/Crown Copyright)

Despite the addition of huge masts and aerials, the converted ships still retained their powerful destroyer appearance. The extent of the changes to the after superstructure are also evident in this port side shot. *(John Brewer)*

31.08.64	Exercised with **Lion**, **Carysfort**, **Diamond** and seven frigates in the Solent.
03.09.64	Attended Royal opening of the Forth Road Bridge.
10.64	Portland.
11.64	Londonderry.
21.11.64	Portsmouth for defects and repairs.
08.01.65	Gibraltar before continuing onto Malta for Exercise *Square Root*.
28.01.65	Sailed via Suez for the Far East.
12.02.65	Singapore.
April 1965	Hong Kong and Exercise Seahorse with **USS Bennington**, **HMAS Melbourne** and **Victorious**.
May 1965	Visited Bangkok.
June 1965	With **Victorious**.
13.07.65	Aden.
21.07.65	Malta.
August 1965	Nice.
03.09.65	Portsmouth.
Autumn 1965	In British waters including Exercise *Totem Pole*.
11.65	Exercise *Calpurnia*.
01.66	Exercise NATO *Matchmaker II*.
14.03.66	Plymouth.
20.04.66	Esberg.
20.05.66	Chatham.
Summer 1966	'Meet the Navy' tour of British ports that started in London, Sunderland and Newcastle, then fourteen more ports before arriving at Portsmouth on 1 July 1966.

12.09.66	Commander P. R. D. Kimm took command of the destroyer, which was in refit at Portsmouth.
03.03.67	Refit completed.
28.09.67	Commander G. M. K. Brewer took command.
October 67	In Operational Reserve at Portsmouth. A fire broke out whilst in reserve in the main switch board room. Later *Agincourt* was laid up in the big basin by Fountain Lake and used as an accommodation ship.
1972	Placed on the disposals list.
1973	Sold to H. Kitson Vickers (Sheffield).
October 1974	Towed by *Typhoon* to Hudson Dock in Sunderland for demolition.

Agincourt Memories

Peter Beale joined *Agincourt* in March 1951 when she was part of the Home Fleet (4th Destroyer Flotilla). He recalls that 1951 was the year of the Festival of Britain. "*Agincourt* *"showed the flag" at Southend between 18 and 25 July before moving onto South Shields and Glasgow in August. Later we were seconded to the Mediterranean Fleet and journeyed to the Persian Gulf with stops at Gibraltar, Malta and Cyprus. Whilst at Cyprus the crew practiced landing parties at Larnaca. We proceeded to Port Said where they refused to refuel us so Captain Evans sent away a landing party, took over the fuel station and pumped our own oil. I remember there was a dockyard strike and I believe that about this time, the statue of Ferdinand de Lesyps - the builder of the Suez Canal was tipped over. We helped berth merchant ships who were waiting to pass down the Suez Canal. We eventually reached Port Suez and entered the Red Sea but we were then recalled arriving back in Portsmouth in March 1952.*"

Mr. Murphy remembers the *Agincourt's* ships dog during his time onboard the destroyer between 1956 and 1957. The dog was called Black and was a very good sea dog. *"This dog would always be the first off the ship in all ports and the first back and throughout Europe enjoyed the canine delight of each destination. However, when the ship visited Naples Black trotted off the destroyer and visited one of the poorest cities in Italy where they still ate dogs. Black never came back onboard the Agincourt."*

Whilst in reserve at Portsmouth a fire broke onboard the destroyer. Regarding the fire on *Agincourt* one former member of her crew recalls "All I remember is that it was in the main switchboard room in early 1967. Rumour was pretty strong at the time that it was sabotage but nothing was ever proved. We had a lot of 'Jocks' onboard who joined together from *Cochrane* and with the refit being extended they were a bit disgruntled. Anyway the upshot was that with the age of the ship and radar pickets being made obsolete by Gannet aircraft, their Lordships decided it was not cost effective to make good the damage. We laid her up in the big basin by Fountain Lake where she stayed for a couple of years as an accommodation ship.

HMS AISNE

An early image of **HMS Aisne** *with her original pennant of I22.* *(Portsmouth Royal Naval Museum)*

3.43	Ordered from Vickers Armstrong, Naval Yard, Walker.
26.08.43	Laid down.
12.05.45	Launched at 1700 by Mrs Morse, wife of Rear Admiral H. Morse, ASC, CBS.
12.03.46	Lieutenant P. R. S. Brayn took command.
12.02.47	Commissioned into service.
06.03.47	Dedicated by Right Reverend Lord Bishop of Newcastle, Dr Noel B. Hudson.
Early 1947	Exercised off Gibraltar with *Vanguard* and *Superb*.
17.04.47	Chatham.
Spring 1947	Portsmouth before visiting Copenhagen with *Superb*.
22.07.47	Clyde Fleet Review at Greenock.
13.08.47	Chatham.
1947/1948	In Home waters and the Mediterranean.
28.08.48	Commander W. A. Juniper DSO, DSC, took command.
09.48	Visited Portland and Jersey.
09.48	Caribbean cruise to islands such as Trinidad, Montego Bay, Jamaica, Belize, Nassau and the Azores.
13.12.48	Chatham.
24.01.49	Saile from Chatham to Portland to go onto the Mediterranean.
Spring 1949	Visited Malta, Famgusta, Dhekelia, Beirut, Larnaca and Limassol on 10 April.

04.49	Visited Rhodes, Lindos and Kyrenia.
23.04.49	Port Said.
02.05.49	Chatham.
30.06.49	Penzance for Exercise *Verity*.
22.07.49	Chatham via Weymouth and Torbay.
07.49	Western Union Combined Manoeuvres with the aircraft carrier ***Implacable***.
04.08.49	Commander J. C. A. Ingram DSC took command.
Autumn 1949	In Home waters.
22.11.49	Sheerness.
13.01.50	Chatham for repairs.
24.01.50	Portland before onward journey to the Mediterranean.
02.50	Off Gibraltar.
03.50	Visited Palma Bay and arrived Gibraltar on 13.3.50.
31.03.50	Arived Chatham to enter Reserve Fleet.
05.05.51	Commander M. G. Haworth DSC took command.
12.05.51	Left Chatham.
18.07.51	After visiting Portland, anchored off Southend.
26.07.51	Chatham.
05.09.51	Sailed for Invergordon.
05.10.51	Chatham in preparation for Abadan oil crisis, which thankfully passed by without the need for the destroyers of the 4th DS.

HMS Aisne *comes alongside another ship to conduct a light jackstay transfer.* *(Jim Ashby)*

HMS Aisne *with a full battery of close range AA mountings and a single 4.7-inch gun aft of the funnel.*

(Maritime Photo Library)

19.10.51	Sailed from Plymouth for Gibraltar.
09.12.51	Off Port Said and relieved ***Agincourt*** and ***Corunna*** on station.
01.52	Off Gibraltar for Exercise *Grand Slam*.
07.03.52	Chatham Dockyard.
16.05.52	Sailed to Portland.
06.52	Exercise *Castinets* that ended with a visit to Falmouth.
07.52	Visited Lorient and returned to Chatham.
19.08.52	Left to take part in Exercise *Mainbrace*.
01.10.52	Rosyth followed by Invergordon and Londonderry.
01.12.52	Sheerness and later the same day Chatham Dockyard.
19.01.53	Sailed to operate in Home Waters.
27.03.53	Commander J. R. G. Trechman took command at Chatham.
5.5.53	Sailed from Chatham.
06.53	Paid a visit to Rosyth before taking her position at Spithead for the Coronation Review.
23.07.53	Chatham Dockyard.
12.10.53	Left Chatham.
17.10.53	Portland.
10.53	Royal Search and Rescue duties off Cape Farewell for HM Queen Elizabeth. Met with mountainous seas.
28.10.53	At the end of SAR duties returned to Londonderry. At Londonderry ***Barrosa*** collided with ***Aisne*** and smashed ***Aisne***'s starboard whaler to matchwood.

Aisne had been secured alongside (Portside to) when ***Barrosa*** nipped in from the starboard quarter and dug

*her bows into the boiler room leaving a slot about two foot wide across the edge of **Aisne**'s iron deck. **Barrosa** quickly backed off - too quickly in fact as a merchantman was then passing astern of her - which entailed full ahead to avoid a collision, so back she came, this time smashing **Aisne**'s starboard whaler to matchwood. Debris from the collision was scattered around **Aisne**'s decks and the whaler was destroyed, whilst the motor boat was pushed to a position where it was seen to be attempting to climb the starboard forecastle ladder. The ship was immediately moved to another berth and divers and welders set to work. Welders and burners were onboard within twenty minutes and then worked almost to midnight. The damage was sufficient that the destroyer sailed back to Chatham for a full assessment of the repairs necessary to be undertaken.*

11.12.53	Chatham Dockyard.
25.01.54	Sailed for Spring Cruise to the Mediterranean.
10.02.54	Gibraltar.
17.02.54	**Barrosa** again collided with **Aisne** whilst at Gibraltar.
26.02.54	Casablanca before returning to Gibraltar.
04.04.54	Chatham. 25th MAR: 54 JOINED.
07.05.54	Portsmouth.
08.05.54	At Torbay to escort **Britannia** up English Channel to Portsmouth on 14 May.
15.05.54	Sailed for Portland.
05.54	In Scottish waters.
11.06.54	Scapa Flow.
19.06.54	Aberdeen for 4-day visit.
26.06.54	Helsinki. A firework display went badly wrong and missiles fired in all directions. The gun deck became an inferno. Three people were seriously injured including two civilians.

A former crewmember recalls. "The whole harbour was packed for a 'farewell firework display'. I had a good position on the bridge looking down on the fireworks on 'B' gundeck. That's when things went wrong. As we fired the first rack of rockets the backflash ignited around 150 rockets, ready for the next rack, which exploded and went shooting off in all directions. The gundeck caught fire and in seconds was a blazing inferno. However, the fire was quickly brought under control as the fire parties on the upperdeck had been standing by with hoses turned on - the water going over the ships' sides. One rocket went straight through the window of a harbour side house, through two doors and lodged in the wall on the opposite side of the house. Luckily there was no one home, and our fire parties had to break into the property to put the fire out. There were two serious injuries onboard; and one in the crowd. The one in the crowd was a woman who was hit on the head by a passing rocket, sustaining a deep gash and being knocked unconscious. Apparently there was blood everywhere. Of the two injuries onboard, one was standing beside the rockets when they went off and caught the full force of the blast. As he fell from the gundeck he was caught by the fire hoses, which put out his clothing, which was on fire. His hands and feet took the full force of the blast and were in a horrible state - with pieces of burnt flesh hanging from the bones. The second casualty, also standing near the rockets, ran and dived over the gundeck guardrails, and landed on his chest on the deck below. He smashed ribs and was still unconscious when taken to hospital. The first ambulance reached the ship within two and a half minutes of being called and all three casualities were rushed to the Helsinki Military Hospital."

03.07.54	Sailed from Helsinki.
07.07.54	Rosyth.
20.07.54	Arrived at Chatham via Portland.

In the autumn of 1954 Arctic clothing was "de rigeur" for anyone working on the upperdeck during Exercise Morning Mist off Norway
(Jim Ashby)

30.08.54	Arrived at St Helens Roads.
01.09.54	Portsmouth.
Late 9.54	Exercise *Morning Mist* off Norway.
01.10.54	Bergen.
04.10.54	Liverpool.
11.10.54	Arrived Chatham to pay off.
01.12.54	Re-commissioned under the command of Commander A. Gray DSO.
11.12.54	Arrived Portland and joined *Agincourt* and *Corunna* en route to Gibraltar.
22.12.54	Malta.
14.01.55	Large tactical exercise called Operation *Catchcan* before returning to Malta.
Spring 1955	Visited the Lebanon and Beirut before returning to Malta and visited Famgusta.
02.55	Exercise *Gradient Easy*.
02.55	At Malta's dockyard to change gun barrels and work on faulty boilers.
10.03.55	Exercise *Lancex* and later in the month escorted *Britannia* into Malta with Duke of Edinburgh onboard.
22.03.55	All ships from the exercise sailed to Naples and then onto Civitavecchia before returning to Malta.
13.04.55	Sailed from Malta to operate around Cyprus and a visit to Tripoli. *Aisne* then returned to Malta for a refit.
25.09.55	Left for United Kingdom via Gibraltar.
03.10.55	Chatham Dockyard.

Late 10.55	Rosyth for exercises off Cape Wrath.
11.11.55	Liverpool.
Late 11.55	Visited Londonderry for training then Irish Sea and Rothesay.
08.12.55	Chatham Dockyard.
16.01.56	Sailed to Portland for Exercise *Spring Six Able* en route to Gibraltar.
01.56	Visited Ceuta before returning to Gibraltar to refit.
01.56	Exercise *Spring Six Baker* with **Tyne** en route to Valencia.
Mid 3.56	Combined Fleet Exercises around Naples.
03.56	Cyprus Patrol.
24.03.56	Malta. *29th May '56 Drafted.*
05.56	Tripoli and returned to the United Kingdom.
01.06.56	De-stored and later laid up in the Reserve trots at Folly Point. She was later towed to Chatham Dockyard.
30.10.61	Work started to modernise the destroyer into a radar picket ship.
01.62	Commander W. Noble DSC, AFC, took command.
10.01.62	Returned to sea for sea trials, which lasted until summer 1962. She then joined the 7th DS in the Mediterranean.
09.08.62	Exercise *Ripetide II* off Gibraltar that included **USS Forrestal** and **USS Enterprise**. At the end of the exercise the British ships visited Lisbon.
09.62	Visited Lemnos, Larnanca and Haifa.

HMS Aisne *taking it green after her conversion to a Radar Picket Ship.*   *(MoD/Crown Copyright)*

12.10.62	Mersin for five-days before sailing onto Beirut.
27.10.62	Malta
31.10.62	Sailed for Izmir and to take part in Exercise *MEDASWEX*
11.11.62	Malta
20.11.62	Sailed for Cartagena in Spain and Exercise *Spanex* until the end of the November.
12.62	In and around Malta
05.01.63	Went to the aid of the cruise liner **Canberra** with **Scorpion** after a fire in her main generator room. In the event the liner was able to put out the fire and restored power herself.
19.01.63	Taranto with **Dunkirk** and **Scorpion.**
30.01.63	*Aisne* struck *Trafalgar* whilst manoeuvring in Malta's busy harbour. *Aisne* suffered minor damage.
04.02.63	Squadron sailed for Naples.
02.63	Cyprus patrol.
23.02.63	Sailed for Beirut and onward journey to Suda Bay.
Late 3.63	Exercises off Tobruk.
30.03.63	Sailed through Suez Canal to relieve **Corunna** in Persian Gulf.
Spring 1963	Visited Aden, Mombasa and Zanzibar.
24.05.63	Sailed through the Suez Canal.
26.05.63	Malta for two-week maintenance period that was completed on 11 June.
06.63	Visits in June included Palma, Ajaccio and Bordighera.
30.07.63	Portsmouth for a refit.
04.11.63	Refit completed and following trials *Aisne* joined the 30th Escort Squadron.
12.63	Operating between Portsmouth and Portland.
02.01.64	Commander M. J. Garrett took command.
12.03.64	Sailed from Portsmouth to Birkenhead and onward to Greenock.
08.04.64	Aberporth.
11.04.64	Portsmouth.
15.05.64	Gibraltar.
Summer 1964	Visits included Malta, Argostoli, Bari and Venice.
13.07.64	Malta.
11.08.64	Villefranche.
09.64	Sent to Far East after extra weapons were fitted for the Indonesian conflict.
10.64	Arrived at Singapore and went on war footing for confrontation patrols. *Aisne* remained in the Far East until early 1965 before returning to Chatham.
05.03.65	Left Chatham for 5-day visit to Bergen with **Cassandra**.
17.03.65	Portsmouth.
06.04.65	Chatham.
11.04.65	After exercises with Falmouth visited Barrow-in-Furness.
18.05.65	Chatham.
25.05.65	Portsmouth for repairs.
12.06.65	Left with **Falmouth.**
17.06.65	Gibraltar for four-days.
29.06.65	Southbound transit of Suez Canal.
16.07.65	Following visits to Aden and Gan arrived at Singapore.
04.08.65	For the next nine days operated with **Ark Royal** and took part in Exercise *Guardrail*.

HMS Aisne prepares to take another warship in tow. The loss of all her secondary AA armament is evident. The conversion made provision for the installation of the Seacat AA missile system.
(MoD/Crown Copyright)

21.09.65	Hong Kong.
30.09.65	Sailed for Singapore.
10.65	Visited Penang and returned to Singapore for a maintenance period that lasted until 8 November.
12.11.65	Bangkok for a goodwill-visit.
22.11.65	With *Falmouth* in company started journey home to the United Kingdom.
05.12.65	Northbound transit of Suez Canal.
11.12.65	Gibraltar.
15.12.65	Portsmouth.
17.12.65	Chatham where Commander A. Gray took command.
30.12.65	Entered into long refit at Chatham.
06.05.66	Refit completed.
08.05.66	Returned to sea for trials.
27.05.66	Portsmouth.
10.06.66	Declared operational to the fleet.
13.06.66	Left Portsmouth for Portland.
12.08.66	Portsmouth.
04.09.66	Commander W. S. Gueterboak took command.

10.66	Off Portland working up.
18.10.66	Gibraltar.
01.11.66	Southbound transit of Suez Canal.
13.11.66	Gan.
19.11.66	Singapore for maintenance period.
28.11.66	Exercise *Twin Top* that finished on 9 December.
12.66	Hong Kong in time for Christmas.
02.01.67	Singapore.
01.67	Operated with the aircraft carrier **Victorious** and had a nine-day stopover at Hong Kong.
11.02.67	In Dockyard hands at Hong Kong.
27.02.67	Sailed from Hong Kong to Ililo for Exercise *Siyasat* until 18 March.
21.03.67	Singapore.
03.04.67	Gan.
04.67	Returned to Portsmouth for a refit.
03.07.67	Refit completed.
13.07.67	Plane guard to **Eagle** in Bristol Channel.
20.07.67	Official visit to Oslo for five-days.
16.08.67	Rejoined **Eagle** as plane guard.
26.08.67	Portsmouth.
02.10.67	Sailed to Gibraltar.
11.10.67	Visited Palma en route to Malta.
10.67	Visited Lorient before returning to Chatham.
04.01.68	Left Portsmouth for a Caribbean cruise.
08.01.68	Ponto Delgada in the Azores.
01.68	Visited Terceria, Barbuda, St Thomas, Tobago and Montserrat.
02.68	Visited Chaguarama.
09.02.68	Port Canaveral for four-days before visiting Freeport.
23.02.68	West Palm Beach.
02.03.68	Key West before taking up Bahama's Patrol duties.
08.03.68	Freeport before resuming Bahama's Patrol.
03.68	Bermuda before crossing the North Atlantic to the United Kingdom.
28.03.68	Portsmouth.
22.05.68	Portland before sailing to Scottish waters for an exercise which was cancelled due to poor visibility. Remained at Rosyth until 24 June when she sailed for Londonderry.
16.07.68	Visit to Halsingborg, which was followed by Exercise *Forthex*.
07.68	Western Fleet Assembly off Rosyth.
02.08.68	De-commissioned at Portsmouth.
Summer 1970	Sold for scrap.
23.06.70	Towed from Portsmouth.
26.06.70	Arrived at T.W. Wards at Inverkeithing for breaking up.

Aisne Memories

Aisne was at Venice between 6-11 July 1964. David Cook recalls *"On a trip from Malta to Venice, the Captain was persuaded to take with us our own Maltese dhaigsa, the Maltese version of the gondola. The boat was hoist-*

ed inboard complete with Charlie, it's owner-operator. Charlie messed in one of the JR's messes. We used him in Venice as a liberty boat - much, much cheaper than gondolas. We anchored off St Mark's square and I was on duty when a sailor swam off and had to be given numerous injections, given the state of the water he was swallowing."

September saw *Aisne* being sent to the Far East. David Cook takes up the story. *"We were in the Mediterranean berthed at* **HMS St Angelo** *when we received a signal to proceed at best speed to Singapore for Indonesian Confrontation period. It seemed serious at the time and I recall that we had to write home and explain to families as we were meant to spend the summer in the Mediterranean. The ship was brought up to a 'war footing' with extra Oerlikons fitted. After some careful calculations, the Captain decided to proceed all the way at 25 knots. This speed made things a little tense in the engine room and boiler rooms, one could not relax at that power."*

"I remember we bent the jackstaff in a gale after leaving Malta - almost to a right angle. The Captain would not go through Suez with nowhere to put the jack, it was too large to repair in the ship. I was put ashore with a seaman, and the bent staff, at Tobruk, the ship sailed away overnight and returned the next day. We were picked up by a truck from RAF El Adem who had offered the use of their aircraft repair workshops. The first thing I managed to do was rip a vice off the bench trying to straighten the staff. I fixed it eventually by cutting and welding it and returned to the ship after a few pints and little sleep."

"In the Far East, I remember on arrival in the Malacca Straits we were inspected by an aircraft of the Indonesian Air Force prompting us to go to action stations. The ship did two weeks on patrol between Malaya and Indonesia trying to catch insurgents crossing into Malaya at night. After two weeks we were on standby for two weeks either in Singapore or on visits to Hong Kong or Penang and then it was back for two weeks of patrols. Whilst preparing to fuel off Singapore, we suffered a tragedy. A bolt fired across from the tanker, bringing the first line over, became snagged or ricocheted causing the bolt to become lodged in the head of one of the fuelling party taking cover behind one of the 4.5-inch gun turrets. He was only a youngster. The forecastle party built some cover from the sun for him on the upperdeck and tried to hold him still as he trashed about with the bolt sticking from his skull. The ship went rapidly to full power and headed toward Singapore where en route we were met by a helicopter bringing a doctor from **HMS Terror**.*"*

"The kid died shortly after the doctor removed the bolt whilst still on the upperdeck. I remember the silence throughout the ship - I had never heard it so quiet"

"We stopped numerous ships for searching during the confrontation which was a bit dangerous as one was never sure if someone would appear on deck and throw a grenade or open fire. The upperdeck was always cleared for these little forays. I remember days and days at 10 knots interspersed with high speed runs when our massive 965 radar picked up a tiny dot miles away. That radar on a Battle class always looked like a large clockwork key sticking out of the top of the ship!"

HMS ALAMEIN

HMS Alamein *running full power trials in 1947.*   *(Maritime Photo Library)*

03.43	Contract awarded to Hawthorn Leslie.
01.03.44	Laid down.
28.05.45	Lady Margaret Alexander, wife of Field Marshall Alexander launched the ship.
06.04.48	Lieutenant Commander H. T. Harrell took command.
21.05.48	Completed.
Early 48	Trials.
08.48	In Scottish waters with **Barrosa.**
18.09.48	Portland to prepare for cruise to Africa.
05.10.48	Freetown with **Agincourt.**
08.10.48	Takoradi.
18.10.48	Arrived at Simonstown.
26.10.48	Sailed for Port Elizabeth with exercises en route.
02.11.48	Durban.
11.11.48	Cape Town.
16.11.48	Sailed on return leg of voyage.
26.11.48	Freetown.

12.48	Devonport.
03.02.49	Left for Gibraltar with *Vanguard* for exercises with *Superb*, *Aisne*, *St James*, *Solebay* and *Jutland*.
03.03.49	Visited Tangiers.
14.03.49	Sailed from Gibraltar for Lisbon where she was joined by the battleship *Duke of York*, *Diadem* and three destroyers.
24.03.49	Devonport.
04.04.49	Sailed for Mediterranean where she spent the summer operating out of Malta.
10.49	Devonport.
10.49	Exercise *Porcupine* with *Vengeance*, *Cleopatra* and *Jutland*.
21.11.49	Devonport.
09.01.50	Commander I. M. Clegg took command.
24.01.50	Portland.
28.01.50	Sailed to Gibraltar on training cruise with *Vanguard*, *Victorious*, *Implacable* and *Vengeance*.
02.02.50	Gibraltar.
03.50	Visited Philipeville and Villefranche with *Agincourt* and *Barrosa*.
31.03.50	Plymouth for maintenance.
06.50	Rosyth.
04.07.50	Sailed for exercises in Dornoch Firth.
10.07.50	Kristiansund Sound.
17.07.50	Larvik.
28.07.50	Arrived Portsmouth to enter reserve. Later towed to Plymouth and laid up in River Tamar.
Early 1954	Started re-activation. Towed to Rosyth for the major part of the work.
21.03.56	Work completed and destroyer started sea trials.
07.05.56	Sailed for Chatham.
10.05.56	Arrived at Chatham.
25.05.56	Re-commissioned.
28.05.56	Sailed for Portland.
02.06.56	Sailed to Gibraltar and onward journey to Malta.
11.07.56	Visited Tripoli in Libya on courtesy visit to British Army there in particular the 3rd Royal Horse Artillery.
16.07.56	Returned to Malta.
21.07.56	Visited Port Augusta (Sicily).
07.56	Visited Messina and then Cyprus for anti terrorism patrol around the island.
21.08.56	Beirut.
Late 1956	Operation *Musketeer* - Suez Canal assault. Operated with the British aircraft carriers.
25.12.56	Returned to Sliema Creek on Malta at 0700. She remained in the Mediterranean until March 1957.
03.05.57	Chatham Navy Days.
05.05.57	Chatham Dockyard for a refit.
05.57	Exercises off Scotland.
28.05.57	In Moray Firth for HM The Queen's inspection of divisions onboard the aircraft carrier *Albion* from the Royal Yacht *Britannia*.
Summer 1957	In British waters.

01.11.57	Returned to Chatham Dockyard for brief reserve.
25.11.57	Sailed to the Mediterranean with visits to Venice, Civitavecchia and a period in dry-dock at Gibraltar. Also took part in the Cyprus Patrol during her stay in the Mediterranean.
09.58	Visited Barcelona with 4th DS.
09.58	Stripped turbine en route from Malta and made a slow 4 knot voyage on one shaft to Gibraltar and onto Chatham.
23.10.58	Arrived at Chatham Dockyard.
05.11.58	Wardroom caught-fire causing severe damage.
25.03.59	Refit was completed.
Spring 1959	Operations in Home waters.
18.06.59	Arrived Chatham.
01.09.59	Sailed to Plymouth to join the Reserve Fleet.
Autumn 1964	Approved for scrapping. Sold to Hughes Bolckow at Blyth for breaking up.
01.12.64	Arrived at Blyth for demolition to commence.

Alamein Memories

Martin Bird recollects joining the ship at Chatham on 18 November 1957. *"I was an Acting Sub Lieutenant as Correspondence officer and TASCO (Torpedo and Anti Submarine Control Officer), I got my watch keeping certificate during my time onboard. **Alamein** replaced **Aisne** in the 4th Destroyer Squadron."* On 25 November **Alamein** sailed from Chatham. Martin Bird remembers *"During our time in the Med we were based at Malta and apart from a period in dry dock at Gibraltar we visited Venice on our own and Civitavecchia with **Corunna**.*

HMS Alamein *approaching Grand Harbour. Note the awnings from the funnel right aft.* (Steve Bush Collection)

We also spent several periods carrying out the Cyprus patrol, attempting to catch gun runners, and sent members of our landing platoon ashore (including myself) to carry out patrols with the army whilst there. We joined the 'Suffolk's' in Nicosia for this purpose. Army personnel spent the same period on board in a sort of exchange programme."

"Our main patrol area in Cyprus was the northwest sector where we had a close liaison with the Argyll's and a number of our officers were dining with them one night when their transport park was set alight by terrorists. We also had an exciting steering gear failure rounding Cape Karavostai early one morning when the steering gear jammed heading us towards rocks 2 cables (400 yards) distant at 18 knots when I was on the watch. Fortunately it had happened to me a week earlier in more open seas so we survived!"

"We had one serious incident whilst on patrol; we had sent a boarding party to board a fishing boat late one night and were hoisting the boat using the forward capstan when one of the falls broke. It had been incorrectly rigged in the darkness, and instead of passing over a roller on the breakwater it bore against a sharp edge, which caused the fall to part when levelling the boat at the davit head. The occupants of the boat were tipped into the sea and one man, the radio operator who still had his set strapped on, was drowned."

"During our time in the Med, Field Marshall Viscount Montgomery, who was due to retire, was making arrangements for his farewell tour of NATO and asked that **Alamein** transport him in the Eastern Med (Lebanon to Turkey). All was agreed between Lord Mountbatten and Admiral Sir Charles Lamb but it was not to be. War blew up in the Eastern Med, the tour was cancelled and the fleet sailed to the east. We sailed on our own for some reason and about 12 or so hours out of Malta the Sick Berth Attendant diagnosed that a member of the ship's company had a brain tumour. It was then 27 knots for Cyprus while ships with doctors on board converged on us. About 6 hours later we jackstayed a doctor from **Ausonia** while another arrived by helicopter from the cruiser **Cumberland**. There was also a carrier in the vicinity. Pretty good service. The patient had a migraine as far as I recall!"

"I believe it was in about September that the 4th DS was to visit Barcelona, prior to returning to the UK, and we were on our way from Malta in fairly bad weather, doing about 18 knots, when **Alamein** stripped a turbine. So for us it was 4 knots on one shaft to Gibraltar and subsequently, a very long and slow passage back to Chatham where we arrived on 23 October. On 5 November the wardroom caught fire causing quite severe damage to the compartment and surrounding areas."

HMS BARROSA

HMS Barrosa in 1947 shortly after completion. The pennant letter (flag superior) was not changed to "D" until 1948.
(Portsmouth Royal Naval Museum)

03.43	Ordered from John Brown on Clydebank.
28.12.43	Laid down.
17.01.45	Launched.
14.02.47	Completed.
03.47	Trials in Scottish waters.
1947	Spent inactive due to oil price crisis with USA.
1947	Used during filming of movie '*The King's Navy*.'

George Brown joined the ship in March 1947 as part of the Commissioning Company shortly after she had 'slipped' in John Brown's yard on the Clyde. "On completion we commenced working up trials in and around the Northern Irish Sea and amongst the Western Isles. Winter 1947 was a very severe one and **Barrosa** *responded to requests from the community of Portree on the North East coast of the Isle of Skye for provisions to eke out their immediate needs. I also recall the mad scramble in the Bar of one of the two pubs in Tobermory when the last bottle was held aloft, a gift by the Landlord in appreciation for hosting most of the off duty watch."*

1947 was a bad year for the Royal Navy when due to a dollar crisis the price of oil meant that there were widespread restrictions on the use of fuel. This had the knock on effect that many warships spent many months alongside in semi-mobilised states, **Barrosa** *included. The inactivity meant, however, that the ship could be used for other purposes as Tony Hall recalls. "While at Portsmouth* **Barrosa** *was in a film called "The King's Navy". The film went on general release in 1948."*

04.48	Re-activated.
7-11.06.48	Worked up in the English Channel.
21.06.48	Plane guard to *Theseus.*
07.07.48	Devonport via Portland.
11.07.48	Sailed for Dartmouth Naval College.
13.07.48	Portsmouth.
14.08.48	Sailed from Portsmouth at 0800 to rendezvous with *Vengeance* off Portrush.
16.08.48	Mull of Kintyre.
18.08.48	Sailed to Northern Ireland.
19.08.48	Rescued pilot from *Vengeance* who crashed into the sea.
19.08.48	Visited Bangor and anchored offshore.
20.08.48	Travelled up Victoria Channel to Belfast and secured on *Vengeance* at old Airport Jetty.
Late 08.48	Red Bay, Lamlash and Brodick Bay.
27.08.48	Greenock with *Vengeance.*
01.09.48	Portsmouth for five-days and onwards to Portland.
09.09.48	Left Portland for exercises with *St Kitts* and *Astute.*
23.09.48	Sailed on Caribbean cruise with the battleship *Duke of York.*
09.10.48	San Fortin.
10.48	Visited San Fernando, Tobago, St Vincents, St Lucia, Souffriere, Montserrat, Virgin Islands and Bermuda.

This port quarter view shows to advantage the two twin 40mm STAAG mountings on the after deckhouse and the single twin 40mm mounting further forward. The single 4.5-inch gun sited abaft the mast is trained forward in its usual stowed position.
(Maritime Photo Library)

Duncan Mackenzie recalls his time at Tobago. "To the best of my recollection the whole fleet arrived off the Island of Tobago, whereupon it was decided to land a large number of sailors on the island to attack a supposed rebel fort. Large numbers of motor launches, towing whalers from every ship, all crammed with sailors armed to the teeth made for the shore where we stormed a medieval fort. Needless to say everyone joined in the fun, however, following the exercise, someone decided we all needed some company drill. This drill actually took place in the sweltering heat, close to the old fort. The drill was then followed by a route march on the Island of Tobago; believe me I have never forgotten it. We all eventually collapsed on the beach, where the locals cut open coconuts for us. I recall on that occasion falling out of a grapefruit tree onto some wild pigs while pinching grapefruits!"

28.11.48	Sailed Bermuda.
06.12.48	Horta in the Azores.
07.12.48	Operation *Sunrise*.
12.12.48	Portsmouth.
18.01.49	With ***Theseus*** for flying operations off Sandown on the Isle of Wight.
21.01.49	Returned to Portsmouth.
25.01.49	With ***Theseus*** again for one-day of flying operations.
27.01.49	Portland.
31.01.49	Sailed to Gibraltar.
04.02.49	Gibraltar.
09.02.49	Mock torpedo attack on ***Theseus.***
10.02.49	Malta, where she spent the rest of February.
01.03.49	Gibraltar.
04.03.49	Malaga.
09.03.49	Gibraltar.
14.03.49	Sailed for Lisbon with ***Sluys*** for a four-day visit.
25.03.49	Portsmouth for refit.
03.05.49	No 9 dock.
04.07.49	Sailed from Portsmouth for Portland to conduct trials.
09.07.49	With ***Agincourt*** at Ostende.
14.07.49	Anvers via the Schelde Channel.
22.07.49	Portsmouth.
04.09.49	Lizard area.
05.09.49	With ***Vengeance.***
07.09.49	Portland.
08.09.49	Sailed for Invergordon with ***St James***, ***Agincourt***, ***Cleopatra*** and ***Implacable***.
03.10.49	Spey Bay to exercise with ***Thermopylae***.
03.10.49	Gentle collision with ***Jutland***, slight damage to both ships.
10.49	Londonderry.
10.49	Londonderry, Irish Sea and Brodick Bay and Exercise *Artichoke* and Exercise *Tangible*.
24.10.49	Exercise *Healthy*.
Late 10.49	Loch Boisdale and Londonderry.
07.11.49	Portland for Operation *Porcupine*.
22.11.49	Portsmouth where she stayed until the end of the year.
24.11.49	Lieutenant Commander A. A. Diggens DSC took command.

23.01.50	Sailed to join *Implacable* in the Solent and at Portland.
28.01.50	Sailed to Gibraltar with *Victorious*, *Vengeance* and *Implacable*.
02.02.50	Gibraltar, where she spent most of February.
27.02.50	Sailed to Palmas Bay with *Aisne* for a three-day visit.
03.50	Visited Leghorn and Cagliari.
22.03.50	Gibraltar for five-days.
27.03.50	Sailed for the United Kingdom.
31.03.50	South Slip Jetty, Portsmouth.
15.05.50	Moved to B-lock and was struck by a dockyard crane.
20.06.50	Transferred to Reserve Fleet with administration of *Barrosa* being taken over by the cruiser *Sirius*.
04.52	At 48 hours notice for steam.
02.05.52	Commander I. M. Barfour, MBE, RN took command.
12.05.52	Returned to sea for three-days of post commissioning trials.
05/06.52	Visited Portland, Plymouth and Teignmouth.
01.07.52	Nantes for a 6-day visit.
08.07.52	Portsmouth.
19.08.52	Sea trials.
21.08.52	Sailed for Dornoch Firth and Invergordon.
09.52	Exercise *Mainbrace*.
25.09.52	Korsor before returning to Rosyth.
08.10.52	JASS Course off Londonderry.
02.11.52	Invergordon.
14.11.52	Rosyth before an Arctic Cruise with the battleship *Vanguard*.

One former crew member recalls his time onboard during this cruise. "We had prepared the ship for a voyage of experimentation into the northern waters by greasing its outer paintwork to protect it from the anticipated hard weather exposure. The ship looked dull and depressive as we sailed down the Firth of Forth, and out to sea. The day was bleak and wet. As we reached the open seas the waves began to lift our bows. Thirty hours out we rendezvoused with **Vanguard.**

"We steamed northwards in company. A general appraisal of our mission was to make various experiments with equipment that might be used should there be an Arctic war. The cold war was in full spate. One experiment was to test a specially designed ship aerial attached to the port side of Q gun deck. Much of the upper works of the ship were iced over and the ship was rolling heavily in the big troughs. The battleship **Vanguard** *meanwhile was coping well with the conditions being much larger and also having the benefit of an enclosed bridge."*

01.12.52	Portsmouth.
18.12.52	Commander T. W. Best took command.
20.01.53	Portsmouth to Portland.
31.03.53	Gibraltar.
02.03.53	Exercise *Cross Bar* and Exercise *Ginblast*.
11.03.53	Escorted Yugoslavia's Marshall Tito in his yacht *Galeb* across the English Channel to London.
16.03.53	Portsmouth.

*This picture serves well to illustrate the spread of the A/S projectiles fired from the ahead firing Squid mounting as **Barrosa** steams over the site of the attack shortly after the bombs exploded!*
(Martin Feather)

23.03.53	Sailed for exercises for 3-days before returning.
05.05.53	Portland for Exercise *Annals IV*.
29.05.53	Penzance for Queen's Coronation.
04.06.53	Left Penzance for Spithead Review.
18.06.53	Rosyth and entered No 2 dock until 26 June.
Summer 53	Exercised with 4th DS at Invergordon, Loch Eriboll and Cape Wrath.
09.07.53	Rosyth for Captain D inspection.
12.07.53	Off Harwich for Exercise *Garage 5* for six days.
18.07.53	Broadstairs for 4 days.
22.07.53	Portsmouth for a refit.
26.10.53	Refit completed and sailed for trials in the Solent.
05.11.53	Sailed for two days with *Eagle* in English Channel.
08.11.53	Portsmouth followed by exercises.
17.11.53	In Mid Atlantic as SAR for Royal Flight to Canada.
27.11.53	Londonderry.
28.11.53	Collided with *Aisne.*
09.12.53	Left Northern Ireland and headed for Portsmouth via Plymouth.

26.01.54	Sailed for Portland.
02.54	Exercise *FLODAS* off Gibraltar.
03.54	Casablanca and *Exercise Toughline*.
Easter 54	Portsmouth.
14.05.54	Escorted **Britannia** carrying HM Queen Elizabeth II.
05/06.54	Invergordon.
19.06.54	Sailed for Flushing.
07.54	Visited Douglas and Rothesay.
5-10.09.54	Moray Firth area and took part in Exercise *Dawn Haze*.
13.09.54	With **Eagle** in Mull of Galloway.
09.54	Exercise *Morning Mist*.
04.10.54	Liverpool for a 7 day visit.
18.10.54	Plymouth via Newport.
21.10.54	Sailed for Gibraltar and Exercise *Southbound*.
26.10 - 06.11.54	No 1 Dock at Gibraltar for self maintenance.
21.11.54	Re-commissioned at Portsmouth and returned to the Mediterranean.
20.12.54	Gibraltar.
01.55	Off Malta and Exercise *Catchcan*.
Summer 55	Visited Malta, Cyprus, Tripoli, Marmaris and Izmir.
Early 07.55	Sailed for Exercise *Adexo*.

HMS Barrosa and sistership **Agincourt** in Venice 1955.   *(Alan Ashworth)*

08.07.55	Venice.
07.55	Exercise *Ajax* off Split.
23.08.55	Malta.
10.09.55	La Pallice.
16.09.55	Invergordon for Exercise *Sea Enterprise* for 8-days. At its completion **Barrosa** sailed to Norway and the city of Trondheim.
03.10.55	Portsmouth.
26.10.55	Left for Rosyth where she arrived two days later.
03.11.55	Left to visit Liverpool via the north of Scotland.
11/12.55	Visited Belfast, Londonderry, Lamlash and Firth of Clyde.
08.12.55	Portsmouth.
16.01.56	Sailed to Portland and then onto Gibraltar.
02.56	Visited Valencia.
03.56	Exercise *Cascade* and Exercise *Dawn Breeze* before returning to Portsmouth.
26.03.56	London and moored at Greenwich for 4 days.
01.05.56	Portland before visiting Lorient.
09.05.56	North Shields.
29.05.56	Re-commissioned at Portsmouth.
06.56	Returned to Mediterranean.
07.56	Visited Tripoli in Libya and took part in Exercise *JULEX*.
Summer 56	Visited Augusta, Messina, Cagliari and Gibraltar for a refit.
07.11.56	Refit completed.
Mid 11.56	Returned to Maltese waters.
Mid 11.56	Operation *Salaid* off Port Said in support of British troops ashore.
15/16.12.56	Limassol.
27.12.56	Port Said for Operation *Harridan*.
01.57	Cyprus Patrol and visited Famgusta.
01.57	Visited Malta and Naples.
03.57	Exercise *Springex* and visited Genoa and Cannes.
28.03.57	Gibraltar.
04.04.57	Portsmouth.
14.04.57	Sailed to Rosyth to be present during a visit by HM Queen to Moray Firth.
04-07.06.57	Weapons training at Loch Eriboll.
06.57	Visited Den Helder, Horsens, Kiel Canal and Little Belt.
01-05.07.57	Exercise *Fairwind 2*.
Summer 57	Visited Douglas and Rothesay.
17.09.57	Exercise *Strikeback* before Greenock and Portsmouth.
14.10.57	Exercise *Pipe Down* before visiting Bordeaux.
19.11.57	Paid off and re-commissioned at Portsmouth.
29.11.57	Sailed from Portland to Gibraltar.
Spring 58	Highlights included *JANEX 1 & 2* off Malta, Exercise *FEBEX* and Exercise *MARJEX*. **Barrosa** also visited La Spezia, Messina and Naples.
03.58	Cyprus Patrol.
08.05.58	Capri.
09.06.58	Arrived Gibraltar for refit that started 17 June.

Autumn 58	On completion of refit returned to UK waters.
24.11.58	Clyde as target for submarine commanders course with *Eastbourne* and *Paladin* off Rothesay.
25.11.58	Camperdown.
28.11.58	Lamlash.
12.58	Londonderry.
12.12.58	Portsmouth.
01.59	Icelandic Fishery Patrol.
Mid 02.59	Returned to Portsmouth.
02.59	Visited Vigo with *Agincourt* and cruiser *Gambia* after which sailed to Gibraltar.
03.59	Exercise *Dawn Breeze 4*.
15.03.59	During exercise collided with *Corunna* and received damage to the starboard quarter and after end of the STAAG deck. *Barrosa* returned to Gibraltar to make initial repairs.

Barrosa had been part of the bent line screen made up of several destroyer escorts. Corunna being in the outer starboard position and Barrosa travelling ahead to port in an anti submarine screen. The orders to turn to port were read too early by Corunna and, therefore, closed to Barrosa at a rate of knots - 14 knots approximately. Lieutenant Pritchard, TAS Officer who was Officer of the Watch (Middle Watch) was aware of the approach and he ordered the helm hard over to port. By this action he avoided a collision amidships. A/B 'Tug' Wilson, starboard look out, had reported to the bridge 'Corunna getting near - Corunna getting very near' before contact was made aft.

*HMS Barrosa heads for Gibraltar following her collision with **Corunna**. Notice the gash on the starboard quarter just ahead of the Squid mounting.*
(Maritime Photo Library)

HMS Barrosa *with a full armament fit.* (Maritime Photo Library)

Mick Hutchins recalls the events of the day. "We were in three watches and I had had the first, and by then, had got my head down. Next I realised the lights were on and the Gunnery Officer, Lieutenant Outhwaite, was shouting for everyone to go to their abandon ship stations. My reaction was 'not pleased' and I told him to 'go away' as I had the morning watch! Realising both messes were cleared I joined him reluctantly.

"There were 9 frames damaged on the starboard side aft and, worse, the spirit compartment was flooded. This was solved by a jackstay transfer of rum from Agincourt."

27.04.59	Princes Pier, Greenock.
27.04-12.05.59	Icelandic Cod War.
12.05.59	St Helier for a three day visit.
19.05.59	South Railway Jetty, Portsmouth.
25.05.59	Sailed for Exercise *Shop Window* with **Victorious**.
End 05.59	Plymouth for reconstruction to Radar Picket.
11.12.61	Commander P. F. R. Corson took command.
05.03.62	Compass swinging in Plymouth Sound.
02.05.62	Re-commissioned at Devonport.
05.62	Sea trials.
25.05.52	Portsmouth.
28.05.62	Sailed to Portland.
Late Spring 62	Sea trials continued.
11.09.62	Sailed to Gibraltar from Devonport.
23.09.62	Suez Canal.
27.09.62	Refuelled at Aden.
01.10.62	Sir Abu Nuair Island with **Bulwark** and **Carysfort**.

13.10.62	At Aden.
19.10.62	Port Victoria in Seychelles for a 3-day visit.
10.62	Visited Providence Island, Farquar Island and Mombasa.
25.10.62	Visited Aldabra Island before returning to Aden.
19.11.62	Left Aden to sail to Singapore via Addu Atoll.
30.11.62	Singapore until 7 December.
20.12.62	Indonesian Patrol off North Borneo.
01.63	Exercised with US Navy off Subic Bay followed by visit to Hong Kong.
04.02.63	Sailed to North Borneo for Indonesian Patrol.
12.02.63	Caught suspect pirate craft but AB Charles Alan Sutherland was killed in the incident.

*Whilst operating in the Alice Channel 30 miles off North Borneo **Barrosa** had caught a suspected pirate craft. Thirteen men on board the craft jumped overboard and began swimming for the shore. The ship's whaler gave chase and four of the men were seized. The moon which had been quite bright clouded over and one of the pirates saw an opportunity to fight. He fired his weapon and mortally wounded twenty six year old A.B Charles Alan Sutherland. **Barrosa's** Commanding Officer Commander P.F.R Corson ordered the ship to abandon the chase and speed towards hospital facilities to get AB Sutherland much needed medical care. Regrettably he subsequently died of his injuries.*

Mid 02.63	Visited Tawau, Lahatdatu and Sandakan.
17.02.63	Bombardment practice off Balambangan island for 2 days.
Spring 63	Indonesian Patrol and Exercise *Jet 63* held between 11-17 March in the Bay of Bengal.
18.03.63	Singapore.

HMS Barrosa at sea following her conversion into a "Radar Picket" ship. As well as the obvious changes to the mast and after superstructure, the bridge has also been widened enclosing the space previously used by the bridge wing gun mountings.
(MoD/Crown Copyright)

28.03.63	Gan until 6 April before returning to Singapore.
11.04.63	Exercised with the destroyer *Caesar*.
23.04.63	Lifted dry in *AFD31* for maintenance until 10 May.
24.05.63	Visited Sasebo and berthed on *HMAS Vampire*.
06.63	Visited Matsuyama and Yokohama in Japan.
10.06.63	Exercise *Home Run*.
22.06.63	Singapore.
25.06.63	Plane guard to *Hermes* with *Loch Killisport*.
07.63	Exercise *FOTEX 63*.
13.08.63	Sandakan.
Late 08.63	With *Duchess* en route to Hong Kong.
26.08.63	Arrived at Hong Kong.
02.09.63	Sailed for Tawau with frigate *Plymouth*.
06.09.63	At Tawau.
10.63	Self maintenance at Singapore.
20.10.63	Commander J. A. G. Evans took command.
25.10.63	Re-commissioned.
Autumn 63	Indonesian patrol.
24.12.63	Arrived back at Singapore for a boiler survey and minor repairs.
11.02.64	Repairs and survey completed.
Late 02.64	Sailed to Port Dickson after sea trials.
06.05.64	Visited Chinkae in South Korea.
Mid 05.64	Exercise *Willow Pattern*.
30.05.64	Manila Bay.
27.06.64	In *AFD31* for refit that lasted until 10 October in Singapore.
24.12.64	Hong Kong.
05.01.65	Sailed for Singapore.
15.01.65	Re-commissioned under command of Commander D. L. G. James.
01.65	Patrols in Malacca and Singapore Straits
26.03.65	Exercise *Show Piece* off Langkawi.
27.03.65	Singapore.
03.04.65	Sailed to Hong Kong.
07.04.65	Hong Kong for an 18-day visit.
01.05.65	Started patrol off Belawan in Sumatra.
04.05.65	Singapore.
Summer 65	Visited Hong Kong and Tawau.
Late 08.65	Alongside Heavy Repair Ship *Triumph* at Singapore.
22.09.65	Sailed to Borneo for exercises with *Albion.*
01.10.65	Penang for a four day visit.
04.11.65	In Coral Sea for Exercise *Warrior* until 24 November.
Late 11.65	In Australian waters.
12.65	Visited Providence Bay, Sydney, Hobart and Williamstown for Christmas celebrations and repairs.
27.12.65	Sailed from Williamstown for Singapore via fuelling at Fremantle.
08.01.66	Arrived back at Singapore and entered *AFD31* to have bottom scraped.

Mid 02.66	South East Jahore and Singapore Patrols.
05.03.66	Visited Remunia Shoal.
06.03.66	Sultan Shoal.
Spring 66	Visited Loyang, Hong Kong and Pulau Tioman.
05.66	Visited Pulau Upeh, Pulau Besar, Pulau Hanyot and Gan.
04.06.66	Northbound transit of Suez Canal.
09.06.66	At Gibraltar.
12.06.66	Sailed for the United Kingdom.
16.06.66	Arrived at Devonport.
27.06.66	Refit at Devonport.
04.07.66	Commander J. A. F. Lawson took command.
13.01.67	Sailed for trials.
03.02.67	Re-commissioned followed by sea trials.
18.03.67	Sea trials were interrupted by the ***Torrey Canyon*** disaster. ***Barrosa*** was used to spray detergent onto the sea to try to break up the massive oil spill.

*The destroyer had been refuelling in Plymouth Sound at the time of the disaster and immediately put to sea along with the minesweeper **Clarbeston**. Both ships had onboard large quantities of detergent with which it was hoped to deal with the escaping crude oil.*

*The following day saw **Barrosa**'s crew spraying the detergent over the most badly affected areas. Reports indicated that the crude oil was incredibly smelly and sticky. It coated everything it touched in a thick layer and some wags thought that the destroyer's hull looked like old fashioned camouflage painting. The deck of **Barrosa***

*Laid up at Portsmouth awaiting disposal, **Barrosa** was one of the last of the class to be towed to the breakers yard.*
(Ken Harrow)

was increasingly, however, becoming treacherous to work on as the oil and detergent mixed to make a very slippery surface to walk on.

Such was the scale of the disaster that huge quantities of detergent were necessary and the **Barrosa** had to replenish her supplies frequently usually at Crow Sound in the Scilly Isles. One incident that could have added to the **Torrey Canyon** disaster was mercifully avoided however. A press aircraft flying over the stricken oil tanker flew into the flight path of a Buccaneer strike aircraft flying at over 500 knots. The pilot of the Buccaneer successfully avoided the press aircraft but the manoeuvre the pilot achieved was said to be spectacular. Following this incident air control in the area was handled by the **Barrosa**. March 21 saw the arrival of a fleet of craft to assist the **Barrosa** and **Clarbeston**. These included tugs, fishing boats and small craft. Each carried onboard detergent spraying equipment to aid the spraying campaign. **Barrosa** had by this time plotted the area most affected by the slick and stationed the fleet to the best advantage. The destroyer **Delight** joined the other two Royal Navy vessels on March 23. Eventually, the decision was taken to bomb the **Torrey Canyon** with napalm on 30 March in an effort to destroy the risk of any further leaks from the shattered hull. **HM Ships Aurora**, **Eskimo**, **Daring**, and **Carysfort** joined **Barrosa** and **Delight** in forming 'a ring of steel' at a distance of five miles radius around the tanker and watched the spectacular explosion when the bomb hit the crude oil.

31.03.67	Plymouth for self-maintenance.
11.05.67	Portsmouth.
16.05.67	Portland.
23.06.67	Two-day visit to Southampton.
28.07.67	Sailed on first leg of voyage to East of Suez.
09.08.67	Gibraltar.
08.67	Visited Saint Raphael and Theoulue.
20.08.67	Malta.
11.09.67	Sailed for Gibraltar to make her way round the Cape.
25.09.67	Freetown in Sierra Leone.
04.10.67	Simonstown.
11.10.67	Beira Patrol.
29.10.67	Maintenance period at Mombasa alongside *Triumph*.
21.11.67	Left Beira Patrol to take part in Operation *Magistrar* off Aden.
25.11.67	Naval Review of Task Force 318, of which *Barrosa* was a part.
10.12.67	Escorted *Bulwark* with *Devonshire* off Masirah for withdrawal form Aden.
17.12.67	Sailed from Bandar Riscuit area for Massawa.
20.12.67	Massawa.
27.12.66	Towed RFA tanker *Tidespring*, which had suffered boiler problems back to port in Massawa.
01.01.68	Returned to Aden.
07.01.68	Refuelled at Gan.
12.01,68	Singapore.
18.01.68	Entered *AFD31* for a refit.
11.02.68	Left *AFD31*.
25.02.68	Arrived at Hong Kong.
21.03.68	Sailed for Subic Bay areas.
08.04.68	Chimonoseki in Japan and later Nagasaki.
29.04.68	Subic Bay.
05.05.68	Singapore.

10.05.68	Sailed to Aden via Gan, Astore Island and Port Louis in Mauritius.
03.06.68	Mombasa for 12 days.
20.06.68	Beira Patrol.
28.06.68	Simonstown.
21.07.68	Plymouth Sound.
25.07.68	Devonport Dockyard.
05.09.68	Sailed.
06.09.68	Chatham Dockyard.
09.09.68	Left to take part in Exercise *Silver Tower* on 19 September.
18.09.68	Rosyth.
01.10.68	Sailed for Portsmouth.
21.10.68	Exercise *FRANCEX*.
25.10.68	Gibraltar.
28.10.68	Sailed for Toulon for Exercise *Eden Apple*.
17.11.68	Naples for a four-day visit before sailing onto Malta.
29.11.68	Arrived at Gibraltar.
01.12.68	Sailed for Plymouth.
04.12.68	Arrived in Plymouth Sound.
05.12.68	Sailed into Devonport wearing her paying off pennant.
12.68	Moved to Portsmouth.
1970	Put on Disposal List but used as static stores hulk.
02.08.78	Sold for breaking up.
12.78	Demolition completed at Blyth.

Barrosa Memories

David Lee remembers his time onboard **Barrosa**, *"I joined the **Barrosa** in Plymouth in April 1962. She was an extremely hot ship to live on under operational conditions out in the Far East. Most of the crew suffered from extreme sweat rash, prickly heat and salt loss. But, it did give me an education in life that civilian life could never have given me."*

Trevor Harman remembers the problem of terrorism in the area during his time onboard. *"A lot of our time during our 18 months in the Far East was taken up with operations along the West coast of Malaya. The Indonesian confrontation was well advanced by this time and along with other naval units we were required to patrol the seas around the coast of Malaya in an attempt to prevent incursion by hostile groups of Indonesian terrorists, regular soldiers and saboteurs. They would normally travel by night and used small wooden boats called kumpits to carry arms, explosives and intelligence information. The kumpits were usually crewed by one, two and sometimes three personnel and our job was to stop and search. Occasionally we would anchor off one of the small islands and all those not required for duty onboard would take to the boats for a banyan ashore. The most popular island being Pulau Tioman. This was a small sandy beached paradise with a few local residents and some coconut palms. The sea was very clear, ideal for swimming and snorkelling. I don't know what the local residents thought about as we would only borrow their island for a couple of hours I suppose they were happy to tolerate us."*

HMS CORUNNA

A fine aerial view of **HMS Corunna**. *(MoD/Crown Copyright)*

03.43	Ordered from Swan Hunter & Wigham Richardson Ltd.
12.04.44	Laid down.
27.05.45	Launched.
06.06.47	Completed.
16.06.47	Chatham Dockyard.
19.06.47	Sailed to continue trials throughout autumn 1947.
Christmas 47	At Chatham Dockyard.
29.04.48	Spent months at Chatham with brief periods at sea.
26.08.48	Commander T. D. Herrich took command.
09/10.48	At sea with *Vengeance* en-route to South Africa.
05.10.48	Freetown.
07.10.48	Simonstown.
10.48	A visit was made to East London.
11.48	Visits made to Durban and Cape Town.
26.11.48	Freetown.
12.12.48	Sheerness to unload ammunition.
15.12.48	Chatham for brief refit and leave.
23.02.49	Sailed Chatham to operate in Home Waters before returning to Chatham on 25 March 1949.
02.05.49	Sailed to Gibraltar.
07.05.49	Gibraltar and onward to Malta and Suez Canal.

28.05.49	Aqaba where she stayed until 12 June.
14.06.49	Northbound transit of Suez Canal.
16.06.49	Left Port Said for Kyrenia and Famgusta on Cyprus.
06.49	Cyprus.
28.06.49	Malta.
07.49	Visited Phaleron and Syros.
08.49	Visited Poros, Trieste and Venice.
26.08.49	Squadron arrived at Gibraltar en route to United Kingdom.
02.09.49	Chatham Dockyard.
05.09.49	Commander F. J. Cartwright took command.
11.10.49	Sailed Chatham for home waters.
23.11.49	Returned to Chatham.
19.01.50	Sailed Chatham.
28.01.50	Portland.
02.02.50	Gibraltar.
03.50	Visited Palmas Bay, Rapallo with the cruiser *Superb* on 8 March for a five-day stay.
03.50	Jijelli and on 22 March a return to Gibraltar.
31.03.50	Sheerness and later the same day Chatham Dockyard.
09.05.50	Sailed Chatham to escort the aircraft carrier *Implacable*.
12.06.50	Searched for crashed Sea Hornet from the carrier.
06.50	Very rough seas in English Channel meant that destroyer had to proceed to Portsmouth for repairs.

*With all guns trained to port, **Corunna** is seen during a firepower demonstration.*   (MoD/Crown Copyright)

07.50	With *Implacable* in Moray Firth areas before sailing to Norway with visits to Trondheim and Malmo.
27.07.50	Returned to Chatham for summer leave.
05.09.50	Sailed with *Solebay*, *Gabbard* and *Crossbow*.
09.50	Summer cruise to the Mediterranean with *Vanguard*, *Cleopatra*, *Swiftsure* and *Vengeance*.
18.10.50	Sal Rei before going onto visit Casablanca on 27 October 1950.
04.11.50	Gibraltar.
16.11.50	Sheerness.
17.11.50	Chatham for brief refit.
End of 01.51	At Gibraltar.
02.51	Ajaccio and St Maxime.
15.03.51	Gibraltar before returning to Chatham.
24.03.51	Chatham Navy Days for 3 days berthed inboard on *Broadsword*.
16.04.51	Commander R. H. C. Wyld DSC took command. A week later she sailed for Sheerness and onwards to Portsmouth for C-in-C Home Fleet Inspection by Admiral Vian.
26.04.51	Sailed from Portsmouth bound for Bangor in Northern Ireland. Later she carried out training around Loch Ewe/Loch Eriboll and Burghead Bay.
05.51	Training at Invergordon, Plymouth and Portland.
18.05.51	Portsmouth.
22.05.51	Plymouth.
Late 05.51	Visited St Ives, Torquay and then arrived Devonport on 31 May.
Early 06.51	Exercise *Progress*, which started at Penzance and finished at Cherbourg on 7 June.
09.06.51	Left Cherbourg for Weymouth and Lamlash on 15 June.
1951	Festival of Britain cruise with *Swiftsure*, *Agincourt*, *Aisne* and *Jutland* took her to Glasgow. The cruise took *Corunna* to Oban, Ayr and Bangor.
16.07.51	Sheerness and Chatham for a short refit.
04.09.51	Refit completed and made for Portsmouth.
08.09.51	Sailed to St Andrews for Royal SAR duties for HM King George VI.
09.51	Operating off Invergordon.
Late 09.51	Abadan Oil crisis called for the squadron to sail to Persian Gulf, but this was later cancelled.
08.10.51	Sailed from Chatham for Penzance, Plymouth and Gibraltar.
05.11.51	Sailed to Malta and secondment to the Mediterranean fleet.
10.11.51	Guard ship at Port Suez.
21.11.51	Sailed to Port Said and later Ismailia
02.12.51	Port Said.
12.51	Off Egypt.
19.01.52	Sailed for Malta.
28.01.52	Sailed from Malta for Larnaca and Kyrenia.
11.02.52	Sailed from Kyrenia.
02.52	Malta, Palermo and Gibraltar.
07.03.52	Sheerness and Chatham for refit.
15.05.52	Refit completed.
20.05.52	Portland.
06.52	Exercise *Castinets*.
27.06.52	Anchored half a mile off Hastings for six days.

07.52	Visited Spithead and La Harve with **Indomitable** and **SS United States** on 10 July with a return to Chatham on the same day.
07.52	Refit at Chatham.
18.08.52	Refit completed.
21.08.52	Commander J. N. Kennard relieved Commander Richard Herbert Chelcroft Wyld DSC and Bar.
18.08.52	Left Chatham to ammunition at Sheerness.
08.52	In Northern Irish waters.
09.52	Crossed Irish Sea to Greenock at start of Exercise *Mainbrace*.
13.09.52	Start of exercises that took the ships to the Arctic. Bad weather forced **Corunna** to head to Trondheim. Later in the exercise **Corunna** also visited Esjberg.
01.10.52	Sailed from Esjberg to Rosyth to make repairs.
11.11.52	Left Rosyth for Londonderry before returning to Rosyth at the beginning of November.
17.11.52	Sailed for Exercise *Autumn Bear* off Jan Mayen Island with temperatures of -30°C.
30.11.52	Sheerness.
01.12.52	Chatham for refit.
19.01.53	Sailed to operate in Home Waters.
27.03.53	Returned to Chatham for maintenance until 07.05.53.
06.53	Coronation Review at Spithead moored between **Solebay** and **Aisne**.
09.53	Exercise *Mariner* in Denmark Straits with **Vanguard**, **Eagle**, **Swiftsure** and **USS Iowa**.
02.11.53	Chatham.
25.01.54	Left for the Solent.
05.02.54	Left Portland for Gibraltar.

HMS Corunna's *original armament layout before her conversion to a Radar Picket Ship.* (Maritime Photo Library)

26.02.54	Casablanca.
03.54	Exercise *Ginblast* en route to Gibraltar.
14.03.54	Gibraltar.
19.03.54	Exercise *Toughline*.
28.03.54	Sailed for Chatham and Operation *Loyalty* en route.
02.04.54	Chatham for a maintenance period.
06.05.54	Sailed from Chatham.
05.54	Visited Brixham and Torquay.
14.05.54	Escorted **Britannia** and **Triumph**.
14.05.54	Portsmouth.
24.05.54	Sailed for Invergordon.
End 05.54	Summer Cruise with **Vanguard**, **Implacable** and **Indefatigable**.
17.06.54	Scapa Flow for Fleet Regatta.
21.06.54	Flushing with **Barrosa** and onward journey to Antwerp.
20.07.54	Chatham for Navy Days.
30.08.54	Sailed for Invergordon and NATO Exercise *Morning Mist* for a fortnight including a visit to Bergen.
11.10.54	Morecambe and Heysham.
10.54	Visited Cardiff and Falmouth.
21.10.54	Gibraltar.
11.54	Operated off Gibraltar.
23.11.54	Chatham Dockyard.
01.12.54	Commander R. A. Begg took command.
06.12.54	Sailed from Chatham for Sheerness.
07.12.54	St Helens.
16.12.54	Gibraltar.
18.12.54	Sailed for Malta.
21.12.54	Malta.
Early 55	Visited Beirut and Cyprus.
28.03.55	Gibraltar for refit.
End 06.55	Casablanca.
07.55	Returned to Malta.
07.55	Visited Venice and Split in Yugoslavia.
03.08.55	Malta.
08.55	En route to UK visited La Pallice in France.
09.55	Chatham Dockyard.
09.55	Invergordon and NATO Exercise *Sea Enterprise*.
03.10.55	Chatham Dockyard.
26.10.55	Sailed to Rosyth.
11.55	Visited Liverpool, Londonderry and Rothesay.
08.12.55	Chatham to be dry-docked until 16 January 1956.
Early 1956	Operated in Home waters.
26.03.56	Chatham.
26.04.56	Visited London as Headquarters ship for Easter Navy Days.
30.04.56	Sailed from London.

04.56	Portland and Lisbon and Corunna in Spain.
15.05.56	Chatham.
29.05.56	Re-commissioned.
28.08.56	Malta.
10.56	Gibraltar.
10.56	Return visit to La Corunna. 10,000 people toured the destroyer during five-day stay.
23.12.56	Took post to Syracuse.

*On 23 December the merchant packet that normally brought mail from Sicily to Malta cancelled its call and the Maltese post office appealed to the Navy for help. **Corunna** sailed to Syracuse. There they arranged for the train with the mail to be shunted close to the ship's berth and the bags taken onboard. **Corunna** reached Malta with seven Maltese passengers and 15 tons of mail at five o'clock on Christmas Eve. The destroyer wore a large notice saying Royal Mail and for good measure the one of the ship's company paraded the upper deck dressed as Santa Claus with a bag of Yuletide mail on his back.*

24.12.56	Returned to Malta with 7 Maltese passengers and 15 tons of mail.
1957	Started exercises around Malta.
05.04.57	Chatham.
10.05.57	Sailed from Chatham.
18.05.57	Northeast Coast of England to escort **Britannia** during visit to Hull. Together with **Diamond** and **Duchess**, **Corunna** escorted the Royal Yacht on a visit to Copenhagen.
21.05.57	Copenhagen.
25.05.57	Left to return to Home Fleet Inspection in Moray Firth two days later.
26.07.57	Chatham.
30.08.57	Sailed to operate in Home Waters.
31.09.57	Chatham.
11.57	Re-commissioned for service in Mediterranean.
Christmas 57	Malta.
1958	In Mediterranean.
12.12.58	Chatham.
19.01.59	To sea, reurning to Chatham 16.02.59.
23.02.59	Sailed with 4th DS to visit La Corunna.
05.03.59	Gibraltar to take part in Exercise *Dawn Breeze 4*.
15.03.59	Collided with **Barrosa**. **Corunna**'s damage was extensive and required her to steam stern first to Gibraltar and was steered by main engines. Once at Gibraltar most of her bow was sliced off and a temporary new bow fitted. **Corunna** was then taken to Rosyth.
Late 1959	Refit started to convert the destroyer into Radar Picket. Refit took two years to complete and totally altered her appearance. A huge radar set was mounted on a new mainmast, a Seacat missile launcher was fitted and a new deck house built at a cost of £2.5 million.
09.12.61	First sea trials post refit.
10.12.61	Some compartments damaged by flooding to a depth of 8 feet.
02.01.62	Commander O. N. A. Cecil took command
Early 62	Worked up off Portland before joining 7th DS in the Mediterranean.
22.06.62	Clyde.
12.07.62	Exercise *Shop Window*.

*Damage caused by the collision with **Barrosa** is evident in this view taken after the accident.   (Maritime Photo Library)*

*Not the most elegant of repairs! **Corunna** was fitted with a temporary bow at Gibraltar following her collision.*
(T. Ferrers-Walker Collection)

HMS Corunna *following her conversion into a Radar Picket Ship.* (*Maritime Photo Library*)

21.07.62	Portsmouth.
09.08.62	*Corruna*, *Centaur* and *Hermes* sailed from Gibraltar to take part in *Exercise Riptide III* with US aircraft carriers *USS Forrestal* and *USS Enterprise*.
16.08.62	Portuguese port of Estoril at the mouth of the River Tagus.
08.62	Exercise *Alfex* in the Gulf of Lions.
27.08.62	With *Hermes* and *Scorpion* off Malta.
Early 63	Joined Escort Squadron.
08.63	Portsmouth Navy Days.
End of 1963	Rosyth for refit.
13.12.63	Commander B. K. Shattock took command.
01.02.64	Re-commissioned at Rosyth.
11.03.64	Sailed for Portsmouth and onward journey to Portland.
03.64	During work-up collided with tanker *RFA Tidepool* went to Devonport for repairs to this damage and her boilers.
Early 64	During trials suffered a boiler room fire.
02.11.64	Sailed from Portsmouth.
01.12.64	Gibraltar and onward journey to Suez, Aden and Gan, where she refuelled.
21.12.64	Refuelled from *RFA Retainer*.
23.12.64	Penang.
27.12.64	Sailed to Singapore to join anti-terrorism patrols in Indonesia.
Early 02.65	Hong Kong and exercises with *Victorious*.
27.02.65	Singapore for 3-week maintenance period.
17.03.65	Sailed for Exercise *FOTEX* with *Eagle* and *Victorious*.

Early 65	Langkawi before returning to Singapore.
Early 05.65	With **HMAS Melbourne** and **USS Bennington** to Manila for Exercise *Seahorse*. The exercise ended with a visit to Bangkok.
08.65	Hong Kong - also rode out Typhoon Babe in South China Sea with the destroyer **Cambrian**.
08.65	Exercise *Windy Weather* prior to arriving at Singapore. **Corunna** was escort to the assault carriers **Albion** and **Bulwark**.
23.08.65	Chatham Dockyard.

*Ken Mowatt recalls "I was on the **Blackwood** in Rosyth Dockyard, and the **Corunna** was in the basin. One evening, when we were doing sunset, there was no one on the **Corunna**'s ensign. Suddenly a person in overalls came out the aft superstructure with an axe, chopped the ensign staff so it and the ensign fell into the basin and then he disappeared back into the superstructure, it turned out that that was her last day in commission."*

09.65	Refit at Rosyth.
04.67	Operational Reserve at Portsmouth.
1972	Placed on disposal list.
20.11.74	Arrived at Sunderland under tow of **Roysterer**. Breaking up was, however, delayed.
11.09.75	Ship towed to Blyth to complete destruction.
23.11.75	Breaking up was completed.

HMS Corunna *in the Far East with the aircraft carrier* **HMS Victorious.**   *(Steve Bush Collection)*

T. E. Warden recalls that he joined **Corunna** at Chatham Dockyard on 18 November 1957. *"When she re-commissioned on what was then the last of the old General Service Commissions. At the time I was the Yeoman of the Signals and her Captain was Commander T. T. Lewin DSC (Later Admiral of the Fleet the Lord Lewin KG).*

"Our new captain was Commander Cecil Gordon DSC who was a submariner returning to general service. He was a good Captain and highly thought of by our ships company. **Corunna** *was the Divisional Commander in the 4th Destroyer Squadron, the other ships being* **Agincourt**, **Alamein** *and* **Barrosa**.*"

"All four ships left the United Kingdom shortly after re-commissioning for the Mediterranean carrying out only a very brief work up at Portland. We arrived in Malta just in time for Christmas. We spent a reasonably happy time in the Mediterranean with the usual activities of a fleet destroyer, mainly on the Cyprus patrol at first. Later in the hum drum role of dogs-body in Fleet exercises which as the ship's Yeoman of Signals - I very much enjoyed. Apart from my usual duties, there was a 4.7-inch gun just aft of the funnel on the port side and this was very rarely used but our ship's Gunnery Instructor PO(GI) Ernie Davis made up a scratch guns crew of stokers and other odd bods - including me as Captain of the gun. We enjoyed the few occasions when we got to fire this gun as it was really designed as a star shell gun for the main armament."

"On completion of our time in the Mediterranean we returned to the United Kingdom and became a home based unit once more at Chatham together with sister ship **Alamein**. *The most memorable activity we did whilst in the Home Fleet was on Fishery protection duties in the Icelandic Cod War."*

HMS DUNKIRK

*An early view of **HMS Dunkirk**, still with her original pennant number of I09.*   *(Ben Warlow Collection)*

19.07.44	Laid down by Alexander Stephens and Sons, Glasgow.
27.08.45	Launched.
03.46	Lieutenant Commander J. Smallwood took command.
27.11.46	Completed.
End of 1946	Joined 4th DF and went to the Mediterranean for the next two years.
22.07.47	Clyde Fleet Review at Greenock.
02.49	Decision taken to place **Dunkirk** in reserve.
03.49	Paid off at Londonderry and taken to Devonport .Whilst at Devonport, **Dunkirk** was used as the stokers training ship for **HMS Raleigh**.
20.5.58	Re-commissioned at Portsmouth with **Jutland** and **Trafalgar** with Commander J. Nash DSC in command.
07.06.58	Sailed for Mediterranean via Gibraltar.
01.07.58	Suffered a boiler room fire.
04.07.58	Off Famgusta for Cyprus Patrol, which included a visit to Beirut.
08.08.58	Civatavecchia and onward to Istanbul before resuming Cyprus patrol.
27.11.58	Visited Haifa with **Sheffield** and **Trafalgar**.
02.12.58	Malta.
Mid 12.58	Exercises off Palmas Bay.

HMS Dunkirk *and her sistership* **Trafalgar** *at Monaco in February 1959.*   *(Douglas Busby)*

20.12.58	Malta.
30.12.58	Collided with *Jutland* causing slight damage.
01.59	Visited Monaco.
28.01.59	Their Serene Highnesses Prince Rainier and Princess Grace of Monaco onboard.
02.59	Visited Tripoli and took part in Exercise *FEBEX*.
02.59	Cyprus patrol.
23.03.59	Malta.
08.04.59	NATOs 10th Anniversary celebrations at Malta.
05.59	Istanbul.
Summer 59	Returned to the United Kingdom.
08.59	Plymouth Navy Days.
26.08-11.09.59	Icelandic fishery patrol.
13.09.59	Rosyth.
21.09.59	With *Victorious*, *Armada* and *Trafalgar* for Exercise *Blue Frost* and Exercise *Barefoot*.
02.10.59	Rosyth.
Late 1959	Icelandic fishery patrol.
Late 1959	Visited Gothenburg and Amsterdam.
23.11.59	Commander Henry C. Leach took command.
24.11.59	Re-commissioned.
12.59	Arrived off Plymouth.
06.01.60	Portland.

22.02.60	Plymouth.
Mid 03.60	Exercise *Dawn Breeze V* off Gibraltar.
Mid 03.60	Joined 7th DS in Mediterranean which was composed of **Trafalgar**, **Jutland**, **Scorpion** and **Broadsword**.
1960	Visited Palmas Bay, Cyprus Patrol, Naples, Messina and Tripoli on 7 October.
19.11.60	Toulon before returning to Malta.
11.60	Exercise *Royal Flush IV*.
13.12.60	Malta.
23.01.61	Toulon for Exercise *MEDASWEX 42* in the Gulf of Lions.
02.61	Visited La Spezia, Heraklion and Souda Bay.
12.02.61	Exercise *Inner Circle*.
15.02.61	Piraeus and Souda Bay.
22.02.61	Malta.
08.03.61	Alicante.
18.03.61	Brest for start of Exercise *Dawn Breeze VI*.
24.03.61	Devonport.
27.3.61	Portland.
07.06.61	Weymouth Bay area with **Trafalgar**.
Mid 08.61	Bantry Bay.
1961	Tour of South America for four months with the cruiser **Lion** and frigates **Leopard** and **Londonderry** and **RFA Wave Prince**. The ships visited Rio de Janeiro, Buenos Aires, Mar

HMS Dunkirk *in 1961. Other than a revised pennant number, she appears little changed from when originally completed in 1946.*
(Steve Bush Collection)

*A splendid view of **HMS Dunkirk** from the air showing the layout of the weapons to good effect.*

(MoD/Crown Copyright)

	del Plata and Commodore Rivadavia in Argentina.
17.01.62	Sailed from Valparaiso for port of Callao.
29.01.62	Panama Canal.
02.62	**Dunkirk** stayed with **Lion** and visited San Juan before crossing the Atlantic to the Azores and the port of Ponta Delgada.
21.02.62	Plymouth.
02.62	Leave before heading to the Mediterranean and a small refit at Malta.
06.03.62	Exercise *Dawn Breeze*.
05.04.62	Malaga.
05.62	Exercised with the aircraft carrier **Centaur**.
06.05.62	Corfu for four days.
01.06.62	Barcelona and Palma.
06.62	Sorrento before onward journey to Malta.
27.06.62	Left Malta to exercise with **Hermes** and submarine **Tiptoe** off Tobruk.
Summer 62	King Hussein of Jordan and Princess Muna-al-Hussein visited the ship along with singer Gracie Fields.
07.62	Leghorn.
19.08.62	Malta after visits to San Remo and Theoule in France.
30.09.62	Visited Lemnos and Zanguldak.
09.62	Exercise *Falltrap* with Italian and US warships in bad weather, so bad that the programme was abandoned.

01.10.62	Plane Guard to aircraft carrier *Centaur*.
06.10.62	Larnaca.
09.10.62	Haifa.
15.10.62	Mersin.
18.10.62	Beirut.
23.10.62	Sailed from Beirut bound for Malta.
26.10.62	Malta.
31.10.62	Sailed from Malta for Izmir and Exercise *MEDASWEX*.
11.11.62	Malta.
11.62	Cartagena in Spain for Exercise *SPANEX* before returning to Malta.
15.12.62	Exercised with *Corunna* and *Lion*.
12.62	Was due to return to the United Kingdom, but *Broadsword* developed a fault and *Dunkirk* stayed in her place in the Mediterranean.
17.01.63	Sailed from Malta for Taranto arriving after 2-days at sea.
02.63	Visited Naples, Cyprus, Beirut and Souda Bay.
03.03.63	Malta.
12.03.63	Gibraltar.
18.03.62	Arrived Plymouth for final time.
1964	Used as extra accommodation at Devonport.
11.65	Towed away from Plymouth.
22.11.65	Arrived at Shipbreaking Industries Faslane for breaking up.

*A very smart looking **HMS Dunkirk** leaving Malta on a sunny day.* (Steve Bush Collection)

Dunkirk Memories

Bill Campbell remembers his first impression of **Dunkirk**. *"I had just finished an engineering course on the old **Alaunia** that had lasted from April to July, 1952 and got a draft to **HMS Raleigh**. But instead of going to my old Alma Mater in Torpoint, I went onboard the **Dunkirk** which happened to be alongside the **Alaunia**. Evidently, the **Dunkirk** was the stoker's training ship for **Raleigh** and I was one of the small ships' company allocated to help with their training. It was a cushy number and we had plenty of free time after daily duties - although our trips ashore were via the **Alaunia** which meant falling in on her quarterdeck to be inspected, not always welcome. The odd time we could hitch a ride on our own motor boat, cutting out a lot of red tape. It could be handy sometimes if we wanted to avoid passing through the dockyard gates where we may be inspected for having illegal tobacco. A craft run in the motor boat across to the Cornwall shore could be a Godsend at times. A bus to Torpoint then the ferry over to Devonport and we were in Plymouth without loosing too much time. I was on the **Dunkirk** for almost a year and at the time never imagined she would ever go to sea again, but evidently she did, although I never saw her again."*

Terry Stevenson recalls joining **Dunkirk**, *"On joining **Dunkirk** we had a four month tour showing the flag all around South America."* **Dunkirk** was part of a powerful force assembled by the Royal Navy that comprised the cruiser **Lion**, the frigates **Leopard** and **Londonderry**, the **Dunkirk** and the oiler **RFA Wave Prince**."*

Ivor Rich recalls this South American trip with fondness. *"In South America we visited Rio De Janiero in Brazil, Buenos Aries, Mar Del Plata and Commodore Rivadavia in Argentina."* He also remembers Christmas Day 1961. *"I was under arrest on Christmas Day in Buenos Aries for coming back to the ship inebriated and taking a police horse from a paddock across from the ship and trying to get it onboard, with the ridiculous intention of putting it in the Coxswain's cabin."*

HMS JUTLAND

HMS Jutland prepares to come alongside at Capetown, South Africa.   *(Maritime Photo Library)*

1943	Contract awarded to Alexander Stephens and Sons, Glasgow.
27.11.44	Laid down.
20.02.46	Launched as *Malplaquet*.
1947	Renamed *Jutland*.
30.4.47	Completed.
12.05.47	Arrived at Chatham at start of trials.
22.07.47	Clyde Fleet Review at Greenock.
1948	Joined the 4th Destroyer Flotilla.
12.12.48	Arrived back at Chatham.
02.49	Operated with *Vanguard* and *Superb* off Gibraltar.
24.06.49	Exercise *Verity* in Western Approaches.
08.49	Visited Scotland, Invergordon and Northern Ireland then onto the Mediterranean with visits to Gibraltar and Calgari.
18.10.49	In Scottish waters and intercepted a suspected Soviet Spy Ship.

Tom Watson recalls: "This was to be kept secret but I can remember the sea was very rough when we caught up with the Russian ship. We went alongside her shining light from fore to aft, the crew onboard seemed to be dashing for cover, one of our officers was shouting out instructions to the Russian ship which I couldn't hear very well. After the incident, which lasted about half an hour, we sailed away from her and shadowed her for a few days."

16.11.49	Arrived at Chatham.
02-03.50	Exercise *Verity*.
22.05.50	Exercise *Activity* with Dutch and French ships in Dourarenez Bay.
08.50	Arrived Portsmouth.
17.08.50	Arrived at Chatham to be reduced to reserve.
23.04.51	Re-activated.
05.51	Off Bangor, Loch Ewe, Loch Eriboll or Burghead Bay.
24.10.51	Off St Ives then onto Torquay and Plymouth.
02.06.51	Exercise *Progress* in Bay of Biscay.
06.51	Festival of Britain cruise with visits to Lamlash, Oban and Ayr.
10.07.51	Arrived at Chatham.
18.07.51	Festival of Britain Cruise at Southend on Sea with **Vengeance**.
26.07.51	Arrived Portsmouth before going onto Chatham.
04.09.51	Left Chatham for training in Scottish waters. The Abadan Oil Well Crisis caused a change in plans and the 4th DS was told to prepare to sail to the Persian Gulf. The decision was rescinded after a few days however.
10.51	Exercise *Assess* off Gibraltar and then onto Malta.
10.11.51	Sailed from Malta for duties as Port Said guardship, where she stayed throughout November.
25.12.51	Christmas was spent at Malta before returning to Port Said.
1952	Visited Larnaca, Kyrenia and Palermo before returning to the United Kingdom.
06.03.52	Arrived at Portsmouth for a short refit.
05.52	Fire broke out onboard in dry-dock.
05.52	Refit completed **Jutland** returned to Chatham.

HMS Jutland *at a fleet gathering prior to fleet exercises. The three King George V class battleships of the Training Squadron are visible in the background.* *(Steve Bush Collection)*

*This stern view of **HMS Jutland** shows the different AA mountings carried aft.*   (*MoD/Crown Copyright*)

1953	Decision taken to reduce the destroyer to reserve at Portsmouth.
18.05.53	Brought forward from reserve for Coronation Review. Positioned on Line E between *Trafalgar* and ***Obdurate***. When the Review was over ***Jutland*** was returned to the dockyard for another refit and placed in reserve again.
09.57	Taken to Chatham for a major refit.
05.58	Refit completed.
20.05.58	Formed part of the 7th DS with ***Dunkirk*** and ***Trafalgar***, with all the ships commissioning together at Portsmouth.
07.06.58	Work ups at Portland, then passage to Gibraltar and Malta.
Summer 58	Anti-terrorism patrols off Cyprus.
28.05.59	Exercise *Fairwind*.
12.06.59	At Rosyth storing up for Cod War duties off Iceland.
07.07.59	Londonderry.
01.08.59	Chatham Navy Days.
21.08.59	Sailed from Chatham Dockyard.

11.09.59	Off Invergordon with *Bermuda*, *Camperdown*, *Saintes*, *Armada* and *Trafalgar*.
22.09.59	Trondheim for exercises.
Autumn 59	Returned to Cod War Patrols off Iceland.

Jim Welford recalls his times onboard. "We were involved in the first cod war and spent, I think, a month up there in August patrolling round and round Iceland. We only entered harbour to refuel at the Shell jetty in Reykjavik, obviously no shore leave so we spent our time fishing over the side in the harbour. We were amazed at the amount of flatties we caught, your line hardly reached the bottom before you had one, not that we wanted them as our fishing fleet kept us so well stocked with fresh fish of every variety. We had, four gash bins lashed to the upper deck. Every time we rendezvoused with a trawler because she was either inside the limit or was having trouble with her radar in which case we sent a radar bod over to her to repair it, they always filled our inflatable with fish before it returned to us. My officers' galley was always full of stokers after I had finished the evening meal, busily frying their fish, there was so much fish nobody bothered with chips. Now I know why the wardroom at RNB Chatham asked us to keep our frozen provisions store low - so we could top up with fish on our return for them."

07.11.59	Relieved on Cod War Patrols.
09.11.59	Visited Gothenburg.
18.11.59	Arrived home to Chatham.
22.11.59	*Jutland* re-commissioned with Commander R. P. Fitzgerald DSC in command.
02.12.59	Sailed from Chatham for Portland.

HM Ships Jutland, *Dunkirk* and *Trafalgar* *steaming in line abreast.*   *(MoD/Crown Copyright)*

HMS Jutland *at speed.*   *(John Brewer)*

25.12.59	Arrived at Chatham for maintenance.
10.03.59	Sailed from Chatham for Mediterranean.
Spring/Sum 59	Visited Palmas, Valetta, Crete and Naples.
10.60	Exercises *Water Gap 1, Full Cry II* and *MEDASWEX 40.*
Late 11.60	Visited Barcelona for five days.
12.60	Exercise *DECEX.*
12.60	Exercise *Royal Flus*h off Malta.
01.61	Exercise *JANEX* before sailing to Toulon, which was visited again on 1 February.
10.02.61	Sailed through Straits of Messina before visiting Olympia, Navaro and Patras.
15.03.61	Left Gibraltar.
18.03.61	Arrived at Brest to take part in Exercise *Dawn Breeze VI.*
25.03.61	Arrived at Chatham.
27.04.61	Left Chatham for Portland to carry out crew training.
17.05.61	Returned to Chatham.
22.05.61	Commander J. D. Honeywill became the destroyer's, last commanding officer.
23.05.61	Ship re-commissioned.
05.06.61	Sailed from Chatham.
24.08.61	Chatham for refit.
28.09.61	Refit completed.
05.10.61	Left Chatham for Kiel in Germany. Collided with oiler in Loch Eriboll during a storm. Crushed bow was repaired at Rosyth.

Jim Welford remembers that "the weather was atrocious so it was pot mess every day. The Americans decided it was too rough to continue so we all anchored in Loch Eriboll and our captain decided to oil at sea instead of in the loch to show the Yanks how it should be done. Things, however, didn't go quite to plan as we collided with the oiler while we were taking on fuel, so the exercise was off for us and we limped back to Rosyth for repairs to our bows."

*Whilst at Rosyth, two members of **Jutland**'s crew got into trouble with the local police. The two men, missed the liberty boat back to their ship and had walked across the Forth using the tiny catwalk, which had no safety rails, that was strung at a height of 500 feet above the river between the towers of the new road bridge then being built. At Dumfermline Sheriff Court they were fined £3 each for 'causing a breach of the peace by putting two night watchmen on the bridge in a state of fear.*

07.12.61	Returned to Chatham for seasonal leave.
15.01.62	Left Chatham.
16.01.62	Arrived at Portland for CASEX with *Trafalgar*.
17.02.62	Arrived at Portsmouth.
28.02.62	Left Portsmouth for Cherbourg and Exercise *Dawn Breeze 7*.
04.62	Visited Lamlash and Greenock.
09.04.62	Arrived at Chatham.
8.05.62	Sailed from Chatham.
06.62	Paid off at Portsmouth.
Spring 1963	Moved to Chatham and entered Reserve Fleet.
12.05.65	Sailed from Chatham for the last time.
14.05.65	Arrived Hughes Bolckow at Blyth for breaking up.

Jutland Memories

Tom Watson joined **Jutland** in August 1949 at Chatham. *"On my first trip to sea the ship patrolled in the North Sea, Irish Sea and the Atlantic calling into Sheerness, Scotland, Invergordon and Northern Ireland before returning to Chatham on 2 September. After a short spell in dock we sailed for the Mediterranean calling at Gibraltar and Calgari. During my daily morning chores I can remember all the waste had to be disposed of down the chute at the stern of the ship. After cleaning out the mess I threw the rubbish over the side amidships, we were doing around 25 knots at the time and the rubbish blew into the face of the Chief Petty Officer who was furious. I just bolted but he caught up with me and told me to report to him at 1800 hours that day which I did. He gave me a very small brush and told me to scrub the decks while he paraded up and down the ship keeping an eye on me. I never knew if I was scrubbing it clean or not because the waves kept coming over the sides washing the soap away. I must have done a good job because after a couple of hours he relieved me."*

Tom Watson also remembers that the **Jutland** *"reached the final of the Flotilla Football cup, which I played although we lost. I played for Newcastle United prior to being called up and while on her I was selected to play for the combined services against a Spanish side and later an Italian eleven."*

HMS MATAPAN

HMS Matapan was the last of the RN Battle class to be completed and is shown here during her sea trials in September 1947. She went into reserve almost immediately afterwards and remained there, virtually a brand new ship, until 1969, when she was earmarked for conversion to a trials Ship. *(John Brewer)*

11.03.44	Laid down at John Brown's yard.
30.04.45	Launched.
05.09.47	Finally Completed.
22.09.47	Arrived at Chatham Dockyard followed by sea trials in River Medway and Thames Estuary. Later used as a depot ship and then prepared for the reserve fleet having only steamed for 150 hours.
28.10.47	Left Chatham and laid up in Gillingham Reach on the River Medway for a few months.
02.07.48	Entered Chatham Dockyard to prepare for the tow to Devonport.
20.07.48	Left Chatham.
07.48	Arrived at Devonport and placed into reserve.
1961	Decision taken to convert the destroyer into the Royal Navy's Underwater Trials Ship. Was to be fitted with the Type 2016 sonar for trials. However, lack of funds meant that she remained at her River Tamar mooring.
05.01.70	Entered No 14 Dry Dock at Portsmouth at the start of her refit. A special 13ft high plinth was placed underneath the destroyer to support her whilst the sonar dome was fitted. The ship was completely rebuilt and bore little resemblance to her destroyer heritage. All weapons were removed and replaced with sophisticated equipment and a flightdeck. Her displacement rose to 3,835 tons.

01.11.71	Left No.14 dry dock at Portsmouth.
08.05.72	Commander W. H. H. McLeod took command.
27.07.72	Began sea trials.
02.02.73	Re-commissioned.
28.04.75	Spent time at Portland and in Scottish waters. Whilst off Scotland the sonar housing flooded after which *Matapan* spent a period in dry dock at Devonport undertaking repairs.
Early 1976	Back at sea and sonar trials off east coast of the United States and in the Caribbean.
08.77	Paid off and laid up at Portsmouth.
18.05.79	Sold to H. K. Vickers at Blyth.
11.08.79	Arrived Blyth for demolition to start.

Of the Battle class destroyers the dubious honour of the ship with the shortest active career goes to *Matapan*, and her career was spent as a sonar trials vessel. The ship was originally constructed as a standard Battle class destroyer but her completion was severely delayed by the end of the war and when finally completed there appeared, at first, to be no active role for the new ship to play. *Matapan's* history started when John Brown ship-yard received the contract for the destroyer's construction. The new ship was given the yard number 616 and was duly laid down on the slipway on 11 March 1944. Construction of the destroyer progressed well and was readied for her launch on 30 April 1945. The urgent need for the ship had disappeared with the end of the war in Europe and further progress on *Matapan* slowed to a crawling pace. Her hull, superstructure and fittings were finally completed on 5 September 1947.

M. Gilmour recalls the time he spent onboard *Matapan* after having spent fifteen months at *HMS*

HMS Matapan *during sea trials in her original configuration.*   *(MoD/Crown Copyright)*

HMS Matapan *stretched her legs as a destroyer for a very short period, never being commissioned as such.*
(Ben Warlow Collection)

Collingwood undertaking a course in radar mechanics. *"I was sent to Chatham before being posted to **Matapan**. At the time no one knew the whereabouts of the destroyer. A few days later it was discovered that she was new and nearing completion at John Brown's shipyard at Clydebank. On arrival I was informed that it was the Bank Holiday fortnight and everyone had gone on leave, so I joined them."*

"On my return I was joined by a radar mechanic colleague, a fellow Scot called Cant from Carnoustie. The ship was crawling with shipyard workers doing the finishing touches. From there we sailed to the Tail of the Bank at Greenock." These builder's sea trials were conducted over Taylour Bank, Gourock. Her stopping time from full speed ahead was recorded as 95 seconds. He continues, *"There followed daily journeys in the Firth of the Clyde for about a week, testing everything possible but still with shipyard personnel onboard."*

"From there we set sail round the south of England before arriving at Chatham on 22 September. Again sea trials were carried out in the Medway and Thames estuary. Following that we were tied up to a depot ship and the process of going into reserve was instigated. This as far as I was concerned was sealing off all radar installations with various materials which was very time consuming." **Matapan** had only steamed for 150 hours under her own power but with no need for the ship in the active fleet the Admiralty had decided that it was best to place the destroyer in reserve for possible future use

Matapan left Chatham Dockyard on 28 October 1947 passing through the dockyard's North Lock at 1030 and sailed to Gillingham Reach in the River Medway and was then laid up in reserve. A few months later the decision was taken to move the ship to Devonport and **Matapan** was taken into Chatham Dockyard on 2 July 1948 to be prepared for the tow. Eighteen days later on the 20 July **Matapan** left Chatham for the last time. Under tow the destroyer arrived a few days later at Devonport where the process of storing the ship in reserve continued. Everything possible was preserved or removed from the ship and the hull and superstructure was dehu-

This overhead view shows that, although destined to go into reserve immediately, **HMS Matapan** *was completed with a full armament fit.*

(MoD/Crown Copyright)

midified. Once complete *Matapan* was moved into the River Tamar and joined the Reserve Fleet.

7 June 1949 saw *Matapan* being moved alongside sister ship *St James* within Devonport dockyard at 1540. Three days later the destroyer *Onslow* secured alongside *Matapan*. The three ships stayed in this position for the next three days until on 13 June *Matapan* and *Onslow* exchanged positions. *Matapan* was, however, destined to return to her moorings in the River Tamar on 20 June when at 1330 she was towed back up the river.

The following year together with other ships in the fleet *Matapan* was affected by a spate of malicious damage caused by discontent and low pay, although in *Matapan's* case no serious damage was done to the ship. *Matapan* stayed in reserve in the River Tamar for the next nine years before being moved back into Devonport for 1959's Devonport Navy Day's held that August. During the two day event *Matapan* was displayed along with her sister ship *Dunkirk*.

In 1961 the decision was taken that the *Matapan* should be converted and re-commissioned into service as the Navy's Underwater Trials Ship in order to conduct trials on new sonar systems such as the Type 2016. The conversion meant that the old sonar trials ship *Verulam* could finally be retired. The decision stated that the ship would require substantial refitting and that this would inevitably cost a large amount of money. Perhaps this was one of the reasons why for the next six years *Matapan* remained firmly in the trots at Plymouth with only an occasional visitor.

Eventually, however, after twenty two years in the River Tamar *Matapan* was towed to Portsmouth for the extensive conversion. She edged her way into No 14 Dry Dock on 5 January 1970 and docked down on a 13 foot high plinth. This unusual arrangement was necessary to construct the deep skeg on the bottom of the ship. As work progressed so the plinth was cut away transferring the weight of the ship to a new bottom line several feet below her docking line. On 18 January 1970 Eng Lt Commander (SD) D.E Holloway was appointed as *Matapan's* commanding officer. In addition to commanding the ship he was also MEO of the ship.

In addition to the deep skeg other alterations made to *Matapan* included replacing all the ship's structure forward of No 11 station with a bulbous bow thus making *Matapan* the first Royal Navy warship to have such a bow. The forecastle deck was further extended to aft in the ship. Under this extension new compartments were added. The superstructure was also radically altered in appearance. A new enclosed bridge and a forward superstructure was built over the area former-ly occupied by the 'A' and 'B' gun turrets. A new plat-ed mast was also provided for navigational radar sets and communication equipment. An additional funnel was fitted for the sonar generators exhaust gases and there was also a brand new deckhouse aft that incor-porated a helicopter platform, although there was no provision for a hangar for any aircraft. Some indica-tion of the extent of the work carried out on *Matapan* can be gauged from the fact that parts of three decks had to be strengthened to take fly wheel generator sets.

The process of modernising *Matapan* caused a fair degree of problems for the Portsmouth shipyard work-ers. When welding the new design to the old structure this caused a large number of rivets to loosen all of which had to be replaced or tightened. Essentially the wartime riveted hull was retained more or less as designed but above the upperdeck the whole of the ship was brand new. Another aspect of the conversion work was that the entire ship had to be completely rewired to comply with new standards. The pro-gramme of works also included the fitting of air com-pressors, air piping, gearing and shaft modifications, new propellers and one pair of non retractable sta-bilisers.

During this first docking period about 70 tons of concrete was poured into the after end of the ship to maintain her trim. Displacement increased from 1775 tons to 3835 tons, draught increased from 8.6 feet to 22 feet with the large sonar dome. Additional accom-modation was also provided for scientists that also included a number of women a fact that D. Moore remembers well. *"Two cabins were allocated for the female scientific staff and the scuttles of those cabins were the shiniest onboard. My lads used to spend hours polishing them just so they could talk to the*

In this overhead shot following conversion **HMS Matapan** *is barely recognisable from her former destroyer lineage. (MoD/Crown Copyright)*

ladies."

During her time in No 14 dock within Portsmouth Dockyard *Matapan* was visited by Rear Admiral Nathan Soneshein, Commander US Naval Ship Systems Command and Rear Admiral Healey, USN. Of the *Matapan* Admiral Sonestein said, *"I still marvel at the boldness of this concept and will continue to monitor that programme in the months ahead."*

Coming out of dock 1st November 1971 the refit would continue for some months. On 8 May 1972 Commander Holloway was replaced by Commander W.H.H. McLeod as the ships commanding officer. *Matapan* started her sea trials on July 27 1972 and she was found to handle well despite the large sonar dome giving a large amount of lift on occasions. With the trials programme complete *Matapan* finally re-commissioned on the second day of February 1973.

4 June 1974 Lt Commander D.J. Leach was appointed as acting commander of the sonar trials ship. He remained in command for three months until Commander R. E. Hoskins returned to *Matapan* on 20 January 1975. Upon the commander's return to the trials ship Lt Commander Leach resumed his duties as the ship's executive officer.

D. Moore joined *Matapan* on 28 April 1975 as the Petty Officer T.A.S.I (Torpedo and Anti submarine Instructor) and he remembers that within two hours of arriving onboard the ship sailed for Portland for a four week workup period.

"After work-up the ship spent a number of months in Scottish waters, especially tied up between four buoys in Loch Fyne carrying out sonar trials. The noise from the sonar was very loud and ear defenders were de

An amazing transformation. A new bow, bridge, superstructure, flush deck, second funnel and flight deck have removed all traces of the ship's former identity. The only tell tale sign is the original forward funnel. The underwater conversion was even more substantial with draught increasing from 8.6 to 22 feet!
(Tim Meredith)

rigueur wear for hours on end. Just to produce the power for the sonar set needed two special generators each with a five ton flywheel. Another aspect of the electrics onboard was that there was an AC switchboard for all the modern gear fitted, but the original DC switchboard was still in use to run some of the older electronics. We did go to sea on trials as well as being between the buoys and during one of these we lost all pressure in the Skeg. This was the housing for the sonar and went over two thirds of the length of the ship. One of the fibre glass panels (we called them windows) had lost about a 20 foot length and we were trying to pressurise the ocean. This meant we needed emergency dry docking to fit a new window which was about 120 foot long and the only place that could take us at short notice was Devonport dockyard. Upon arrival we were put into dry dock and it was quite funny to see the look on the dockies faces as they drained the dock. We only went down a few feet and our upper deck was just above the level of the dockside when we were on the blocks and the dockies couldn't understand why the dock was draining, but we were not going down any lower. They were amazed to see the ship when she was fully exposed in a dry dock as it really was a feat of engineering how she was constructed. One of the drawbacks of being in a dry dock was that the hull below the water line was fitted with anecoic tiles and these had to kept from drying out, so every couple of hours they had to be hosed down by the duty watch. Another problem was getting the replacement window from Portland to Devonport by road. A 120 foot load took some manoeuvring on the roads under a police escort."

"We eventually got back to sea and the early months of 1976 were spent in the Atlantic carrying out more sonar trials and then it was off to the USA to operate with the **USS Tullibee***. We spent a great deal of time operating with her and part of the process prior to the trials commencing was to attach a barrage balloon to the submarine. This was done by passing a 1000 foot tow to the submarine which she connected just aft of her fin. At the other end of this tow we attached an Oropesa minesweeping float and then from a barrage balloon on a 200 foot wire. The balloon carried loads of electronics which enabled the scientists carrying out the trials to triangulate the positional data from the sonar and keep a check on the accuracy of the readings. We also attached a White Ensign to the balloon which meant that* **USS Tullibee** *was flying the flag of the Royal Navy and not the Stars and Stripes. Unfortunately, if* **USS Tullibee** *dived a little too steeply the screw cut the tow and we would then have to go on a balloon hunt and start all over again reattaching the gear to the submarine. This happened quite a lot and I suspect sometimes it was done on purpose as they didn't appreciate our sense of humour by making them fly the White Ensign. The crew of* **USS Tullibee** *claimed that having our sonar ping them was like having a metal bucket on your head and someone hitting it with a sledge hammer. We had to limit the time of each trial to about six hours and then give them a couple of hour's break, before starting again. During this period of trials* **Matapan** *claimed the longest period of time at sea for any ship."*

With *Matapan* reaching warmer climbs in the Caribbean upper deck activities took on a new life. Competitions included one for the best rubber band driven racing car and a drag beauty contest with the winner being crowned "*Miss Matapan*!"

Commander Hoskins was replaced in command by Commander R G Evans on 2 August 1976. *Matapan's* executive officer, Lt Commander Leach, was also replaced on the same day by Lieutenant D E Whitehouse.

D. Moore remembers that around this time *Matapan* had been operating off the coast of the United States. *"We had some good runs ashore then we came back to this side of the pond and continued trials in and around UK waters for the rest of the year and into 1977. The ships final port of call was Liverpool during the Queen's Silver Jubilee and then it was home to Portsmouth a week later for paying off."*

August 1977 *Matapan* paid off for disposal as she sailed into Portsmouth her paying off pennant was suspended from a large balloon together with the Stars and Stripes representing the American involvement in her final program.

Throughout the remainder of 1977 and into 1978 *Matapan* was laid up at Portsmouth whilst her fate was decided. On 18 May 1979 she was sold to H.K Vickers at Blyth for breaking up. The Underwater Trials Ship

Previous page: **HMAS Anzac** *comes alongside the aircraft carrier* **HMS Vengeance** *in a choppy sea.*

(Steve Bush Collection)

HMAS ANZAC

Showing the classic lines of a British destroyer, **HMAS Anzac** *shortly after commissioning and prior to having her raked funnel cowling fitted.* (*Royal Australian Navy*)

Built at Williamstown Naval Dockyard in Victoria *Anzac* was laid down on September 23 1946 and launched on 20 August 1948 by Mrs A. Collins, wife of the Chief of Naval Staff. On 14 August 1950 the Australian government announced that the STMG Mk II would be fitted in *Anzac* and her sister ship *Tobruk*. The destroyer was commissioned at Williamstown Dockyard on 14 March 1951 under the command of Commander John Plunkett Cole, RAN, although the ship was not accepted by the Royal Australian Navy from the dockyard until 22 March.

Anzac left Sydney on 30 July to join the United Nations Forces in Korea and arrived at Sasebo on 14 August, after a short visit to Hong Kong. Ten days later the destroyer departed Sasebo as a unit of Task Element 95.11 screening *USS Sicily* off the west coast of Korea. On 2 September *Glory* relieved *USS Sicily* as the operational carrier and four days later *Anzac* detached and sailed to an area off Haiju (Western Korea) to bombard selected targets on the coastline.

This was the first opportunity for the new destroyer to fire her guns in anger and the 4.5-inch rounds started raining down on Korean positions at 1815 on 6 September. Targets included the suspected Communist headquarters in the area. With the operation completed *Anzac* returned to Sasebo.

On 12 September *Anzac* proceeded to Wonsan, eastern Korea, where she assumed the duties of Commander Task Element 95.22. Two United States warships the *Thompson* and the *Naifoh* joined *Anzac* in this task. The ships were to blockade of the east coast of Korea from a point 23 miles south of Songjin to latitude 41° 50'N, being some 34 miles south of the Korean Siberian border. Operations with TE 95.22 continued until 26 September when after firing her one thousandth round of 4.5-inch ammunition against the enemy *Anzac* parted company with her consorts and sailed for Kure, ending her first tour of duty in Korea. From Kure the Australian destroyer made her way to Hong Kong from where she left on 30 September escorting the aircraft

carrier **Glory** for Australia and together with the British ship entered Sydney Harbour on 20 October. **Anzac** had been away from home for almost three months and some steamed some 23,000 miles.

Following a refit at Williamstown, completed on 14 December 1951, **Anzac** spent four months in home ports and east coast exercises. Command was transferred in February 1952, the new commanding officer being Captain G.G.O. Gatacre DSC.

In May 1952, in company with **Australia**, she visited Papua New Guinea, New Britain, Manus and the Solomon Islands. Whilst in June she was again in dockyard hands at Williamstown completing her second refit of the year on 25 July. August was spent exercising and on her shakedown period before her planned return to Korean waters. On 1 September 1952 **Anzac** departed Sydney for Sasebo to begin her second tour of duty in the war zone. Singapore was reached on 10 September and Hong Kong six days later, where she relieved **Bataan** on the station, proceeding to Sasebo on 27 September. The following day **Anzac** joined the British six-inch gun cruiser **Newcastle** and **HMNZS Rotoiti** at Paengyong Do to begin a coastal patrol of the area. **Anzac** would spend the next six days with the West Coast Bombardment and Blockade Group followed by nine more on patrol with the aircraft carriers.

On 4 October **Anzac** completed her period of patrol and proceeded to operate on the screen of **Ocean**, relieving the Dutch warship **HNMS Piet Hein** and **HMCS Nootka** and **USS Vammen**. She stayed with the aircraft carrier until 13 October when the entire group sailed for Sasebo and onto Kure for some rest.

On 29 October with Lieutenant Commander W.O.C. Roberts in temporary command **Anzac** returned to the eastern coastline of Korea as a unit of Task Unit 95.12. The Task Units role was the defence of the islands of Sok To and Cho Do. Cho Do Island housed a vital radar station and Tactical Air Defence Centre. The multi-national task group comprised **Anzac**, **HMCS Crusader**, **Comus** and **USS LSMR 412** plus some small vessels

*Unlike the Royal Navy, the Australian Navy chose to equip her two Battle class destroyers with the MkVI twin 4.5-inch turret as clearly seen in this image of **HMAS Anzac**.* (Steve Bush Collection)

of the South Korean Navy. Whilst on patrol on 16 November 1952 *Anzac* was shelled by a battery on the mainland causing no damage to the destroyer. *Anzac's* period of patrol and bombardment came to an end on 17 November, when the duties of CTU 95.12.1 were turned over to Captain (D) 8th Destroyer Squadron in *Cossack*.

Ten days later after a suitable rest period for the crew, *Anzac* returned to active duty on the west coast where she screened the carrier *Glory*. The Dutch *HNMS Piet Hein* and the American *USS Hickok* joined the Australian destroyer in this task. On 7 December, *Anzac* detached, relieved *HMCS Crusader* and resumed bombardment and patrol duties in the vicinity of Cho Do and Sok To islands. Five days later *Anzac* was relieved by the British destroyer *Comus*. Rear Admiral Clifford (second in command, Far East Station) joined the destroyer as she sailed into Sasebo Harbour on 13 December 1952.

The crew were allowed rest and relaxation ashore but after six days the destroyer sailed on 19 December for her last patrol of the year and headed for Korea's east coast as a unit of Task Element 95.22. *Anzac*, joined US ships *The Sullivans*, *McNair* and *Evansville* and replaced the Canadian *HMCS Haida* in the force. Operations were centred on the defence of the island of Yangdo. Commenting on this phase of Anzac's Korean service, which ended on 3 January 1953, Commander W.O.C. Roberts stated, *"This tour of duty on the east coast has introduced the ship to a naval aspect of the Korean War greatly differing from that on the west coast. Enemy batteries were numerous and very hostile; navigational worries were few, tides almost non existent. Moreover, there has been the experience of working in what is almost an entirely American force. The weather alternated between heavy snowfalls and days of bright sunlight"*. On 5 January 1953 *Anzac* berthed at Kure and her crew were again permitted runs ashore.

The 21 January saw *Anzac* return to Korea's west coast patrol and in particular the destroyer was tasked with defending Sok To and Cho Do areas. On 25 January *Anzac* was relieved on the battle line by the cruiser *Birmingham* and herself relieved *Cockade* as CTU 95.1.4, then comprising *Anzac*, *Cockade* and *USS Quapan*. Operations of this group followed the usual pattern with destroyers being allocated daily for gunfire support against the mainland. Many of the planned activities had to be abandoned due to severe wintery conditions throughout the winter of 1953. *Anzac* shelled positions ashore on Australia Day raising morale as she did so. She left soon after and sailed for Sasebo where she arrived on 29 January.

On 5 February 1953 *Anzac* headed back to sea and left port to escort *Glory*. The Australian crew of *Anzac* then began a period of eleven weeks of nearly continuous service on the Korean west coast patrol. Only brief stops at Sasebo or Kure allowed the crew some time to unwind before returning to the patrol. Captain J.S Mesley DSC took command of *Anzac* in April 1953. The destroyer's tour ended on 23 April, when she left Yongpyong Do for Hong Kong where she remained until 7 May 1953.

12 May saw *Anzac* joining TU 95.2.2 with the American warships *Gurke* and *Maddox*. For this *Anzac's* second period of duty on the east coast she was based on Yangdo where routine roles included the protection of the island and the blockade and shelling of traffic on the north and east coastal railways. *Anzac* left the area on 26 May and sailed for Japan. *Anzac* arrived with *Mounts Bay* in Tokyo Bay where she represented Royal and Commonwealth Navies at a ceremony marking the Coronation of Queen Elizabeth II. After the celebrations *Anzac* left Tokyo and set course for Sasebo where the destroyer arrived on 7 June and stayed for only two days before sailing in company with *Ocean* for her final patrol on the Korean conflict. Six days later at 1845 on 13 June 1953 *Anzac* was relieved by *Cockade* bringing to an end her part in operations in Korean waters. After an absence from home waters of 305 days *Anzac* sailed into Sydney harbour and was welcomed by large crowds on 3 July 1953 having steamed 57,865 miles.

Three days later *Anzac* arrived at Port Phillip and began a refit at Williamstown which would see her in dockyard hands until 16 September. Exercises with *Sydney* and transport of National Service trainees occupied sea time between September and October with more exercises with *Vengeance* in November. A second refit began

at Williamstown on 12 November, the ship remaining there until 6 January 1954. Later in the month there were further aircraft carrier exercises along Australia's east coast. February 1954 saw *Anzac* acting as escort vessel during the visit of HM Queen Elizabeth and HRH the Duke of Edinburgh. In March 1954 *Anzac* visited the Great Barrier Reef and the following month she was in Papua New Guinea waters. For fifteen days starting on 13 May *Anzac* was heavily involved in group exercises with *HMNZS Black Prince*, the Royal Navy submarines *Telemachus* and *Thorough* and a number of Australian warships including the aircraft carrier *Vengeance*. May also saw the arrival on board of the destroyers' latest commanding officer, Captain I. H. McDonald RAN who oversaw the refitting of the destroyer.

Anzac was refitted at Williamstown between 4 June and 11 August 1954, Commander G. B. Crabb DSC RAN was appointed as the new commanding officer in August 1954 in time to take the ship out of dockyard hands and to be tested on anti-submarine exercises in September. In October *Anzac* took part in joint exercises in the Manus area with the Flag Officer Commanding the Australian Fleet flying his flag in *Sydney* and Rear Admiral Gladstone flying his flag in the cruiser *Birmingham*. The exercises ended on 27 October when the combined force returned to Sydney. During the first week of November there was the annual arrival in Port Phillip, with a return to Sydney in mid-month. The remainder of the year was taken up with weapons training exercising off the New South Wales coast.

New Year's Day, 1955, found *Anzac* self refitting at Cockatoo Dockyard, Sydney, work which continued until 13 February. The closing days of the month were chiefly occupied by joint anti-submarine exercises and joining company with *Sydney* on 28 February for passage to Fremantle.

Anzac spent a week at Fremantle between 4 and 11 March before arriving at Melbourne on 18 March. She then proceeded to Sydney to take part in further fleet exercises which continued intermittently until 19 April when *Anzac* detached for New Caledonia for an eleven day goodwill visit.

On 17 May *Anzac*, in company with *HMNZ Ships Black Prince* and *Pukaki* and *HMA Ships Quadrant*, *Arunta*, *Tobruk* and *Warramunga*, the destroyer proceeded to sea to begin ANZEX exercises which were to last until late July. Units of the Royal Navy led by *Newcastle* (flying the flag of Flag Officer Second in Command, Far East Station, Rear Admiral E F Elkins, CB, CVO, OBE) were eventually joined en route Darwin to Singapore on 1 June 1955. Following the conclusion of the joint exercises *Anzac* departed Singapore with her sister ship *Tobruk* on 2 July for a brief stop at Sydney before sailing for Melbourne and a refit at Williamstown dockyard.

The two and a half month refit was completed on 7 October 1955, with Commander E. Peel DSC RAN taking command of the destroyer at its completion. Williamstown was left behind on 7 October when *Anzac* sailed for Sydney where she remained for the next five weeks.

On 16 November, in company with *Tobruk*, *Anzac* departed Sydney for Singapore via Freemantle to become part of the Strategic Reserve on the Far East Station with the pair arriving at Singapore on 1 December. Two weeks were spent alongside before *Anzac* left the port on 15 December and sailed to Hong Kong for naval exercises which would occupy the ship and crew until 16 January. On 15 February 1956 *Anzac* sailed from Hong Kong to arrive at Bangkok on 16 February. Two days were spent ashore in the city before the destroyer sailed for Singapore to become part of the Malayan patrol on 21 February. During March 1956 *Anzac* participated in Exercise *Welcome* in the waters around Singapore before returning to the port on the 5 March. With the exercise over *Anzac* stayed in nearby waters until 15 March when she left Singapore. On 19 March 1956 the destroyer arrived at Hong Kong and left the same day. Three days later *Anzac* arrived at Hong Kong for exercise Sea Dragon. The next day dawned with another exercise, Exercise *Monsoon*. On 26 March with the exercise over the warship left Hong Kong. *Anzac* stayed in Hong Kong waters until 9 April when she sailed for Japan. During her time in Japan she toured a number of cities including Yokosuka, Kure and Nagoya before arriving at Paenyong on 5 May 1956. During May *Anzac* went onto make visits to Yong Pyong Do and Inchon

The introduction of the MkVI turret on the Australian Battles resulted in the bridge being raised to afford a view over the roof of "B" turret. *(Steve Bush Collection)*

before returning to Kure on 10 May for naval exercises. Once successfully completed *Anzac* left on 14 May and headed for Hong Kong where she arrived eight days later. *Anzac* stayed in Hong Kong and awaited dock-yard space for a refit period to commence on 31 May 1956.

July 1956 was a very busy month for the destroyer. After completing her refit on 3 July she left Hong Kong on 6 July. Five days 13 later off Singapore *Anzac* took part in Exercise *Mango* before sailing on 25 July for Kualapahang a three day visit to this ancient and mysterious city. On 30 July *Anzac* returned to Singapore where she stayed until 7 August when she left the port. August was also a particularly busy month for the destroyer with visits to Penang, Port Dickson, Pangker Island, Port Swettenham, Singapore and Tawau. On 1 September 1956 *Anzac* arrived at Sandakan for a two day visit before arriving back at Singapore on 7 September.

Hong Kong welcomed the warship on 14 September for a ten day visit. The problems of Malaysian terrorists meant a recall for the destroyer to Singapore where she arrived on 29 September together with her sister ship *Tobruk*. In the first of only two offensive actions undertaken by Royal Australian Navy ships during the Malayan Emergency (1948-1960) Anzac and *Tobruk* bombarded terrorist positions south of Jason Bay in Johore State. The same day *Anzac* returned to Singapore where she stayed until 2 October 1956 before sailing for a four day visit to Bangkok. The crew were amazed by the city with its mix of ancient and modern and rich and poor. On 12 October the destroyer sailed from Bangkok and spent the next twelve days at sea before she

arrived at Saigon. Three days were spent alongside before she sailed for home calling at Darwin and Brisbane before arriving at Sydney on 12 November. *Anzac* was scheduled for another refit and after destoring she left on 15 November to sail to Williamstown to dock down and commence the short refit. On 30 November *Anzac* sailed from Williamstown upon the refit's completion sailed for Melbourne where she saw out the remainder of the year.

Commander P. Stevenson RAN took command of *Anzac* in January 1957. On 15 February 1957 *Anzac* left Melbourne and conducted sea trials in the Bay for the next five days. The next day she visited East Coast Tasmania where she stayed until the first day of March.

Exercise *Trade Wind* occupied the ship and crew for eight days in the Indian Ocean from the 10 April before she returned to Singapore on 18 April 1957 to begin another tour of duty on the Malaysian patrol off Palau Tioman. *Anzac* took part in Exercise *Astra* in early May 1957 before heading back to Hong Kong for eight days until 15 May.

The destroyer sailed from Hong Kong to Manila to participate in the multi-national Exercise *Sea Link* which took place in mid May. At its completion *Anzac* sailed for Hong Kong where she arrived on 31 May. From Hong Kong *Anzac* sailed to Singapore where between 13 June and 27 June *Anzac* participated in a series of naval exercises off Singapore. Then between 27 June and 2 September *Anzac* visited a great many ports of call across the region including Pulau Tioman, Langkawi, Penang, Miri, Tawau, Sandakan, Jesselton before arriving at Singapore on 2 September. She refuelled and replenished and left the same day heading for Hong Kong and a refit. Hong Kong was reached on 7 September and the destroyer stayed in the port until 7 October 1957.

The remainder of October saw port visits to Yokosuka, Kobe, Tokyo and Inchon, whilst in November Anzac went onto visit Yong Pyong Do, Pusan, Sasebo, Kagoshima before entering Hong Kong on 15 November. Just over two weeks later on 2 December the destroyer left the British colony and headed towards Bangkok, Singapore and Pulau Tioman. Christmas 1957 was spent alongside at Singapore. New Year's Day 1958 saw the destroyer slip out of the Naval Base at Singapore and headed for home waters pulling into Fremantle, Adelaide and Williamstown before arriving at Sydney on 8 February 1958 to begin a major refit which kept her in dock-yard hands until October. During this period Commander Stevenson was replaced in August by Commander R. A. H. Millar RAN. *Anzac* herself continued trials until 27 February 1959.

After some time spent around the Australian coast including the Great Barrier Reef *Anzac* in March resumed service as a unit of the Strategic Reserve in the Far East.

April 1959 started with a major fleet exercise off Singapore. Exercise *FOTEX 59* tested ships, men and weapons to the maximum and lasted for five intensive days. As if the rigours were not enough a second exercise had been planned to follow the first. Exercise *Sea Demon* started on 10 April and would last for another four days. On 14 April the destroyer left Singapore and made calls at Johore Straits, Manila, Hong Kong and Singapore before arriving off Borneo for Exercise *Saddle Up* on 9 June. The remainder of June saw visits to Sandakan, Singapore, Swettenham, Penang and on 26 June Bangkor Island for a three day visit. Five days later on 30 June 1959 *Anzac* arrived at Pulan Anak Borau for exercises which were completed by the beginning of July.

On 7 August 1959 the destroyer arrived at Singapore for exercises that would last for five days. *Anzac* then proceeded to Cochin where more exercises were carried out through until 21 August. The remainder of 1959 saw the Australian destroyer visit such interesting places as Trincomalee, Jesselton harbour, Labuan and Yokohama. On the final day of October *Anzac* together with her Australian sister *Tobruk* was in the Japanese port of Yokosuka as escorts for the British aircraft carrier *Centaur*. There the pair joined the British Battle class ship *Lagos* and destroyer *Cavalier*.

Anzac sailed from Hong Kong with a course firmly set for Australia. She required a refit and was put into dockyard hands at Williamstown between 12 December and 22 March 1960.

1960 started with the usual post refit trials and rectifications conducted in and around Sydney and Jervis Bay and also saw the appointment of a brand new commanding officer in March when Acting Commander B. D. Gordon RAN took command of the warship.

The next two months saw *Anzac* in the Pacific Ocean visiting Noumea, the Solomons and Papua New Guinea. The summer of 1960 saw the destroyer exercising throughout August in Platypus Bay, Moreton Bay and in and around Sydney. On 23 October she conducted a three day exercise with other navy units around Spalding Cove. A controversial moment occurred in September 1960 when during these exercises *Anzac* fired a shot into sister ship *Tobruk* whilst undertaking gunnery exercises off Jervis Bay.

Visits to Garden Island, Devonport and Port Arthur followed in November before the destroyer put into Sydney on 22 November. There the crew and dockyard workers carried out maintenance on the ship through until the last day of January 1961.

Lieutenant Commander D.M. Wogan-Browne RAN took over command of *Anzac* in February 1961. After a spell spent at Melbourne further maintenance of *Anzac* was carried out at Williamstown between 21 February and 7 March. Just days before the completion of the work it had been announced on 1 March 1961 that *Anzac* had become the Fleet Training Ship (seaman training only), with an extra deckhouse aft and the director removed.

March and April saw the officers and seamen under training visiting Spalding Cove, Wallaroo Bay, Adelaide, Whyalla, Port Lincoln, Emu Bay and Kangaroo Island before returning to Jervis Bay on 4 April and a series of trials in the waters around Sydney and Melbourne.

9 August saw *Anzac* participating in Exercise *Tucker Box* through until 17 August around Brisbane. Exercise *Tucker Box* continued until 24 August but had relocated to Hervey Bay. More exercises awaited the crew when

HMAS Anzac *looking remarkably like a Daring class destroyer from the bows.(T. Ferrers-Walker Collection)*

they reached Auckland in New Zealand on 30 August 1961. These were completed by 4 September when after a brief stop at Wellington the destroyer returned to Melbourne on 13 September.

The next big exercise for *Anzac* had been long in the planning and the destroyer was destined to play a large part. Exercise *Shop Window* was planned to start on 20 September in Sydney and would finish thirty days later on 11 October. This multi-national exercise saw warships from Australia, New Zealand, America and the United Kingdom taking part.

The remainder of October and November were spent in home waters before heading again to Auckland on 1 December for a three day visit. Soon afterwards she returned to Australia and resumed her normal operations around the coastline of Australia offering young Australian seamen the opportunity to experience naval life. Some of the more interesting ports of call made through January and February were to Stanley-West Bay, Three Hummock Island, Burnie, Port Arthur and Hobart. Also in January the opportunity was taken to participate in the work up of the aircraft carrier Melbourne. More exercises and trials were carried out around Sydney and Jervis Bay before *Anzac* entered Williamstown again for another refit on 9 April 1962. During this refit the entire ship was fumigated to remove all unwanted parasites and possible sources of infection.

Once the refit was completed on 7 July 1962 the ship again resumed her normal routine of carrying out training around the Australian coast. She did participate in Exercise *Tucker Box II* between 30 August and 6 September around Brisbane before entering Sydney to have her bottom scraped and repainted whilst in dry dock. In October she made visits to Papua New Guinea and the Solomons. November 1962 saw visits to Melbourne, Adelaide and Albany whilst in December exercises around Sydney and Jervis Bay occupied the crew. These lasted into the following January with Christmas spent in the dockyard.

Commander D.A.H. Clarke DSC MVO RAN took command in January 1963. Whilst the next month saw visits to Sydney during the destroyers work up followed by trips to Kangaroo Island and Backy Bay. *Anzac* escorted the Royal Yacht *Britannia* when a Royal visit was made to Melbourne on 23 February 1963. Between 1 April and 24 April 1963 the ship underwent modifications at Williamstown to fit her for a wider training role. A major item was the removal of 'B' Turret and the GI Bofors gun mounting and the installation of a charthouse/classroom in their place. Initially she then became responsible for the training of cadets, ordinary seaman and higher rates. With this refit *Anzac*'s primary task became the training of junior officers and ordinary seamen.

Anzac accepted onboard a number of cadets for sea training at Jervis Bay in May. These cadets sailed with the destroyer and visited Hayman Island, South Molle Island, Lindeman Island, Magnetic Island, Fitzroy Island and Green Island before taking part in some fleet exercises.

The destroyer returned to Sydney on 5 June but was soon taking part in more exercises conducted nearby through until 12 June. Gladstone, Great Keppel Island and Rundle Island were all visited before arriving at Townsville for more exercises with her embarked cadets. Throughout the remainder of 1963 training was of paramount importance and was carried out at every opportunity. The lessons learnt were later tested in exercises such as the one day Exercise *Carbine* which took place off Caloundra on 28 August or the later anti-submarine exercise staged off Sydney between 19 September and 24 September.

During December 1963, while in Tasmanian waters, she received a signal stating that the jetty at Tasman Island was on fire. Fire parties were landed and the fire gradually was brought under control. For their efforts the fire parties received grateful thanks and praise from residents of Tasman Island.

Between 4 January 1964 and 1 April 1964 *Anzac* was again in the hands of dockyard workers who refitted the ship at Melbourne. Following the completion of the refit the destroyer conducted trials shuttling between Jervis Bay and Sydney throughout April and into the first few days of May. On 16 May *Anzac* visited Trobriand Islands for a two day visit before moving onto Talasea-Kimbe Bay. The Governor General, Viscount de Lisle, embarked in *Anzac* on 22 May 1964 and enjoyed the cruise which followed in Papua New Guinea waters.

Places visited during the cruise were Rabaul, Sohano, Losuia, Oro Bay, Esa Ala, Milne Bay, Samarai and Port Moresby.

9 July 1964 *Anzac* arrived at Sydney to take part in *Operation Longex*. This was followed by more exercises around Jervis Bay and a period of self maintenance at Sydney until the middle of August. In July 1964 command of the destroyer changed over to Commander I. H. Nicholson RAN. *Anzac* paid a return visit to New Zealand throughout August and September calling at Wellington, Lyttelton, Dunedin and Auckland before returning to Sydney for self maintenance.

Towards the end of September *Anzac* arrived at Jervis Bay to take part in Exercise *Winchester*. October and November were spent operating around the coastline of Australia before calling at Melbourne on 13 December 1964 for a four month long refit that was completed on St Patrick's Day 1965. Two days later she left after replenishment and headed for Sydney for manoeuvres in the Bay. On 29 March she left Sydney and headed for Jervis Bay only to leave on 30 March.

On 31 March she arrived at Twofold Bay for exercises which finished the following day. On 2 April *Anzac* returned to Sydney where another set of exercises awaited her attention. The second phase of the naval exercises was completed on 5 April. Visits to Platypus Bay, Bundaberg, Percy Island and Refuge Bay took the ship through until the beginning of May. On the 15 May *Anzac* was at Cairns where she participated in CASEX, a two day intensive exercise that this year saw the participation of the giant American aircraft carrier *USS Coral Sea*.

A cruise in Papua New Guinea waters was made in May-June 1965 with the ship making official visits to Wewak, Aitape, Vanimo, Tarangau, Kavieng and Kozwick Island. On 7 June assistance was given to local authorities in locating and rescuing six persons who were stranded when their launch broke down. They were found the following day and taken to MacKay for medical attention.

On 11 June 1965 she arrived at Sydney for self maintenance which lasted just over a month. Between 14 July and 5 August *Anzac* shuttled between Sydney and Jervis Bay conducting trials and training of young cadets and seamen. Another period of self maintenance followed at Sydney before *Anzac* departed on a cruise to Manus, Madang, Lae, Salamaua Harbour, Kokopo and the Solomon Islands in September 1965. November 1965 saw another major naval exercise off the coastline of Australia. Exercise *Warrior* was conducted off Sydney between 8 November and the 11 November and *Anzac* took part.

Anzac arrived at Sydney on 10 December but left eight days later and headed for Melbourne which was reached on 20 December. Christmas leave was granted. Command was changed yet again when in January 1966 Commander I. W. Broben RAN became *Anzac's* latest captain. The warship remained in Melbourne until 22 March 1966 conducting trials. Later in the month the destroyer took part in Exercise *Jig Time* off Jervis Bay.

Another training cruise for seaman under training had been organised for April and *Anzac's* itinerary was organised to give the greatest variety of training possibilities. It was also organised that the ports of call would be as varied and as interesting as possible. The destroyer called at Lombrum, Honiara, Suva, Apia, Pago Pago and Tomba Ko Nandi on Fiji before returning to Australian waters towards the end of May.

The Australian Navy at this time had a pressing need to survey the coastline of Australia and decided that *Anzac* would make an ideal vessel to carry some surveying equipment and whilst at Hobart on 6 June soundings trials were conducted to check the suitability of *Anzac* to perform this task. The equipment would be fitted during an extended self maintenance period between 10 June and 25 July 1966 at Sydney. Before any surveying work was carried out *Anzac* participated in the two day Exercise *Mulga Bill* off Jervis Bay which started on 14 August 1966. More exercises followed that took the ship through to 12 September. Her first surveying duties were undertaken in October and November 1966 when *Anzac* carried out survey duties off the northwest coast of Australia and in particular around Darwin and Port Hedland.

December 1966 saw *Anzac* at Melbourne undergoing a refit that lasted until 21 March 1967 when she left

Melbourne and resumed her training duties. A celebration was organised on board when the 500,000 mile mark was passed in March 1967. The remainder of March was spent at sea conducting training. Whilst on 6 April 1967 *Anzac* arrived at Sydney for Operation Rumbling One. The remainder of April saw the destroyer visit Seeadler Harbour and Port Moresby before arriving at Sydney on 23 April.

Up until 12 May *Anzac* shuttled between Sydney and Jervis Bay. On 12 May 1967 the warship arrived at Chowder Bay and left the next day. The remainder of the month saw visits to Brampton Island, South Molle Island, Maryport Bay and Cleveland Bay outside of Townsville before returning for self maintenance to Sydney. For two days *Anzac* conducted heeling trials in Broken Bay starting on 5 June 1967. These were successful and the ship returned to Sydney upon their completion. Another new commanding officer took up his post in July 1967 in the shape of Commander M Kelly DSC RAN. July was an interesting and varied time for the ships company when between 3 July and 7 July 1967 *Anzac* visited Tonga and represented Australia at the coronation of His Majesty King Taufa'Ahau Tupou IV.

After visits to Suva and Lautoka and self maintenance at Sydney, *Anzac* participated in the Exercise *JUG 66* off Newcastle from 1 September 1967. More exercises followed in and around Sydney until 18 September. *Anzac* was once again called in to conduct survey work on October 2 when she mapped an area around Cairns using her sounding equipment.

Between 11 October and 23 October 1967 *Anzac* was at Sydney for self maintenance. A week later she took part in Exercise *JUG 67* which took up the whole month of October. After visits to Broken Bay, Sydney, Wide Bay and Port Arthur *Anzac* put into Melbourne on 7 December 1967 for another refit.

The refit was completed on 27 April 1968 with the destroyer reverted to her role of Training Ship and resumed her normal shuttling between Jervis Bay and Sydney until the middle of May. On 25 May 1968 *Anzac* arrived

Late in her career **HMAS Anzac** *was converted to serve as a training ship for cadets and young officers.*
(Royal Australian Navy)

at Manus but left the same day after only a few hours. *Anzac* then proceeded to Vietnam in June escorting the troop carrier *Sydney*. Arriving at 1 Vung Tau on 1 June and no sooner had she arrived than she was on the return leg of the journey. June also saw *Anzac's* fifteenth commanding officer welcomed on board, he was Commander B. Snow, RAN. After her escort duties to Vietnam *Anzac* returned to Darwin on 7 June and later called in to Cairns and South Molle Island before returning to her home port of Sydney on 21 June. Whilst alongside the crew undertook a series of self maintenance projects on the ship over the next nine days.

After various port visits to naval bases around the region *Anzac* headed out to Thursday Island on 22 August for a one night stay before moving onto Cape Keer on 24 August.

On 12 September 1968 *Anzac* participated in Exercise *Coralex*. After the exercise ended on 23 September the destroyer headed for Sio Island which was reached on 29 September for a day visit.

Around this time *Anzac's* annual refit was nearing and the destroyer made her way back to Melbourne via Sydney and Adelaide. *Anzac* nosed her way into Melbourne on 28 November 1968 where she stayed until 22 February. *Anzac* resumed her normal routine of running between Jervis Bay and Sydney until the end of April when she visited Adelaide on 29 April.

The final day of April 1969 saw the destroyer making a visit to King Island. Another busy month was registered in May with visits to Devonport, Jervis Bay, Brisbane, Platypus Bay, Gladstone and Sydney on 21 May. *Anzac* stayed in Sydney for almost a month before venturing back to sea on 18 June 1969 and arrived at Cid Harbour three days later.

Cairns, Lae, Madang, Wewak, Kairiru Island, Manus (Lombrum), Kavieng, Rabaul, Honiara, Tulagi, Vovohe Cove, Gizo and Brisbane were all visited during July before *Anzac* spent some time alongside at Sydney for self maintenance to be carried out.

Back at sea mid August *Anzac* left Sydney for Jervis Bay on 18 August to take part in a series of naval exercises until 21 August. Four days later *Anzac* participated in the search for survivors of *MV Moongah* which sank in rough seas off the New South Wales coast on 25 August.

The destroyers' itinerary for autumn 1969 looked like a travel brochure with exotic locations and destinations at every turn. *Anzac*, however, had an important role to play in training future generations of seamen and the destinations visited throughout September and October were just the icing on the cake. After visiting Auckland on the first day of September *Anzac* went on to visit Tahiti, Pago Pago and Apia. She returned to Auckland on 22 September and began a tour of New Zealand ports calling at Nelson and Wellington before returning once more to Auckland.

Anzac returned to Australian waters on 17 October when she arrived at Sydney for a self maintenance period which finished on 10 November. She arrived at Jervis Bay on 15 November to take part in a series of naval exercises. The exercises continued the following day, but by now the warships had moved to an area near Sydney.

The remainder of November and December 1969 saw a tour of East Coast naval bases with calls at Sydney, Fremantle, Melbourne and Jervis Bay before returning to Sydney on 12 December for another period of self maintenance and the granting of Christmas leave. December also saw another new commanding officer in the shape of Commander G. M. Clark RAN.

On 19 January 1970 the destroyer left Sydney and after a brief period in Australian waters sailed for New Zealand where she arrived at Wellington on the last day of January.

The later part of February saw the Australian training ship take her cadets to Waitangi, Moturua Island and back to Auckland before arriving back at Sydney on 16 February. *Anzac* arrived at Melbourne on 23 February 1970 for her annual reft and leave was granted to the majority of her crew. Cadets were also posted to other ships in the fleet for the duration of her refit which lasted until mid May. May and June 1970 were spent around Sydney and Jervis Bay conducting post refit trials and training of a new batch of navy recruits. In July *Anzac*

paid visits to High Peak Island, Mackay, Cairns, Townsville and Brisbane. On 2 August 1970 *Anzac* returned to Cairns but only stayed one night before sailing for Sydney and a ten day stay alongside in the dockyard. On 17 August *Anzac* left Sydney and sailed again to Cairns and then Normanby Sound, Possession Island, Thursday Island, Port Moresby and arrived at Cid Harbour before the end of the month. Eight days were spent in Cid Harbour before sailing on 6 September for Cairns which was reached the following day. From Cairns *Anzac* paid further visits to Wewak, Manus and on 20 September the ship arrived at Rabaul where two members of her crew were taken off the ship and transferred to the local hospital for medical attention. The destroyer, meanwhile, sailed the same day. Back in New Zealand waters towards the end of September, *Anzac* participated in Exercise *Longex* held off Auckland on 27 September.

October's list of exotic and interesting ports of call included Bay of Islands and Whangarei before returning to the familiar sights and sounds of Sydney Harbour on 22 October 1970 where she stayed until 16 November 1970. *Anzac* operated in Australian waters throughout November before arriving back at Sydney on 3 December for maintenance and Christmas leave. The warship stayed alongside until 27 January 1971 when she sailed for Melbourne and another period in dockyard hands. The refit was extensive and saw the replacement of large numbers of worn out or obsolete pieces of equipment and machinery. *Anzac*'s seventeenth commanding officer, Commander I.A. Callaway RAN joined the ship in May 1971. The refit was completed on 25 June 1971 and the ship left port the same day for trials. Two days later *Anzac* arrived at Sydney for machinery maintenance that would continue until 7 July when she left Sydney. The next month was spent in Australian waters before heading off on a summer cruise in the Pacific.

The ship visited a number of islands in the Pacific and during the course of the cruise visited Papua New Guinea when the Papua New Guinea national flag was raised for the first time to celebrate the Territory's national day on 13 September. A number of *Anzac's* company participated in the flag raising ceremony.

The next day a member of the warship's crew was taken ashore at Milne Bay and after medical treatment returned to the ship which resumed its course onto Noumea, Auckland, Moturua Island and Gisborne before returning to Auckland on 15 October where she spent the next three days before sailing for Port Arthur and Hobart.

On 27 October *Anzac* left Hobart and sailed for two days before entering Melbourne where she stayed until 4 November. The following day *Anzac* arrived at Sydney and festive season leave was granted to the some members of the crew whilst others were tasked with conducting self maintenance. It wouldn't be until 1 February 1972 that *Anzac* left port and went onto visit a number of ports around the Australian coastline until 1 March 1972 when she arrived at Port Moresby for Exercise *Planti Manua*. Five days later the destroyer participated in an exercise with ten Royal Australian Navy patrol boats off Milne Bay before leaving the area on 12 March. The next six days saw visits to Port Moresby and on 18 March Brisbane. A three day stay in the city allowed for some runs ashore but *Anzac* was due to arrive back at her home port of Sydney on 23 March 1972 to commence a refit.

Anzac spent the next ten months being refitted and during this period. Commander M. De V. Salmon RAN assumed command of *Anzac* in August 1972. Completing refitting and modernisation *Anzac* was ready to rejoin the fleet on 8 January 1973 and the ship promptly left Sydney for a series of port calls around Australia including Port Melbourne, Port Lincoln, Portland, Devonport, Storm Bay and on 9 February, Hobart.

On 16 February 1973 *Anzac* arrived at Garden Island for self maintenance which lasted for ten days. The ship sailed on 26 February for the Pacific with a course set for Auckland. She arrived on 2 March and stayed for three days before putting into Wellington in mid March.

On 24 March *Anzac* returned to Port Melbourne whilst six days later she paid a brief courtesy visit to Albany leaving the same day. April saw visits to Fremantle, Albany and Port Adelaide before arriving at Garden Island on 27 April for leave and self maintenance. Those crew members on leave returned to the ship and the mainte-

nance was completed in time for her scheduled departure date of 12 June 1973 and *Anzac* sailed for Townsville, Mackay and Refuge Bay where she anchored for two days from 23 June.

Summer 1973 was spent training around the coastline of Australia except for brief spells of self maintenance at Garden Island in mid July and again in late September. Autumn followed a similar pattern before arriving at Garden Island on 23 October 1973 for self maintenance and leave. The destroyer stayed at Garden Island until 7 January 1974 when she left. The next nine days were spent evaluating systems new systems onboard and continuing the training of seamen cadets. On 16 January 1974 *Anzac* sailed from Garden Island and headed for Queen Charlotte Sound in New Zealand for a one night stay. She sailed on 22 January to Port Lyttleton for a seven day stay which ended on 2 February. She returned to Hobart and continued to operate around Australia until April when the destroyer again returned to Auckland on 20 April.

May and June 1974 saw visits to Sydney, Townsville, Mackay and Scawfell Island where *Anzac* anchored in the harbour on 29 June. The ship's programme was filled with port visits so as to allow as many Australian's as possible the opportunity to witness the destroyer as it had been announced that she was being decommissioned and placed in reserve. July's ports of call accordingly included Brisbane, Sydney and Suva. On 2 August 1974 *Anzac* arrived at Lautoka for a four day stopover.

Further goodwill visits to New Zealand were made in January and February 1974 and April 1974. In late July 1974 a visit was made to Fiji. *Anzac* arrived at Garden Island, Sydney on 11 August 1974 to pay off for disposal. *Anzac* had steamed 693,582.1 miles since commissioning.

With the ship in reserve lower grade commanding officers were appointed to supervise her de-storing ready for disposal. Lieutenant Commander P.J Wright RAN took up the role of commanding officer for two months between August and September 1974. With Lieutenant W. F. A. Wilson RAN becoming *Anzac*'s final commanding officer when he supervised the final stages of her decommissioning between September and October 1974.

The ship finally paid off at Sydney on 4 October 1974 and just over a year later on 24 November 1975 she was sold for scrapping to Hifirm Corporation of Hong Kong. *Anzac* was towed from Australian waters to those of Hong Kong on 30 December 1975.

HMAS Anzac's *last voyage to the scrapyards of Hong Kong began on 30 December 1975.*
(Maritime Photo Library)

HMAS Anzac *launched and fitting out at the Williamstown Naval Dockyard in Victoria in July 1949.*
(Royal Australian Navy)

23.09.46	Laid down at Williamstown Naval Dockyard, Victoria.
20.08.48	Launched by Mrs J. A. Collins, wife of Chief of Naval Staff.
14.03.51	Commissioned at Williamstown Dockyard with Commander John Plunkett Cole RAN in command.
22.03.51	Accepted into service with RAN.
30.07.51	Sailed from Australia for service in Korean War.
14.08.51	Arrived Sasebo after short visit to Hong Kong.
24.08.51	Joined Task Element 95.11 with **USS Sicily.**
06.09.51	Bombarded targets near Haiju, after which she returned to Sasebo.
Mid 09.51	With **USS Thompson** and **USS Naifeh**, *Anzac* blockaded east coast of Korea from a point 23 miles south of Songjin to 34 miles south of the Korean Siberia border.
26.09.51	Fired 1000th round of ammunition against Korean targets.
09.51	Visited Kure and Hong Kong.
30.09.51	Sailed from Hong Kong bound for Australia with **Glory.**
20.10.51	Arrived at Sydney Harbour and entered refit.
14.12.51	Refit completed.
Early 52	In Australian waters.
02.52	Captain G. G. O. Gatacre DSC, RAN took command.
05.52	Visited Papau New Guinea, New Britain, Manus and the Solomon Islands.
06.52	Dockyard hands at Williamstown.

25.07.52	Refit completed.
01.09.52	Sailed from Sydney for Korean War duties.
10.09.52	Singapore.
16.09.52	Hong Kong.
27.09.52	Sasebo.
28.09.52	On patrol at Paengyong Do with cruiser *Newcastle* and *HMNZS Rotaitiat*.
04.10.52	Operated with *Ocean* until 13 October when she sailed for Sasebo.
29.10.52	Part of Task Unit 95.12.1 for the defence of the islands Sok To and Cho Do, which housed vital radar units.
16.11.52	Shelled by a battery on the mainland, no damage caused.
17.11.52	Relieved on station by *Cossack*.
27.11.52	Returned to duty screening *Glory*.
07.12.52	Shelled positions near Cho Do and Sok To Islands.
13.12.52	Sasebo.
19.12.52	Joined Task Element 95.22 off the island of Yangdo.
03.01.53	Tour of duty completed.
05.01.53	Kure.
21.01.53	Off Korea again defending Sok To and Cho Do areas.
29.01.53	Arrived at Sasebo.

HMAS Anzac seen from the aircraft carrier *HMAS Sydney* during operations in Korean Waters in 1953. *Anzac* served with her sister ship *Tobruk* and the Bay class frigate *Murchison*. *Anzac's* activities included bombardments including "train busting" and supporting guerrilla style operations involving South Korean marines. (Royal Australian Navy)

05.02.53	Back at sea with *Glory*.
04.53	Captain J. S. Mesley DSC took command.
23.04.53	Sailed from Yongpyong Do for Hong Kong.
07.05.53	Sailed from Hong Kong.
12.05.53	Joined Task Unit 95.2.2 with *USS Gurke* and *USS Maddox* based on Yangdo.
26.05.53	Sailed for Japan where she represented Australia at the ceremony to mark the Coronation of HM Queen Elizabeth II.
07.06.53	Sasebo.
13.06.53	Relieved by *Cockade*.
03.07.53	After 305 days away *Anzac* returned to Sydney harbour having steamed 57,865 miles.
06.07.53	Refit at Williamstown.
16.09.53	Refit completed.
Until 10.53	Exercises with *HMAS Sydney*.
11.53	Exercises with *HMAS Vengeance*.
12.11.53	Refit at Williamstown.
06.01.54	Refit completed.
02.54	Royal escort for HM Queen Elizabeth and Duke of Edinburgh.
03.54	Great Barrier Reef.

*HMAS Anzac as she appeared as an ocean escort for the Royal Yacht **Gothic** in February 1954 during Queen Elizabeth's visit to Australia.*
(Royal Australian Navy)

05.54	Exercises with **HMNZS Black Prince** and submarines **Telemachus** and **Thorough** and other Australian ships.
05.54	Captain I. H. McDonald took command.
04.06.54	Entered refit at Williamstown.
11.08.54	Refit completed.
08.54	Commander G. J. B. Crabb DSC RAN took command.
09.54	ASW exercises.
10.54	Joint exercises off Manus with **HMAS Sydney** and **HMS Birmingham**.
27.10.54	Exercises completed the force returned to Sydney.
Late 1954	Weapons training off New South Wales coast followed by refit at Cockatoo Dockyard.
13.02.55	Refit completed.
28.02.55	Sailed for Fremantle.
18.03.55	Melbourne and onward to exercises.
19.04.55	New Caledonia for 11 day goodwill visit.
17.05.55	ANZEX exercises which lasted until late July.
01.06.55	Singapore.
02.07.55	Sailed with **Tobruk** for refit at Williamstown.
07.10.55	Refit completed and Commander E. J. Peel DSC took command.
07.10.55	Sailed to Sydney, where she stayed for 5 weeks.
16.11.55	Sailed with **Tobruk** for Singapore via Fremantle to become part of the Strategic Reserve on the Far East Station.
01.12.55	Arrived at Singapore.
12.55	At Hong Kong for exercises.
15.02.56	Sailed from Hong Kong for Bangkok.
21.02.56	Arrived at Singapore for Malayan Patrol duties.
03.56	Exercise *Welcome* off Singapore.
19.03.56	Hong Kong for Exercise *Sea Dragon* and Exercise *Monsoon*.
09.04.56	Left Hong Kong waters bound for Japan, where she visited Yokosuka, Kure and Nagoya.
05.05.56	Paenyong.
05.56	Visited Yong Pyong Do and Inchon.
10.05.56	Kure for naval exercises.
22.05.56	Hong Kong.
31.05.56	Refit at Hong Kong commenced.
03.07.56	Refit completed.
06.07.56	Sailed for Singapore to take part in Exercise *Mango*.
25.7.56	Kualapalang for 3 day visit.
30.7.56	Singapore.
08.56	Visited Penang, Port Dickson, Pangker Island, Port Sweetenham, Singapore and Tawau
01.09.56	Sandakan for 2 day visit.
07.09.56	Singapore.
14.09.56	Hong Kong and then back to Singapore for more Malaysian Patrol duties.
29.09.56	Bombarded terrorist positions south of Jason Bay in Johore Strait with sister ship **Tobruk**.
29.09.56	Singapore Dockyard.

*A rare photo of **HMAS Anzac** pictured firing her Squid mortar during fleet exercises.*   *(Royal Australian Navy)*

02.10.56	Sailed to Bangkok.
24.10.56	Saigon.
12.11.56	Sydney after brief stops at Darwin and Brisbane.
15.11.56	De-stored in preparation for refit at Williamstown.
30.11.56	Refit completed.
01.57	Commander J. P. Stevenson RAN took command.
15.02.57	Sailed from Melbourne for sea trials.
21.02.57	Visited East Coast of Tasmania until beginning of March.
10.04.57	Exercise *Trade Wind* in Indian Ocean for 10-days.
18.04.57	Singapore for Malaysian Patrol.
05.57	Exercise *Astra*.
08.05.57	Hong Kong.
mid 05.57	Exercise *Sea Link*.
31.05.57	Hong Kong.
13.06.57	Singapore.
27.06.57	Left for series of naval exercises off Singapore.
Until 09.57	Visited Pulau Tioman, Langkawi, Penang, Miri, Tawau, Sandakan and Jesselton.
02.09.57	Singapore for refuelling and onward journey to Hong Kong.
07.09.57	Hong Kong.
07.10.57	Sailed from Hong Kong.
10.57	Visited Yokosuka, Kobe, Tokyo and Inchon.
11.57	Visited Yong Pyong Do, Pusan, Sasebo, Kagoshima and Hong Kong on 15 November.
02.12.57	Sailed for Bangkok, Singapore and Pulau Tioman.
25.12.57	Christmas at Singapore.
01.01.58	Headed to sea and home to Fremantle, Adelaide and Williamstown.

Seen in her early days as a fleet training ship, **HMAS Anzac** *underway in Sydney Harbour with some of her 21-inch torpedo tubes and 40mm anti-aircraft mountings landed.* *(Royal Australian Navy)*

08.02.58	Sydney for major refit.
10.58	Refit completed then under command of Commander R. A. H. Millar RAN.
27.02.59	Sea Trials completed.
03.59	Great Barrier Reef.
04.59	Exercise *FOTEX 59* off Singapore.
04.59	Exercise *Sea Demon*.
14.04.59	Left Singapore for Manila, Hong Kong and Singapore before arriving off Borneo for Exercise *Saddle Up* on 9 June 1959.
06.59	Visited Sandakan, Singapore, Sweetenham and Penang.
26.06.59	Bangkor Island for 3 day visit.
30.06.59	Pulan Anak Borau.
07.08.59	Singapore before sailing onto Cochin.
Late 1959	Visits included Trincomalee, Jesselton, Labuan and Yokohama.
31.10.59	With *Tobruk* at Yokosuka with **HM ships Centaur**, **Lagos** and **Cavalier**.
12.12.59	Refit at Williamstown.
22.03.60	Refit completed.
03.60	Acting Commander B. D. Gordon RAN took command.
Spring 60	Visited Noumea, Solomon Islands and Papau New Guinea.
Summer 60	Visited Platypus Bay, Moreton Bay and operated around Sydney.
31.08.60	Shelled sister ship *Tobruk* causing slight damage to sister ship.

HMAS Anzac *seen underway during a training cruise.* *(Royal Australian Navy)*

02.61	Lieutenant Commander D. M. Wogan-Browne RAN took command.
21.02-07.03.61	Maintenance at Williamstown.
01.03.61	Announcement that *Anzac* would become Fleet Training Ship and a refit was planned to build an extra deckhouse aft and the director would be removed.
03-04.61	Training cruise off Spalding Cove, Wallaroo Bay, Adelaide, Port Lincoln, Emu Bay and Kangaroo Island.
04.04.61	Jervis Bay.
09.08.61	Exercise *Tucker Box*.
30.08.61	Auckland.
04.09.61	Wellington.
13.09.61	Melbourne.
20.09.61	Exercise *Shop Window* that lasted until 11 October.
Late 1961	In Home waters.
01.12.61	Auckland for 3 day visit.
1-2.62	Training cruise around Australia with visits to Stanley-West Bay, Three Humock Island, Port Arthur and Hobart.
09.04.62	Refit at Williamstown started.
07.70.62	Refit completed.
30.08.62	Start of Exercise *Tucker Box II*.
10.62	Visited Melbourne, Adelaide and Albany.
12.62	Exercises off Sydney and Jervis Bay.
01.63	Commander D. A. H. Clarke DSC, MVO RAN took command.
23.02.63	Escorted Royal Yacht *Britannia* on visit to Melbourne.
01.04.63	Underwent modifications at Williamstown to fit her for her training role. Refit completed on 24 April. The 'B' turret and GI guns were removed and replaced by a charthouse/classroom.
05.63	Visited Hayman Island, South Molle Island, Linderman Island, Magnetic Island and Green Island.
05.06.63	Sydney.
28.08.63	Exercise *Carbine* off Caloundra.
19.09.63	Off Sydney for ASW exercise.
12.63	Fought a fire on the jetty at Tasman Island.
04.01.64	Refit at Melbourne.
01.04.64	Refit completed.
16.05.64	Trobriand Island before sailing onto Talasea-Kimbe Bay. *Anzac* went on to visit Rabaul, Sohano, Losuia, Oro Bay, Esa Ala, Milne Bay, Samarai and Port Moresby.
09.07.64	Sydney at start of Operation *Longex*.
07.64	Commander I. H. Nicholson RAN took command.
08.64	Visited New Zealand.
End 09. 64	Exercise *Winchester*.
13.12.64	Four month refit at Melbourne.
17.03.65	Refit completed.
19.03.65	Melbourne.
Late 03.65	Sydney and Jervis Bay.
04.65	Visited Platypus Bay, Bundaberg Bay, Percy Island and Refuge Bay.

15.05.65	Cairns for CASEX with **USS Coral Sea**.
05-06.65	Cruise in Papua New Guinean waters.
07.06.65	Rescued six people after their launch broke down and took them to safety in Mackay.
11.06.65	Sydney for self-maintenance.
09.65	Training cruise to Manus, Madang, Lae, Salamara Harbour and the Solomon Islands.
08.11.65	Exercise *Warrior* until 11 November.
10.12.65	Sydney.
20.12.65	Melbourne.
01.66	Commander I. W. Broben RAN took command.
22.03.66	Left Melbourne for trials and Exercise *Jig Time* off Jervis Bay.
10.06.66	Survey equipment fitted at Sydney to survey Australia's coastline.
25.07.66	After refit sailed to take up survey duties and took part in Exercise *Mulga Bill* off Jervis Bay.
10-11.66	Surveys off North West coast around Darwin and Port Hedland.
12.66	At Melbourne for refit.
21.03.67	Completed refit and resumed training duties.
06.04.67	Operation *Rumbling One*.
04.67	At Seeadler Harbour and Port Moresby.
23.04.67	Sydney.
05.67	Visited Chowder Bay, South Molle Island, Maryport Bay and Cleveland Bay.
05.06.67	Broken Bay for heeling trials.
07.67	Commander J. M. Kelly DSC RAN took command.

HMAS Anzac *pictured on 12 December 1966 in her final configuration after her 1965 refit, which saw the removal of "B" turret and the construction of a special classroom in its place on B deck.* *(Royal Australian Navy)*

07.67	Visited Tongo for coronation of His Majesty King Taufa, Ahau Tupou IV.
Summer 67	Visited Suva and Lautoka and took part in Exercise *JUG* off Newcastle New South Wales.
02.10.67	Survey work around Cairns.
10.67	Exercise *JUG 67*.
07.12.67	Melbourne for another refit.
27.04.68	Reverted to training ship.
25.05.68	Manus before joining Vietnam confrontation and escorted troop carrier **HMAS Sydney** to Vietnam in June.
01.06.68	Vung Tau and returned to Australia.
06.68	Commander J. B. Snow RAN took command.
07.06.68	Darwin and later Cairns.
21.06.68	Sydney.
08.68	Visited Thursday Island at Cape Keer.
12.09.68	Exercise *Coralex*.
29.09.68	Sio Island for a-day long-visit.
28.11.68	Annual refit at Melbourne.
22.02.69	Refit completed.
29.04.69	Adelaide.
30.04.69	King Island.
05.69	Visited Devonport, Jervis Bay, Brisbane and Gladstone.
21.05.69	Sydney.
21.06.69	Cid Harbour.
07.69	Visited Cairns, Wewak, Gizo, Kavieng, Rabual and Brisbane amongst many others.
18.08.69	Naval exercises off Jervis Bay.
25.08.69	Searched for survivors from **MV Moongah**, which sank off New South Wales in rough seas.
Autumn 69	Ports visited included Tahiti, Pago Pago, Apia, Nelson, Wellington and Auckland.
17.10.69	Sydney.
15.11.69	Jervis Bay.
11.12.69	Tour of East Coast naval bases.
12.12.69	Sydney for self maintenance.
12.69	Commander G. J. M. Clark RAN took command.
19.01.70	Sailed for New Zealand.
02.70	Training cruise to Waitangi, Motuna Island and Auckland.
16.02.70	Sydney.
23.02.70	Melbourne.
07.70	Visited High Peak Island, Mackay, Cairns, Townsville and Brisbane.
Autumn 70	Visited Wewak, Manus, Rabual and New Zealand.
27.09.70	Exercise *Longex* off Auckland.
10.70	Bay of Islands, Whangarei and Sydney on 22 October.
21.01.71	Left Sydney for Melbourne for refit.
05.71	Commander I. A. Callaway RAN took command.
25.06.71	Refit completed.
Summer 71	Summer training cruise in the Pacific.

13.09.71	Papau New Guinea on their national day.
27.10.71	Left Hobart for Melbourne.
04.11.71	Left Melbourne for Sydney.
01.02.72	Left for cruise around Australian coastline until 1 March.
01.03.72	Exercise *Planti Manua* at Port Moresby.
23.03.72	Sydney for a refit.
08.72	Commander M. De.V Salmon RAN took command
08.01.73	Rejoined the fleet and cruised to Port Melbourne, Port Lincoln, Portland, Devonport, Storm Bay and Hobart on 9 February.
16.02.7	Garden Island for self maintenance
26.02.73	Sailed to Auckland and Wellington.
03.73	Visited Port Melbourne and Albany whilst April saw visits paid to Fremantle and Garden Island on 27 April.
12.06.73	Sailed to visit Townsville, Mackay and Refuge Bay.
23.10.73	Garden Island for maintenance.
07.01.74	Left for weapons training.
16.01.74	Sailed for Queen Charlotte Sound in New Zealand.
22.01.74	Auckland.
Spring 74	Visited Scawfell Island, Brisbane, Sydney and Suva.
Late 07.74	Goodwill visit to Fiji.
11.08.74	Garden Island to pay off for disposal.
04.10.74	Finally decommissioned.
24.11.75	Sold for scrapping to HiFirm Corporation of Hong Kong.
30.12.75	Towed away for scrapping.

HMAS TOBRUK

*Early days with **HMAS Tobruk** visiting Brisbane, Queensland in 1950, prior to having her distinctive Australian Battle-class funnel cowling fitted.* *(Royal Australian Navy)*

A part from those navies that bought ex Royal Navy Battle class destroyers Australia was the only other operator of Battle class ships, but in their case they chose to build brand new ships. Two ships constructed were *Anzac* (sic) and sister ship *Tobruk*.

Unlike their British counterparts, these two ships were completed with the newer Mk VI turrets. The added height of these turrets meant that the bridge of the two ships had to be raised slightly to ensure that the crew had sufficient views across the bow.

The first steel for **HMAS Tobruk** was placed upon the construction slip at Cockatoo Docks and Engineering Company on 5 August 1946. Construction progressed well aided by a large amount of technical assistance from Britain. By 20 December 1947 *Tobruk* was complete to the launching stage. Cockatoo Dockyard Engineering prepared the slipway and *Tobruk* for her initial taste of water. The launch ceremony was conducted by Mrs W. F. Riordan, wife of the then Minister for Navy. The destroyer's sea trials were conducted in March 1950 and two months later on 8 May 1950 she was handed over to the Royal Australian Navy at Sydney with Commander T.K. Morrison, OBE, DSC, RAN in command. Total cost of the *Tobruk* was $A4.95 million. From Sydney she headed towards Jervis Bay which was reached on 3 July 1950. *Tobruk* would spend the next few months shuttling back and forth between Jervis Bay and Sydney.

On 8 August *Tobruk* was at Sydney but left the same day for exercises returning to Sydney on 13 August. Four days later the destroyer left Sydney and headed for Cape Moreton reaching the port on 21 August for a flying visit that lasted only a few hours before she headed back to sea. *Tobruk* spent a few days in the Pacific before returning to her home port at Sydney on 23 August. Between 18 September and 26 February 1951 *Tobruk* returned to spending time at sea or shuttling between Jervis Bay and Sydney.

Between 26 February 1951 and 14 March 1951 *Tobruk* was in the Storm Bay Area before heading for Westernport where she spent three days from 16 March. Naval exercises off Adelaide and then Jervis Bay kept the destroyer and her crew busy towards the end of March and into early April. *Tobruk* then resumed her normal routine of shuttling between Jervis Bay and Sydney throughout spring with a two day port visit to Newcastle from 14 April.

On 7 August 1951 *Tobruk* visited Hervey Bay for three days, before moving on around the coast for a visit to Brisbane, *Tobruk* left on 12 August. The following day *Tobruk* sailed into Hervey Bay and Fairfax Island. By 18 August 1951 *Tobruk* was back alongside at Sydney.

Tobruk's entry into service co-incided with perhaps some of the worst fighting in the Korean War and with Australian forces heavily committed to the United Nations led operation it was inevitable that *Tobruk* would serve in the theatre. *Tobruk* initially sailed in August 1951 to Japan where the destroyer joined the United Nations naval forces assembled there. Commander Richard Peek, RAN had by this time replaced Commander Morrison and he took the brand new destroyer to war on 3 October 1951. She was assigned to provide part of the screen of CTE 95.11 centred on the American aircraft carrier *USS Rendova* (CVE-14) with Canadian ships *Athabaskan* and *Sioux* in company.

For the next fifteen days *Tobruk* remained close to the *USS Rendova* as one of her escorts with one exception when she spent a day with TE 95.19 conducting air and bombardment strikes against targets on Korea's east coast. On the 18 October *Tobruk* sailed into Sasebo for some well earned rest.

HMAS Tobruk pictured underway in the early 1950s in Australian waters sporting her full armament of four 4.5-inch dual-purpose guns, eleven 40mm anti-aircraft guns, ten 21-inch torpedo tubes and one Squid anti-submarine mortar.
(Royal Australian Navy)

26 October saw *Tobruk* slip from Sasebo and returned to her role of escorting the *USS Rendova*. Her duties mostly entailed monitoring flight operations and plane guard duties until she was relieved on station on 4 November. *USS Rendova*, *Tobruk* and the RN destroyer *Cockade* all sailed for the Japanese port of Sasebo.

The stop at Sasebo was all too brief for many because after only four days the destroyer once more headed to sea to begin her third patrol. Her destination would be Korea's Eastern coastline while her role would see her use her main gun armament to its fullest. *Tobruk* spent 12 days as part of Task Group 95.2 shelling enemy positions along the coast between Songjin and Chongjin. The highlight for many of her crew was the complete destruction of a freight train on 18 December. Many trains had escaped but on this occasion the target had been derailed which allowed *Tobruk's* gunners to take accurate readings and then to lay down effective fire. The twelve days were very busy ones for *Tobruk's* gunners. Over one hundred targets were attacked and 1,200 rounds of 4.5-inch ammunition were fired.

19 November saw *Tobruk* as part of CTG 95.8 which was centred on the six-inch gunned cruiser *Belfast*. CTG 95.8 was assigned the role of performing a combined two day air sea strike on Hungnam. The aircraft carrier *HMAS Sydney* provided air cover which pounded the town after *Belfast*, *HMNS Van Galen* and *Tobruk* had softened the enemies anti aircraft defences with gunfire. *Tobruk's* records show that over the two days of the operation she fired 321 rounds of 4.5-inch ammunition. After the mission had been deemed a success *Tobruk* broke away and on 21 November she returned to Kure.

On 28 November *Tobruk* began a 26 day patrol and saw a return to Korea's west coastline. Her role was again to act as escort for the American aircraft carrier *Rendova* and later for the Australian *Sydney*. *Tobruk's* partnership with the *Rendova* continued until 6 December when the aircraft carrier left Korean waters. This allowed *Tobruk* to operate independently off Paengyong Do. The next day *Sydney* assumed the role of on duty carrier and operated with *Tobruk* for the next ten days.

Between 17 and 20 December *Tobruk* was attached to Task Element 95.12 and carried out harassment attacks on enemy positions south of Sokto. For this operation the destroyer was joined by the cruiser *Ceylon* and destroyer *Constance* from the Royal Navy, whilst the American contribution was the Cleveland class cruiser *Manchester* and the destroyer *Eversole*.

After celebrating Christmas the crew of *Tobruk* found that the New Year also saw them start the ship's fifth patrol of the War. She relieved the frigate *Whitesand Bay* in the Haeju area and operated mainly in defence of Yongpyong Do. The guns onboard the destroyer were rarely silent as two or three bombardments were carried out daily. On 7 January Chomi Do was heavily attacked by *Tobruk* and other ships to prevent a Communist invasion of Yongmae Do. Two days later on 9 January *Tobruk* was relieved by the Canadian destroyer *Cayuga*.

Seven days later *Tobruk* started her sixth patrol of the Korean conflict when she was absorbed into Task Element 95.11 and provided escort duties to the aircraft carrier *Sydney* once more. During this time the task element spent two days in the Choda Sokto area ready to defend against an invasion. It was expected that any invasion would come at night and the ship was rigged ready to repel this during the hours of darkness. Meanwhile during daylight hours the opportunity was taken to shoot at any enemy positions that could be found. Such gunfire was made all the more impressive because of snow storms and frequent gales in the operating area. *Tobruk* finally sailed for Sasebo on 25 January after completing another highly successful patrol. At the end of her five months of service in the operational areas *Tobruk* had steamed some 39,000 miles and fired 2,316 rounds from her 4.5-inch guns.

Tobruk returned to Australian waters on 22 February 1952 having spent 118 days away in Korean waters. For her crew it was pleasant to spend the next six months in home waters. In September 1952 *Tobruk* escorted the aircraft carrier *Sydney* to Manus Island. October, however, saw *Tobruk* in a high profile role conducting security patrols off the Monte Bello Islands covering the explosion of the first British Atomic bomb. For this role she would identify any ships in the area and escort them away to a safe position. November 1952 to May 1953

was spent operating and training in and around Australian waters.

The continuing conflict in Korea saw *Tobruk* return to the theatre of operations on 26 June 1953 when she joined CTU 95.1.2 centred on the cruiser *Newcastle* at Taechong Do. *Tobruk* was sent to the area to relieve her sister ship *Anzac*. 27 June *Tobruk* became one of the ships assigned to protect the aircraft carrier *Ocean* and stayed with the British carrier until *Ocean* was relieved by the *USS Bairoko* on 5 July.

14 July saw *Tobruk* operating as part of Task Group 95.02 on the Yangdo Blockade. She reached Yangdo and promptly relieved the Canadian destroyer *HMCS Huron*. Two days later *Tobruk* sank a large motor sampan which intelligence reports had suggested was being used to lay a series of minefields. Eight days later and only a few before the end of hostilities, *Tobruk's* last offensive gunfire was directed at a radar post on Musudan Point between Chongjin and Yangdo on 24 July.

Tobruk remained in Korean waters after the ceasefire had been signed. During her second tour of duty in Korean waters she steamed some 26,000 miles (including some 7,000 miles before the end of hostilities). Once relieved on station *Tobruk* returned home for a much needed refit and overhaul. *Tobruk* was at Sydney on 22 February 1954 and stayed there until 17 May when she sailed for Jervis Bay before returning to Sydney. For the next five months *Tobruk* would sail between the two ports conducting trials and exercising the ships' equipment and armament. Brisbane was the next port of call for *Tobruk* when she called into the port on 25 September 1954 for a three day port visit. On the 5 October *Tobruk* entered Manus for fifteen days before returning to Sydney. From Sydney it was a ten day stop at Melbourne which started on 1 November. The next four months would see *Tobruk* frequenting the ports of Sydney and Jervis Bay, spending a few days in each port before moving on. *Tobruk* left Jervis Bay on 22 April 1955 and headed for Newcastle, New South Wales, which was reached the following day. The next month saw the ship paying visits to ports around the coast of Australia including Sydney, Hobart, Townsville and Darwin.

Tobruk then took part in multi-national exercises that took the ship to Singapore on 7 June 1955. Three days in Singapore were followed by a series of gunnery, missile and anti submarine exercises before arriving at Pulau Tioman on 10 June for an overnight stay. Ten more days of hectic training and exercises followed before the next port of call at Bangkok on 21 June. The crew's of the various ships participating in the exercises were allowed some degree of shore leave at Bangkok before the ships left the port on 24 June. Three more days at sea took the *Tobruk* back to Singapore. The exercises completed successfully *Tobruk* returned home to Australia and pulled into Darwin on 8 July. She left the same day and headed for Cairns which was reached four days later. Again *Tobruk* only stayed for a few hours before heading back out to sea. Sydney was reached on 16 July where leave was granted for some whilst others were employed conducting maintenance on the destroyer.

Tobruk returned to sea after three months in dockyard hands on 17 October 1955 and headed for Jervis Bay to take part in the one day Exercise *Dry Salt*. At the completion of the exercise *Tobruk* returned to Sydney only to sail again on 20 October to take part in Exercise *Awkward* which finished on 24 of the month. The warship needed more repairs and some time had been put into the ship's schedule for self maintenance and this was undertaken at Sydney for just under a month.

On 16 November 1955 *Tobruk* once more put to sea and headed for Fremantle for a one day visit which ended on 24 November. Singapore was once again the next port of call, after which the destroyer paid a visit to Penang where she spent Christmas. New Year however was spent at Singapore. *Tobruk* left the Malaysian port on the 4 January 1956 and headed towards Hong Kong to take part in a series of exercises with Australian forces and warships of foreign navies. Before the major exercises *Sea Dragon* and *Welcome* were undertaken off Singapore the opportunity was taken for a two day visit to Bangkok where the crew enjoyed many happy hours ashore. Exercise *Monsoon* was staged off Hong Kong between the 23 and 26 March. At the completion of the exercise *Tobruk's* crew were allowed to enjoy the delights of Hong Kong when she paid a five day visit to the harbour.

The Australian destroyer then headed onto Japan where she visited the ancient port of Yokosuka. She anchored in the harbour on 13 April and was warmly received by her Japanese hosts during the five days she spent at anchor. Such was the success of this visit that the crew couldn't wait to see what sort of reaction awaited them at Japan's capital city, Tokyo which was next on the itinerary of the destroyer. Tokyo was reached on 19 April 1956. True to form the Japanese gave the destroyer an impressive welcome throughout the seven days she spent in the city. During the next two months *Tobruk* would also visit Kure, Paen Yong Do and Chinhae before a return visit to Kure on 10 May 1956. The next four days were spent preparing the ship for the next naval exercise. Exercise *Stop Watch* was to be staged in the waters off Tosa Wan. *Tobruk* completed the exercise successfully on 17 May and headed back to Hong Kong for a period of self refitting which was completed on 16 July 1956. Four days were then spent preparing the ship for sea before *Tobruk* headed for Jesselton Harbour for a three day stop over.

Towards the end of July *Tobruk* visited Labuan and Kuala Belait before again heading for Singapore to take part in *Operation Turnip* from the 1-6 August.

Throughout August *Tobruk* visited a string of Pacific ports including Pangkor Telok Belangor, Langkawi and Penang before arriving on 24 August 1956 at Singapore. Three days later the destroyer left Malaysia and headed for Hong Kong. She arrived on 1 September arrived and prepared to participate in *Operation Nelson's Square*. On 4 September *Tobruk* left Hong Kong but would return three days later and stayed in the British colony for a fortnight before heading out on 24 September and made for Singapore to participate in yet another naval exercise that had been codenamed Exercise *Albatross*.

After a very successful exercise *Tobruk* left Singapore on 2 October. Next port of call was six days steaming

HMAS Tobruk *looking very smart at Sydney. Even so, the lack of flags would indicate that she was laid up.*
(T. Ferrers-Walker Collection)

away, the exotic port of Bangkok and capital of Thailand. Four very enjoyable days were spent in the city before the Australian destroyer left on 12 October and a ten day voyage to Manila. *Tobruk* once more headed to sea after four days ashore on 26 October. A brief stop at Manus followed after which *Tobruk* began preparations for a refit at Sydney. En route the destroyer paid calls at Challenger Bay and Brisbane before finally arriving at Sydney on 12 November 1956. *Tobruk* was to remain in dockyard hands until 20 February 1957 when she commenced a series of post refit trials that saw her shuttling between Hobart, Jervis Bay and Sydney until the middle of March. Having been declared available to the fleet *Tobruk* became part of the forces assembled on 11 March 1957 for Exercise *Shop Window*, held that year in and around the Jervis Bay area. After three days of intensive exercises the crew of *Tobruk* welcomed the chance to return to Sydney which was reached on 15 March. Twelve days later the destroyer slipped and headed towards Fremantle to participate in another exercise entitled Exercise *Tradewind*. From Fremantle *Tobruk* headed back to Singapore to again participate in monitoring the Indonesian crisis in the area.

Between late April and late August 1957 *Tobruk* visited Pulau Tioman, Hong Kong, Seria, Trengganu, Lang Kawi island, Kuala Lumpur, Pangkor Island and Singapore on numerous occasions. She also took part in Exercise *Sea Link* in May off Manila and Exercise *Wealex* off Singapore.

After a brief stop at Singapore to refuel and replenish on 22 August *Tobruk* sailed the same day for Kuala Pahang. Again she left the same day and headed for the neighbouring Pulau Tioman where she stayed for two days. After this visit the destroyer returned once more to the safe and secure confines of the Navy dockyard at Singapore on 26 August. The crew were around this time told of the ship's next ports of call and after a few stops en route *Tobruk* would visit Japan. Japan, however, was in October and a period of self maintenance at Hong Kong awaited the crew before the excitement of Japan.

Tobruk stayed in Hong Kong until 7 October when she put to sea and headed towards Japanese waters around Yokosuka. There the Australian's participated in Exercise *Kosex*. The crew of *Tobruk* were amazed at the warmth of the reception they received in various Japanese ports but especially when they made a return visit to Tokyo for a six day visit on 18 October.

The end of October took the Australian destroyer to waters off Korea again to take part in *Operation Dusky* before again heading back to Japan and visits to Chinhae, Sasebo and Nagasaki in early November. The remainder of the month was spent in Hong Kong which was left on 1 December. *Tobruk's* next destination was Vietnam and in particular the city of Saigon where she arrived on 5 December for a four day visit. The remainder of December saw visits to Singapore and Pulau Tioman before returning to Singapore on 23 December for Christmas leave to be granted.

1958 started with a series of visits to Kuching and Labuan before a return to Singapore on 10 January. *Tobruk* stayed in the Naval base for ten days replenishing stores and generally maintaining the ship before sailing for Australian waters on 20 January. The port of Fremantle welcomed the ship and crew seven days later. Next port of call was a flying visit to Adelaide on 2 February that lasted only a few hours before *Tobruk* left the same day. Two days later she paid a visit to Melbourne before finally entering into Sydney harbour on 8 February for a long planned extended refit. The refit concerned itself mostly with the ship's engines, communications and also replaced or repaired worn out and damaged parts on the ship. On 20 October after eight months work, *Tobruk's* refit was complete and she returned to active duty. Four days later after a brief visit to Jervis Bay, the newly refitted destroyer carried out exercises with other Australian warships in the waters around Sydney that continued into the first days of December 1958. Another spell in dockyards hands occurred between 5 December and 19 January at Melbourne.

Between 21 January and 26 March, *Tobruk* made a tour of Australian ports calling at Sydney, Jervis Bay, Cairns and finally Darwin on 25 March for a one night stay. *Tobruk* left home waters and returned once more to her old stomping ground of Singapore. There she and other units of Australian, American and British navies

*In April 1972, in company with the former **HMAS Quiberon, HMAS Tobruk** is finally towed away to the ship breakers in Japan.*   *(Maritime Photo Library)*

took part in Exercise *Fotex*. A second exercise Exercise *Sea Demon* started eight days later and occupied the ship's time for the next six days. Johore Shoal was next on *Tobruk's* itinerary before a call into the Philippines with a visit to the bustling city of Manila on 28 April. *Tobruk* crossed the sea to Hong Kong and participated in Exercise *Hokex*, which started on 2 May. Experienced sailors who had enjoyed trips to Hong Kong before enjoyed the opportunity to find old haunts in the colony whilst for new crewmembers Hong Kong was truly an eye opener. Many were sad to leave when the ship slipped out of port finally on 19 May 1959.

Summer 1959 was spent either at Singapore or Sandakan where the ship took part in exercises. Later in June she visited Penang before arriving at Dindinga Channel on 26 June where she stayed for three days. On 29]une she arrived at Langkawi island for a flying visit and left the same day before moving onto Kuah - Bass harbour. Whilst at Kuah *Tobruk* took part in a number of exercises through until the 1 July. On 4 July 1959 *Tobruk* paid a brief flying visit to Penang and left the same day before moving onto Singapore the next day. She would spend the next month alongside conducting a self refit. On 3 August *Tobruk* was once again at sea and arrived the same day at Johore Shoal Buoy where she stayed until the following day. 4 August saw the destroyer move into Singapore from where she would participate in that years Exercise *Jet* until 12 August. The officers and men enjoyed a three day break at Trincomalee on 21 August before heading back to sea. However, the lure of the tropical harbour brought the ship and men back again on 27 August. *Tobruk* finally left Trincomalee on 31 August and sailed for Colombo for a planned arrival on 1 September. A hugely successful visit followed before the ship returned yet again to the safe environs of Singapore for a self maintenance period.

On 27 September *Tobruk* sailed into Camranh Bay for a three day port of call. Visits to Subic Bay and Hong Kong followed in October before a nine day visit to Yokohama. Members of the ship's company were allowed leave to explore the area and to learn something of Japanese culture. On 30 October Yokohama was left behind as the destroyer sailed for Singapore calling at Hong Kong along the way. *Tobruk* entered Singapore on 20 November and stayed there for another eight days. The destroyer had been away from home since April and it

was now time to return to Australia. She arrived at Fremantle on 5 December and briefly called into Melbourne before Sydney's naval facilities welcomed her into a berth to commence a period of refit on 15 December. Many of her crew were also granted Christmas leave and dispersed around the country to be with their families.

Tobruk did not return to sea until 21 March 1960 when she left Sydney after having successfully completed her refit. Ten days later she arrived at Jervis Bay to conduct some anti-submarine training (CASEXs 6 & 7). She spent the next two months shuttling between Sydney and Jervis Bay but on 11 April 1960 she did take part in Operation *Awkward*.

On 2 May 1960 *Tobruk* visited Noumea and throughout May visited numerous New Guinea communities such as Vila, Honiara, Rabaul, Manus and Lae before visiting Port Moresby on 23 May.

Spring turned into summer 1960 and *Tobruk's* records shows that she visited Cairns and Brisbane before spending June and July at Sydney for a period of self maintenance and leave. By 2 August she left Sydney and resumed her usual pattern of days spent at Sydney, at sea or at Jervis Bay before calling into Brisbane on 26 August.

On 30 August 1960 the destroyer left Brisbane and headed to Platypus Bay which was reached the following day. Five days were spent there before the destroyer joined other units of the Australian fleet, including her sister *Anzac* at Sydney for *FLEETEX III*. While exercising with the fleet off the east coast of Australia she was accidentally hit by a shell fired from *Anzac*. The damage inflicted on the destroyer was relatively minor but still necessitated a period in dockyard hands at Jervis Bay.

The Australian Navy was at this point developing new and innovative fleet escort replacement plans and *Tobruk* and her sister *Anzac* were initially considered for a major overhaul programme to bring them into line with other members of the fleet but it was eventually decided that such a programme would be too expensive and the two ships would continue more or less as designed until decommissioned. For *Tobruk* this was not far into the future as the decision had been taken to lay up the destroyer. On 17 September *Tobruk* sailed into Sydney to decommission. She eventually entered Reserve on 29 October 1960.

Tobruk languished in reserve for twelve years before the ship was approved for scrapping and sold on 15 February 1972 to Fujita Salvage of Osaka. On 10 April 1972 the Japanese ocean going tug *Sumi Maru No.38* sailed from Sydney for Moji, Japan with *Tobruk* and *Quiberon* under tow.

*Serving with the United Nations forces during the Korean War, **HMAS Tobruk** was an escort to the carrier **HMAS Sydney**, from whom this 1951 photo was taken whilst **Tobruk** carried out a replenishment as sea. During her 1951-52 deployment, **Tobruk** was engaged in bombardments, patrols and blockading and screening duties with aircraft carriers, which were operating against the Communist forces.   (Vic Jeffery Collection)*

05.08.46	Laid down at Cockatoo Docks and Enginerring Company.
20.12.47	Launched by Mrs W. J. F. Riordan.
03.50	Sea trials.
08.05.50	Handed over to Australian Navy with Commander T. K. Morrison, OBE, DSC RAN in command.
03.07.50	Jervis Bay.
08.50	Visited Sydney and Cape Moreton.
09.50 - 2.51	Shuttled between Jervis Bay and Sydney.
03.51	Naval Exercises off Adelaide.
14.04.51	Newcastle, NSW.
08.51	Visited Hervey Bay, Brisbane, Fairfax Island and Sydney.
03.10.51	Sailed to Korea in support of UN forces there. **Tobruk** was assigned to screen CTE-95.11 centred on **USS Rendova** (CVE-114) with **Athabaskan** and **Sioux**.
18.10.51	Sailed to Sasebo.
26.10.51	Back with CTE-95.11 until 4 November and returned to Sasebo.
11.51	On return to Korea, Tobruk joined Task Group 95.2 shelling positions along the coast

between Songjin and Chongjin.

19.11.51	With **HMAS Sydney** for air strike on Hungnam. **Tobruk** fired 321 rounds of 4.5-in ammunition to soften target.
21.11.51	At Kobe.
28.11.51	Start of 26 day patrol on Korea's west coast.
18.12.51	Destroyed a train with gunfire.
01.52	Operated off Yongpyong Do.
07.01.52	Attacked Chimi Do.
09.02.52	Relieved on station by Canadian destroyer **Cayuga.**
16.01.52	Invasion feared at Choda Sokto and **Tobruk** was positioned to repel any such invasion, which never materialised.
25.01.52	Sailed for Sasebo.

HMAS Tobruk *punching through a Southern Ocean swell in the Great Australian Bight.*
(Royal Australian Navy)

22.02.52	In Australian waters.
09.52	Escorted **HMAS Sydney** to Manus Island.
10.52	Monte Bello Islands for the first British Atomic bomb test.
11.52 - 05.53	In Australian waters.
26.06.53	Returned to Korean War and joined CTU-95.1.2 on the cruiser **Newcastle** at Taechong Do. Later also escorted the aircraft carrier **Ocean**.
16.07.53	Sank a large motor sampan that was laying a minefield.
24.07.53	Bombardment of radar post on Musudan Point between Chongjin and Yangdo. **Tobruk** remained in Korean waters for some time after the ceasefire was signed.
22.02.53	Sydney for a refit.
17.05.53	Refit completed and sailed for Jervis Bay.
25.09.54	Brisbane.
05.10.54	Manus for 15-days.
10.54	Visited Sydney and Melbourne on 1st November.
Winter 54	Shuttled between Jervis Bay and Sydney.
22.04.54	Left Jervis Bay to Newcastle NSW.
05.55	Visited Sydney, Hobart, Townsville and Darwin.
07.06.55	Following month of international exercises arrived at Singapore.
10.06.55	Pulau Tioman.
21.06.55	Bangkok.
27.06.55	Singapore.
08.07.55	Darwin and Cairns.
16.07.54	Sydney.
17.10.55	Exercise *Dry Salt* off Jervis Bay.
20.10.55	Exercise *Awkward* off Sydney.
16.11.55	Visited Fremantle before going onto Singapore.
04.01.56	Left Singapore to visit Hong Kong.
01.56	Exercise *Sea Dragon* and Exercise *Welcome* off Singapore.
01.56	Bangkok for 2 days.
23-26.03.56	Exercise *Monsoon* off Hong Kong.
13.04.56	Yokosuka in Japan.
19.04.56	Tokyo before visiting Kure, Paen Yong Do and Chinhae.
10.05.56	Kure for exercise *Stop Watch* off Tosa Wan.
16.07.55	Completed self-refit at Hong Kong.
20.07.56	Jesselton Harbour for 3 days.
07.56	Visited Labuan and Kulala Belait.
01-06.08.56	Operation Turnip off Singapore.
08.56	Visited Pangkor Telok Belangor, Langkawi and Penang.
24.08.56	Singapore.
01.09.56	Hong Kong for Operation Nelson,s Square.
24.09.56	Left Hong Kong for Singapore and Exercise *Albatross*.
08.10.56	Bangkok for 4 days.
22.10.56	Manila.
12.11.56	Sydney for refit.
20.02.57	Refit completed.

Late in her active careesr, **HMAS Tobruk** *as a fleet destroyer with numerous canvas awnings rigged as protection against the tropical sun.* *(Royal Australian Navy)*

11.03.57	Exercise *Shop Window* in Jervis Bay.
03.57	Visited Sydney and Fremantle for Exercise *Tradewind*.
03.57	Singapore for monitor Indonesian crisis.
Summer 57	Pulau Tioman, Hong Kong, Seria, Trengganu, Langkawi Island, Kuala Lumpur, Pangkor Island and Singapore. Also took part in Exercise *Sea Unk* and Exercise *Wealex*.
10.57	Hong Kong and Exercise *Kosex*.
18.10.57	Tokyo for 6 days.
10.57	Off Korea for Operation *Dusky*, before heading back to Japan for port visits to Chinhae, Sasebo and Nagasaki in early November.
11.57	Hong Kong.
05.12.57	Saigon in Vietnam for 4 days.
23.12.57	Singapore for Christmas leave.
20.01.58	Returned to Australian waters.
27.01.58	Fremantle.
02.02.58	Adelaide.

04.02.58	Melbourne.
08.02.58	Sydney for extended refit.
20.10.58	Refit completed.
12.58-19.01.59	Refit at Melbourne.
21.01-26.03.59	Tour of Australian ports.
03.59	Singapore and Exercise *FOTEX* and Exercise *Sea Demon*.
28.04.59	Manila before Hong Kong and Exercise *Hokex*, which started on 2 May.
19.05.59	Left Hong Kong.
Summer 59	Singapore and Sandakan.
26.06.59	Dindingon Channel for 3 days.
29.06.59	Kuah for series of naval exercises.
04.07.59	Penang.
04.08.59	Exercise *Jet*.
21.08.59	Trincomalee.
31.08.59	Colombo.
01.09.59	Singapore for self-maintenance period.
10.59	Visited Camranh Bay, Subic Bay, Hong Kong and a nine-day visit to Yokohama.
20.11.59	Singapore.
05.12.58	Fremantle.
15.12.59	Sydney for a refit.
21.03.60	Refit completed.
04.60	CASEX's 6 and 7 off Jervis Bay.
02.05.60	Novmea and later Vila, Honiara, Rabaul, Manus and Lae.

A 21-inch torpedo test firing whilst alongside in the Garden Island Naval Dockyard, Sydney.
(Royal Australian Navy)

23.05.60	Port Moresby.
Summer 60	Visited Cairns, Brisbane and Sydney.
31.08.60	Platypus Bay for exercises with other RAN units during *Fleetex III*. Sister ship ***Anzac*** accidentally shelled ***Tobruk*** with a round of 4.5-in ammunition. Minor damage was caused, which was repaired at Jervis Bay.
17.09.60	Sailed into Sydney to de-commission.
29.10.60	Entered reserve fleet.
15.02.72	After languishing for twelve years was sold for scrapping to Fujita Salvage of Osaka.
10.04.72	Japanese tug ***Sumi Maru No 38*** took ***Tobruk*** and ***Quiberon*** under tow for Moji in Japan for demolition.

APPENDICES

Previous page: **HMS Corunna** *is seen during a firepower demonstration.*   *(MoD/Crown Copyright)*

BATTLE CLASS BUILD PROGRAMME

1942 Programme

Job No	Name	Builder	Ordered	Laid Down	Launched	Completed
J4583	*Barfleur*	Swan Hunter	27.4.42	28.10.42	1.11.43	14.9.44
J4585	*Trafalgar*	Swan Hunter	27.4.42	15.2.43	12.1.44	23.7.45
J4587	*St Kitts*	Swan Hunter	27.4.42	8.9.43	4.10.44	21.1.46
J4584	*Armada*	Hawthorn Leslie	27.4.42	29.12.42	9.12.43	2.7.45
J4586	*Solebay*	Hawthorn Leslie	27.4.42	3.2.43	22.2.44	11.10.45
J4588	*Saintes*	Hawthorn Leslie	27.4.42	8.6.43	19.7.44	27.9.46
J11707	*Camperdown*	Fairfield	27.4.42	30.10.42	8.2.44	18.6.45
J11708	*Finisterre*	Fairfield	27.4.42	8.12.42	22.6.44	11.9.45
J4681	*Gabbard*	Swan Hunter	12.8.42	2.2.44	16.3.45	10.12.46
J3630	*Hogue*	Cammell Laird	12.8.42	6.1.43	21.4.44	24.7.45
J3653	*Lagos*	Cammell Laird	12.8.42	8.4.43	4.8.44	2 11.45
J3608	*Gravelines*	Cammell Laird	12.8.42	10.8.43	30.11.44	14.6.46
J3615	*Sluys*	Cammell Laird	12.8.42	24.11.43	28.2.45	30.9.46
J11711	*Cadiz*	Fairfield	12.8.42	10.5.43	16.9.44	12.4.46
J11712	*St James*	Fairfield	12.8.42	20.5.43	7.6.45	12.7.46
J11713	*Vigo*	Fairfield	12.8.42	11.9.45	27.9.45	9.12.46

1943 Programme

Job No	Name	Builder	Ordered	Laid Down	Launched	Completed
J4870	*Agincourt*	Hawthorn Leslie	10.3.43	12.12.43	29.1.45	25.6.47
J4876	*Alamein*	Hawthorn Leslie	10.3.43	1.3.44	28.5.45	21.5.48
J4869	*Aisne*	Vickers (Tyne)	10.3.43	26.8.43	12.5.45	20.3.47
J1615	*Barrosa*	John Brown	10.3.43	28.12.43	17.1.45	14.2.47
J1616	*Matapan*	John Brown	10.3.43	11.3.44	30.4.45	5.9.47
J4923	*Corunna*	Swan Hunter	24.4.43	12.4.44	29.5.45	6.6.47
J11603	*Dunkirk*	Stephen	24.4.43	19.7.44	27.8.45	27.11.46
J11604	*Malpaquet*¹	Stephen	24.4.43	27.11.44	20.2.46	30.4.47

1943 Programme - Cancelled Ships[2]

On 25 September 1945 the Admiralty ordered suspension of all work on the last 16 Battle class destroyers. All were cancelled on 15 October 1945.

Job No	Name	Builder	Ordered	Laid Down	Launched	Completed
J4873	*Albuera*	Vickers (Tyne)	10.3.43	16.9.43	28.8.45	
YN075	*Omdurman*	Fairfield	24.4.43	8.3.44		
J4926	*Oudenarde*	Swan Hunter	24.4.43	12.10.44	11.9.45	
J4929	*River Plate*	Swan Hunter	24.4.43	11.4.45		
J11605	*St Lucia*	Stephen	24.4.43	19.1.45		
J11714	*Belle* Isle	Fairfield	24.4.43	10.11.43	7.2.46	
J4922	*Jutland*	Hawthorn Leslie	24.4.43	14.8.44	2.11.45	
J4925	*Mons*	Hawthorn Leslie	24.4.43	29.6.45		
J4928	*Poictiers*	Hawthorn Leslie	24.4.43	9.2.45		
J3694	*Namur*	Cammell Laird	24.4.43	29.4.44	12.6.45	
J3672	*Navarino*	Cammell Laird	24.4.43	25.4.44	21.9.45	
J3651	*San Domingo*	Cammell Laird	24.4.43	9.12.44		
J3633	*Somme*	Cammell Laird	24.4.43	24.2.45		
J1617	*Talavera*	John Brown	5.6.43	4.9.44	27.8.45	
J1618	*Trincomalee*	JohnBrown	5.6.43	5.2.45	18.1.46	
J11716	*Waterloo*	Fairfield	5.6.43	14.6.45		

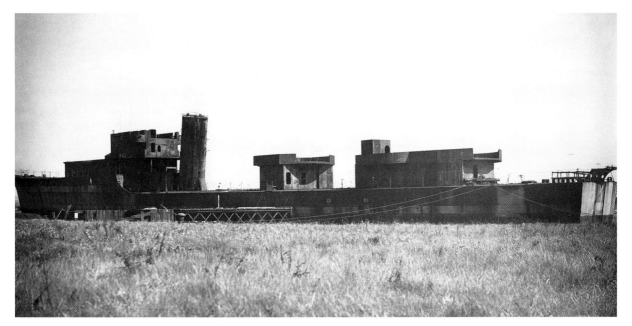

*The incomplete hull of **Namur** pictured awaiting disposal at Barrow in May 1950.*

(T. Ferrers-Walker Collection)

Two further units were ordered but completed as members of the Daring class.

J11717 *Ypres*[3]   Fairfield   5.6.43
J3675   *Vimiera*[3]   Cammell Laird   5.6.43

Royal Australian Navy Battle Class Programme

Name	Builder	Laid Down	Launched	Completed
Anzac	Williamstown Dockyard	23.9.46	20.8.48	22.3.51
Tobruk	Cockatoo, Sydney	5.8.46	20.12.47	8.5.50

Notes:

[1] *Malplaquet* was renamed *Jutland* after launch, once the original *Jutland* was cancelled.

[2] *Mons*, *Omdurman*, *River Plate*, *St Lucia*, *San Domingo*, *Somme* and *Waterloo* were broken up on the slips. *Albuera* was sold for shipbreaking at Inverkeithing on 21.11.50; *Belle Isle* arrived at Troon for demolition in May 1946; *Namur* was surveyed in 1949 for possible completion as a machinery trials ship, however her rusty hull and the projected cost caused the abandonment of the programme. She was sold to T.W. Ward and arrived at Barrow for scrapping in 1951; *Navarino* arrived at Preston for scrapping in 1946; *Oudernarde* was used at Rosyth for destructive testing of the hull. She was sold to Shipbreaking Industries and arrived at Inverkeithing for scrapping in December 1957; *Jutland(i)* was sold to Shipbreaking Industries for scrapping at Rosyth in 1957; *Poictiers* was sold to T. Young in March 1946 and arrived at Sunderland for scrapping on the 29th of the month; *Talavera* was scrapped at Troon in 1946 as was *Trincomalee*.

[3] *Vimiera* and *Ypres* served as fresh development for the Daring class and their contracts were subsequently reawarded as *Danae* and *Delight*. *Danae* was cancelled on 18.12.45 and *Delight* was completed on 9.10.53.

TECHNICAL SPECIFICATIONS

1942 Programme (As Designed)

Displacement:	2,315 tons (Standard)	3,361 tons (Full Load)
Length:	379 ft (OA)	364 ft (WL)
Beam:	40 ft 3 ins	
Machinery:	Two Admiralty Three Drum boilers; 2 shaft Parsons Geared Turbines	
Performance:	50.000 shp; 35.75 knots	
Oil Fuel:	766 tons	
Range:	4,400 nm at 20 knots	
Stabilisers:	*Camperdown* and *Finisterre* only	
Armament:	4 x 4.5-inch guns in 2 MkIV twin mountings	
	1 x 4-inch MkXXIII mounting	
	8 x 40mm AA (4 x twin)	
	6 x 20mm AA (2 x twin; 2 x single)	
	8 x 21-inch torpedo tubes (2 x quadruple launchers)	
	Depth Charge racks and throwers (60 DC)	
Complement:	247 (Leaders 286)	
Leaders:	*Armada; Barfleur; St James; Saintes; Solebay; Trafalgar*	

1943 Programme (As above - except)

Displacement:	2,380 tons (Standard)	3,315 tons (Full Load)
Beam:	40 ft 6 ins	
Armament:	5 x 4.5-inch guns (2 x twin; 1 x single)	
	8 x 40mm AA (3 x twin; 2 x single)	
	10 x 21-inch torpedo tubes (2 x quintuple launchers)	
	1 x Squid A/S mounting	
Leaders:	*Agincourt; Alamein; Corunna; Jutland*	

Radar Picket Conversions

Displacement:	2,480 tons (Standard)	3,430 tons (Full Load)
Armament:	4 x 4.5-inch (2 x twin)	
	1 x Seacat (Quadruple Launcher)	
	1 x Squid A/S mounting	
	2 x 20mm AA (2 x single)	
Complement:	268	

Royal Australian Navy Programme

Displacement:	2,400 tons (Standard)	3,266 tons (Full Load)
Length:	379 ft	
Beam:	41 ft	
Machinery:	Admiralty Three Drum Boilers; 2 shafts Parsons Geared Turbines	
Performance:	54,000 shp; 35.75 knots	
Armament:	4 x 4.5-inch guns in twin MkVI turrets	
	11 x 40mm AA	
	10 x 21-inch torpedo tubes	
	1 x Squid A/S mounting	

Notes:

Similar to the two cancelled RN ships *Vimiera* and *Ypres*, and like them, had the beam slightly increased. The main armament was in two twin MkVI turrets positioned forward and having a maximum elevation of 85°. They reverted to the Mk6 combined HA/LA director as fitted in the 1942 ships, with remote power control of the main armament. The 4.5-inch mountings for *Tobruk* were manufactured in the UK and shipped out, while those for *Anzac* were manufactured locally. The bridge structure was slightly higher than in the RN ships and the funnels were fitted with cowls shortly after completion.

FULL POWER TRIALS

	Speed	Displacement
Barfleur	31.65	2,958
Camperdown	33.58	2,819
Finisterre	33.98	2,757
Hogue	31.40	3,211
Lagos	30.46	3,060
Solebay	32.70	2,905
Trafalgar	32.97	3,094
Cadiz	33.175	2,806
Gabbard	31.663	3,105
St James	32.70	2,873
Saintes	31.82	2,957
Sluys	30.29	3,080
Vigo	33.547	2,757
Agincourt	31.20	3,076
Aisne	32.01	2,850
Barrosa	33.57	2,910
Corunna	31.98	2,787
Dunkirk	32.98	2,816
Jutland	31.44	3,045
Matapan	32.70	2,862

BATTLE CLASS SECONDARY ARMAMENT CHANGES

From initial completion throughout their service lives the secondary armament of the Battle class varied widely between different ships.

1942 PROGRAMME (1st Group)

Upon Completion

Barfleur:
1 x 4-inch HA/LA; 8 x 40mm AA (four twin Bofors Mk4 Hazemeyer mountings, two on the midships gundeck and two on the after shelterdeck); 6 x 20mm AA (twin mountings in the bridge wings and singles abaft "B" turret and on the quarterdeck)

Camperdown; Hogue:
1 x 4-inch HA/LA; 8 x 40mm AA (four twin Bofors Mk4 Hazemeyer mountings, two on the midships gundeck and two on the after shelterdeck); 2 x 2-pdr AA (single mountings on the bridge wings).

Armada; Trafalgar:
1 x 4-inch HA/LA; 8 x 40mm AA (four twin Bofors Mk4 Hazemeyer mountings, two on the midships gundeck and two on the after shelterdeck); 2 x 2-pdr AA (single mountings on the bridge wings). 2 x 20mm AA (single mountings abaft "B" turret and on the quarterdeck).

Finisterre; Lagos; Solebay:
12 x 40mm AA (four twin Bofors Mk4 Hazemeyer mountings,two on the mid ships gundeck and two on the after shelterdeck, four single Bofors Mk3, two abaft the funnel, one abaft "B" turret and one on the quarterdeck). 2 x 2-pdr AA single mountings in the bridge wings).

1945-1946

Armada; Barfleur; Camperdown; Hogue; Trafalgar:
All 20mm mountings landed from *Barfleur*. Two single 40mm AA Bofors Mk3 fitted, one abaft "B" turret and one on the quarterdeck. Two single 2-pdr AA fitted in the bridge wings. *Armada* and *Trafalgar* had the single 20mm mountings abaft "B" turret and on the quarterdeck replaced by two single 40mm AA Bofors Mk3. *Camperdown* and *Hogue* had two single 40mm AA Bofors Mk3 fitted, one abaft "B" turret and one on the quarterdeck.

1947

Solebay as Gunnery Firing Ship:
All previous 40mm AA mountings landed. Two 2-pdr AA retained in the bridge wings.

1948

Finisterre as Gunnery Firing Ship:
All previous secondary armament landed. One twin 40mm AA Bofors Mk2 STAAG mounting fitted on the after shelter deck.

1949

Solebay:
Re-armed after service as Gunnery Firing Ship. Two twin 40mm AA Bofors Mk2 STAAG mountings fitted on the after shelterdeck. Two twin 40mm AA Bofors Mk5 mountings fitted on the amidships gundeck. Six single 40mm AA Bofors Mk3 installed, one abaft "B" turret, two in the bridge wings, two abaft the funnel and one on the quarterdeck.

1951

Barfleur; Lagos:
Barfleur had the 4-inch HA/LA gun abaft the funnel replaced by a single 40mm AA Bofors Mk3 and two single 2-pdr AA in the bridge wings for two single 40mm AA Bofors Mk3. Both had the two twin 40mm Hazemeyer mountings on the after shelter deck replaced by two twin 40mm AA Bofors Mk2 STAAG mountings.

1952

Finisterre:
Twin 40mm AA Bofors Mk2 STAAG mounting landed from the after shelter deck.

Armada; *Hogue*; *Trafalgar*:
Single 4-inch HA/LA abaft the funnel landed and replaced by two single 40mm AA Bofors Mk1. Two single 2-pdr AA in the bridge wings exchanged for the two single 40mm AA Bofors Mk7. All exchanged the two 40mm Hazemeyer mountings on the after shelterdeck for two twin 40mm AA Bofors Mk2 STAAG mountings.

1953

Camperdown:
Single 4-inch HA/LA abaft the funnel landed and replaced by two single 40mm Mk7. Two single 2-pdr AA in the bridge wings exchanged for two single 40mm AA Bofors Mk7. Two twin 40mm AA Hazemeyer mountings on the after shelter deck exchanged for two twin 40mm AA Bofors Mk2 STAAG mountings.

1955

Armada; *Barfleur*; *Finisterre*; *Hogue*; *Lagos*; *Solebay*; *Trafalgar*:
Finisterre re-armed with two twin 40mm AA Bofors Mk2 STAAG mountings on the after shelter deck and five single 40mm AA Bofors Mk7, one abaft "B" turret, two in the bridge wings and two abaft the funnel. The remainder had the two twin 40mm AA mountings on the midships gundeck and the single 40mm AA on the quarterdeck landed. All had the depth charge throwers removed and a Squid A/S mortar fitted on the quarterdeck. *Trafalgar* had the two twin 40mm AA STAAG mountings on the after shelter deck replaced by two twin 40mm AA Bofors Mk5 mountings. *Barfleur*, *Lagos* and *Solebay* had the single 40mm Bofors Mk3 mountings replaced by the Mk7 version.

1956   *Camperdown*
Two twin 40mm AA Bofors Mk2 STAAG mountings on the after shelter deck exchanged for two twin 40mm AA Bofors Mk5 mountings.

1962   *Solebay* as Training Ship:
Two twin 40mm AA Bofors Mk2 STAAG mountings retained on the after shelter deck. Remaining secondary armament and Squid A/S mortar landed.

1942 PROGRAMME (2nd Group)

Upon Completion   *Gravelines*; *St Kitts*:
14 x 40mm AA (four twin Bofors Mk4 Hazemeyer mountings, two on the midships gun deck and two on the after shelter deck. Six single Bofors Mk7, one abaft "B" turret, two in the bridge wings, two abaft the funnel and one on the quarterdeck).

St James; *Sluys*; *Vigo*:
14 x 40mm AA (two twin Bofors Mk2 STAAG mountings, on the after shelter deck. Two twin 40mm AA Bofors Mk5 mountings on the midships gundeck. Six single Bofors Mk7, one abaft "B" turret, two in the bridge wings, two abaft the funnel and one on the quarterdeck).

Cadiz; *Gabbard*; *Saintes*:
6 x 40mm AA (six single Bofors Mk7, one abaft "B" turret, two in the bridge wings, two abaft the funnel and one on the quarterdeck). Due to delays in the supply of the STAAG mountings these three ships entered service without the two mountings on the after shelter deck. They also lacked the two twin 40mm mountings on the midships gundeck. *Cadiz* and *Gabbard* had their armament brought up to the designed arrangement after about four months in service.

1946   *Saintes*:
All secondary armament landed whilst undertaking training and trials duties.

1947   *Cadiz*; *Gabbard*:
Two twin 40mm AA Bofors Mk2 Staag mountings fitted on the after shelter deck in both. Two twin 40mm AA Bofors Mk4 Hazemeyer mountings fitted on the midships gundeck in *Cadiz*. Two twin 40mm AA Bofors Mk5 mountings fitted on the midships gundeck in *Gabbard*.

Saintes:
Twin 4.5-inch DP MkIV turret in "B" position landed and replaced by a twin 4.5-inch MkVI turret installed for sea trials and evaluation.

1948   *Gabbard*; *Sluys*:
Two twin 40mm AA mountings landed from the midships gundeck.

St Kitts:
Single 40mm AA Bofors Mk7 removed from the quarterdeck.

Cadiz:
Twin 40mm AA Bofors Mk4 Hazemeyer mountings landed from midships gundeck.

1949   *Saintes*:
Twin 4.5-inch MkVI turret removed from "B" position and MkIV turret refitted. Secondary armament refitted. Two twin 40mm AA Bofors Mk2 STAAG mountings fitted on the after shelterdeck, two twin 40mm AA Bofors Mk5 mountings fitted on the midships gundeck. Six single 40mm AA Bofors Mk7 installed (one abaft "B" turret, two in the bridge wings, two abaft the funnel and one on the quarterdeck).

1951   *Gabbard*; *Gravelines*:
Single 40mm AA Bofors Mk7 removed from the quarterdeck in both. Two twin 40mm AA Bofors Mk4 Hazemeyer mountings landed from the midships gun deck in *Gravelines*. Two twin 40mm Bofors Mk4 Hazemeyer mountingson the after shelter deck exchanged for two twin 40mm AA Bofors Mk2 STAAG mountings in *Gravelines*.

1951-52   *Cadiz*; *Gravelines*; *St James*; *St Kitts*; *Saintes*; *Sluys*; *Vigo*:
Four depth charge throwers removed from all and a Squid A/S mortar fitted on the quarterdeck. Two twin 40mm AA mountings landed from midships gun deck in *St James*, *St Kitts*, *Saintes* and *Vigo*. Single 40mm AA Bofors Mk7 mountings landed from the quarterdeck in *Cadiz*, *St James*, *Saintes*, *Sluys* and *Vigo*. *St Kitts* exchanged the two twin 40mm AA Bofors Mk4 Hazemeyer mountings on the after shelter deck for two twin 40mm Bofors Mk2 STAAG mountings.

1954   *Vigo* as Firing Ship:
One twin 40mm AA Bofors Mk2 STAAG removed from the after shelter deck, together with the single 40mm AA Bofors Mk7 abaft "B" turret. Remaining 40mm mountings "cocooned".

1957   *Saintes*:
Two twin 40mm AA Bofors Mk2 STAAG mountings on the after shelter deck exchanged for two twin 40mm AA Bofors Mk5 mountings.

Cadiz; **Gabbard**:
Four depth charge throwers removed from Gabbard and replaced by a Squid A/S mortar at the stern. Two twin 40mm AA Bofors Mk2 STAAG mountings on the after shelter deck exchanged for two twin 40mm AA Bofors Mk5 mountings in both.

1962   **Saintes**:
All secondary armament and the Squid A/S mortar landed.

1979   **Badr (**ex-**Gabbard)**:
Two single 40mm Bofors Mk7 abaft the funnel and the after quadruple torpedo tube mounting landed.

1943 PROGRAMME

Upon Completion   **Agincourt**; **Aisne**; **Barrosa**; **Corunna**; **Dunkrik**; **Jutland**; **Matapan**:
The eight ships of this group were completed with a uniform armament of 5 x 4.5-inch DP (two twin MkIV turrets forward and a single 4.5-inch DP MkV mounting abaft the funnel) 8 x 40mm AA (two twin Bofors Mk2 STAAG mountings on the after shelter deck, a twin Bofors Mk5 mounting amidships, between the torpedo tubes and two single Bofors Mk7 in the bridge wings). They also mounted 10 x 21-inch torpedo tubes (in quintuple mounts) and a Squid A/S mortar. With the exception of **Jutland** they retained this armament until they underwent conversion to Aircraft Direction Ships, or, in the case of the unconverted ships, were scrapped.

1959   **Jutland**:
Two twin 40mm AA Bofors Mk2 STAAG mountings on the after shelter deck exchanged for two twin 40mm AA Bofors Mk5 mountings.

ROYAL AUSTRALIAN NAVY PROGRAMME

Upon Completion   **Anzac**; **Tobruk**:
Three twin 40mm Bofors Mk2 STAAG mountings, one on the midships gun deck and two on the after shelter deck. Five single 40mm AA Bofors Mk7, one abaft "B" turret, two in the bridge wings and two abaft the funnel. The torpedo tubes were in quintuple mounts and a Squid A/S mortar was fitted on the quarterdeck.

1960   **Anzac** as Gunnery Training Ship:
Two twin 40mm AA Mk2 STAAG mountings landed from the after shelter deck and both sets of torpedo tubes removed.

1965   ***Anzac*** as Cadets Training Ship
                 Twin 4.5-inch DP turret in "B" position and single 40mm AA Bofors Mk7
                 removed and replaced by a deckhouse/classroom
1970   ***Anzac***:
                 Twin 40mm AA Bofors Mk2 STAAG mounting removed from midships gun deck.
                 Director removed.

PREVIOUS VESSELS OF THE NAME

Agincourt

Camperdown 1797   Egypt 1801   Jutland 1916

This ship commemorates the victory of King Henry V over the French on the battlefield of Agincourt in 1415. There have been five ships with the name of *Agincourt*. The first was a third rate vessel of 1796, which was originally named *Earl Talbot* and was under construction to be an East Indiaman. She was purchased on the building way at Perry in Blackwall and commissioned as *Agincourt* and armed with 64 guns. She became a prison ship on 6]anuary 1812 and was subsequently renamed *Bristol* in 1812. Another third rate followed five years later in 1817. She was Admiral Sir Thomas Cochrane's flagship off China for five years between 1842 and 1847. Forty eight years later the vessel was renamed *Vigo*. Plans had been underway to use the name of *Agincourt* for a new battleship which was completed in 1865 but would eventually end its days as a coal hulk in 1909. Another battleship would follow. Originally this vessel was ordered by Brazil as *Rio de Janeiro* but subsequently sold to Turkey. The Turks renamed her *Sultan Osman I* but with the coming of the First World War theAd,miralty requisitioned the vessel and christened her *Agincourt*. She served with distinction at the battle of Jutland earning one of three battle honours for the name. She was sold for scrap in 1922.

Aisne

This ship commemorates the Battle of River Aisne which was fought in September 1914, when the British Expeditionary Force under the command of General Sir John Pinkstone French successfully held the German advance. The only vessel to bear the name before the Battle class destroyer was a small fishery trawler of 1915.

Alamein

This ship was named after the British victory in the deserts of North Africa when Field Marshall Rommel was defeated by the Desert Rats led by Field Marshall Montgomery in 1942. The Battle class destroyer was the first and only vessel to be named to celebrate this victory.

Armada

The victory this ship celebrates is perhaps one of the best known stories of maritime daring. 1588 the Spanish Armada was bearing down on England and the Royal Navy saw it off with splendid seamanship and outstanding tactics. The name was chosen to celebrate the victory forced upon the Spaniards by Lord Howard of Effingham. There have been two ships of the name. The first *Armada* dates back to 1810 and was a third rate vessel. She was sold in 1863.

Barfleur

Commemorates the victory of the English and Dutch fleets under Admiral Russell over the French led by Comte de Tourville at Cape Barfleur in 1692. Of the Battle class *Barfleur* has the most Battle Honours with nine stretching from 1702 to 1900. There have been four Royal Navy warships that have borne this venerable name. The first was a second rate vessel of 1697, which served for an impressive eighty six years before being broken up. During these years she was flagship of Shovel at Malaga in 1704 and Sir George Byng off Syracuse in 1718. The second vessel was built in 1768 as another second rate and served until broken up in 1819. It would be another seventy three years until the name *Barfleur* was chosen for another warship this time a battleship of the Victorian era that would only serve for eighteen years before being scrapped in 1910.

Barrosa

Benin 1897   South Africa 1899-1900

This name commemorates the Battle of Barrosa which was fought on 5 March 1811 during the Peninsula War. A British force under the command of Lt General Sir Thomas Graham (1748-1843) defeated a much larger force of French troops that was under the command of Marshall Victor. Although the battle was really just a skirmish it was enough to raise Graham to the peerage in 1813 and he became Lord Lynedoch. There have been four ships of this name and between them have secured two battle honours. The first of *Barrosa's* predecessors was built in 1812 as a 5th rate vessel and survived until sold in 1841. The second was a corvette of the Victorian navy constructed in 1860 and scrapped some seventeen years later in 1877. The third ship was a cruiser built in 1889 and sold for scrap in 1905.

Cadiz

There has been only the one *Cadiz* in the Royal Navy and is named after the successful raids by the Royal Navy on the town and port in 1587 and again in 1596.

Camperdown

This ship commemorates Admiral Duncan's victory over the Dutch fleet in 1797. There have been four vessels prior to the Battle class destroyer with this name, the first being a 3rd rate prize, the *Jupiter*. The vessel was taken by the Royal Navy in the battle and renamed to celebrate the victory achieved by Admiral Duncan. The *Camperdown* was sold out of service in 1817. The third ship to bear the name was the former *HMS Trafalgar*, which was renamed *Camperdown* in 1825. She was later renamed *Pitt* in 1882. The fourth *Camperdown* was a battleship built in 1885 and sold out of service in 1911

Corunna

Commemorates the victory of Sir John Moore over the French under Marshall Soult on 16 January 1809. The Battle class destroyer was the first Royal Navy vessel to have this name.

Dunkirk

There have been four ships with the name *Dunkirk* in service of the Royal Navy since 1660. The first was named for the capture of the French town in 1657. She was the 60 gun vessel, *Worcester*, but was renamed in 1660 to mark the Dunkirk escapade. She would survive for another ninety years until broken up 1750. The third *Dunkirk* was formerly the *Dunkirk Prize* and was a 6th rate taken in 1705. However, it would only be another three years before this ship was wrecked and abandoned. Another 60-gun vessel bore the name from 1752 until broken up in 1792. The name lapsed from use for 151 years until it was chosen to commemorate the events leading to the successful withdrawal of thousands of troops from the beaches of Dunkirk in 1940.

Finisterre

Commemorates two naval victories in 1747. The first occurred on 3 May that year when the French led by La Jonquiere were beaten by a force led by Lord Anson. The second event was on 14 October 1747 when Hawke's force destroyed the French led by L'Entenduere. The Battle class destroyer was the first vessel with this name.

Gabbard

In 1653 Monck beat the Dutch admiral Tromp in the battle of Gabbard. *Gabbard* was the first vessel in the Royal Navy to use this name.

Gravelines

Commemorates the second phase of the defeat of the Spanish Armada on 9 August 1588. *Gravelines* was first used as a name on the Battle class destroyer.

Hogue

Baltic 1854-55   Heligoland 1914

Commemorates the second phase of the Battle of Barfleur when Admiral Rooke destroyed the remnants of the French fleet in the Bay of La Hogue in 1692. The first of *Hogue's* two predecessors was a third rate ship built in 1811. She would serve for fifty four years before being broken up in 1865. The second was an armoured cruiser built in 1900. Unfortunately at the Battle of Heligoland in 1914 the ship was torpedoed and sunk.

Jutland

The name Jutland was used to celebrate the victory over the German High Seas Fleet in 1916 when Sir John Jellicoe beat the Germans into a withdrawal. The battle of Jutland is probably best remembered for the remark, "*There's something wrong with our bloody ships*" when the British fleets battlecruiser's blew up during the battle. Even so, the British claimed victory and the name was chosen for a member of the Battle class.

Lagos

Commemorates the victory of Admiral Boscawen over the French fleet under de la Clue in 1759. The Battle class destroyer was the first vessel of this name in the Royal Navy.

Matapan

Named after the famous confrontation between the British and Italian fleets in the Mediterranean on 28 March 1941 when Sir Andrew Cunningham's force beat the Italian squadron sent to destroy them. This was the first use of the name in the Royal Navy.

St James

Commemorates the Battle of St James Day (or Orfordness) when Albermarle defeated the Dutch Admiral Tromp in 1666. The first and so far only use of this name in the Royal Navy.

St Kitts

Commemorates Sir Samuel Hood's brilliant action against the French Admiral De Grasse in Frigate Bay, St Kitts in 1782. The Battle class destroyer was the first time that this name had been chosen for a Royal Navy warship.

Saintes

Commemorates the victory of Admiral Sir George Rodney over the French De Grasse in the West Indies in 1782. The Battle class ship was the first ship of the name in Royal Navy service.

Sluys

Commemorates King Edward III's victory over the French fleet in 1340. The Battle class destroyer was the first vessel to take this name in the Royal Navy.

Solebay

St Kitts 1872

Commemorates the battle between the Anglo French fleet commanded by the Duke of York and the Dutch under Admiral De Ruyter in Southwold Bay in 1672. There have been seven ships of the name the first being completed in 1694. This 6th rate vessel was subsequently wrecked in 1709. The next *Solebay* was another 6th rate of 1711 which was sold in 1748. A third 6th rate vessel followed in 1742 and was sold in 1763. The fourth *Solebay* was a 6th rate vessel of 1763 which was wrecked on 25 January 1782 at Nevis, West Indies. A 5th rate followed in 1785, also being wrecked, this time on 11 July 1809 off the coast of Africa. The sixth vessel, a 5th rate, ex-**Iris**, was broken up in 1833 at Devonport. The seventh *Solebay* was the Battle class destroyer.

Trafalgar

Crimea 1854

Probably the most famous of all Royal Navy battles and the one in which Lord Horatio Nelson was shot and mortally wounded onboard his flagship **HMS Victory**. There have been five vessels in the Royal Navy to bear the name starting with a 2nd rate of 1820 and stretching though to the present day nuclear hunter killer submarine of the name. The first *Trafalgar* was a 2nd rate launched on 26 July 1820 at Chatham Dockyard, but was later renamed *Camperdown*. The second vessel with the name spent some sixteen years on the construction slip and eventually became a 1st rate sailing ship constructed at Woolwich Dockyard being launched on 21 June 1841. At the siege of Sebastopol she took part in the first naval battle in which all ships that went into action under steam propulsion, although *Trafalgar* being a sail ship was towed into action by the steam tug *Retribution*. By 1885 *Trafalgar* had been converted to steam power. By 1870 she was in use as a training ship and three years later in 1873 she was renamed *Boscawen*. An 11,940 ton battleship followed in 1887. Constructed at Portsmouth Dockyard and launched on 20 September 1887 she spent most of her service life in the Mediterranean. After 1897 she became a guard-ship at Portsmouth. The 20th century saw the ship in reserve at Devonport in 1905. From 1907-1909 *Trafalgar* became a training ship for turret and torpedo tube crews at Sheerness dockyard. She was sold for scrap on 9 May 1911 having been outclassed by the latest Dreadnought design. The fourth *Trafalgar* was the Battle class destroyer of the name. The fifth *Trafalgar* is the current Trafalgar class nuclear powered hunter killer submarine that was built at VSEL in Barrow in Furness. This submarine fired Tomahawk missiles into Afghanistan in 2001 during the War against terrorism and returned home in February 2002 flying the traditional Skull and Crossbones.

Vigo

Commemorates Admiral Sir George Rooke's destruction of the Spanish plate fleet and the French ships guarding it in Vigo Bay in 1702. There have been four ships called *Vigo* in the Royal Navy. The first was a prize captured after the battle of Vigo Bay in 1702. She was actually the former *Dartmouth* which had been captured and taken in 1695. She was called *Vigo Prize* but this was subsequently shortened to *Vigo*. Unfortunately she would only serve for another year until she was wrecked in 1703. The second vessel was a third rate of 1810 which was sold in 1865. Another third rate ex *Agincourt* was renamed *Vigo* in 1865 and sold in 1884. The fourth vessel was the Battle class destroyer that was completed in 1945.

Anzac

Korea 1951-53

Commemorates the Australian and New Zealand Army Corps of World War One and in particular the men who fought the Gallipoli campaign. The first *Anzac* was built under the British government's emergency War Programme. Commissioned in April 1917, she became leader of the 14th Destroyer Flotilla based at Scapa Flow. In 1919 she was presented to the Australian Government with the five 'S' class Destroyers *Tattoo*, *Swordsman*, *Success*, *Stalwart* and *Tasmania*. *Anzac* departed Plymouth on 26 February 1920, arriving at Sydney via Singapore and Thursday Island on 29 April 1920. She was the only destroyer in the RAN that was kept in commission during the Great Depression. Except for visits to New Guinea, New Britain and the Solomons in 1924, 1926 and 1930, the remainder of her sea going service was spent in Australian east coast waters. The ship was paid off on 4 August 1926 and re-commissioned on 10 January 1928. She was again paid off on 30 July 1931 and was sold for £1,800, before being scuttled off Sydney on 7 May 1936 when used for target practice. She never saw active service. The second *Anzac* was the Battle class destroyer. A third *Anzac* is the lead ship in a class of modern frigates for the RAN and Royal New Zealand Navies. The present *Anzac* has been involved in many police actions including the War against Terror.

Tobruk

Korea 1951-53

This ship was named after the battle of Tobruk during the North African campaign of 1941-42 during the Second World War . The Battle class destroyer was the first Australian warship to bear the name. The second is a large amphibious landing ship based on the British 'Sir' class landing ships. She entered into service in 1981 and has seen extensive use around the world especially in humanitarian work.

SQUADRONS AND FLOTILLAS

The cruiser **HMS Bermuda** *in company with the destroyers of the 1st Destroyer Squadron,* **Saintes** *(nearest)* **Finisterre**, **Camperdown**, **Solebay** *and* **Aisne**.   *(Alan Duke)*

The Battle class ships usually operated as part of flotillas or squadrons and throughout the course of their service with the Royal Navy the ships switched between squadrons. The annotated list below shows the ships that served in the various squadrons and flotillas during all or part of their careers.

19th DF

Armada, Barfleur, Camperdown, Hogue, Lagos, Trafalgar

Barfleur joined the British Pacific Fleet in time to see service in the war against Japan. After VJ Day she was joined by the remaining five ships to form the 19th Destroyer Flotilla. Two other ships intended for this flotilla, *Solebay* and *Finisterre*, were retained in home waters. Early in 1947 the 19th DF was withdrawn from the Far East and all six ships were placed in reserve.

1st DS

Solebay, Hogue, Lagos, Finisterre, Camperdown, Saintes

The Ch class destroyers of the 1st DS were replaced in May 1957 by the newly refitted and recommissioned *Solebay*, *Hogue* and *Lagos*. The Squadron spent the next 18 months in the Home/Mediterranean Fleet. Recommissioned in November 1958 the squadron deployed to the Far East in April 1959 - the first Battles on that Station since 1947. The deployment was marred by *Hogue's* collision with the cruiser *Mysore* in August

HM Ships Armada, *Barfleur* and *St Kitts* of the 3rd Destroyer Squadron.   *(Ray Lambert)*

*Ships of the 4th Destroyer Squadron, led by **HMS Agincourt** (nearest),* ***Barrosa***, ***Aisne*** *and* ***Corunna***.
(Jim Ashworth)

1959. **Hogue** was replaced by **Finisterre** in April 1960. In May the Squadron was bolstered by an amalgamation with the ships of the 3rd DS. As a result **Lagos** was paid off. Led by **Solebay**, **Finisterre**, **Saintes** and **Camperdown** completed a final two year commission as 1st DS at Home and in the Mediterranean before reducing to reserve in April 1962.

3rd DF/DS

Armada, Barfleur, Camperdown, Gravelines, St Kitts, Saintes, Vigo

This Flotilla was formed in July 1949 when initially, **Saintes**, **Armada**, **Vigo** and **Gravelines** replaced the V class in the Mediterranean. In 1953 **Barfleur** replaced **Gravelines** and **Armada**. The Squadron returned home in December 1954. In 1954 **Vigo** was replaced by **St Kitts**. The Squadron returned to the Mediterranean in October 1955 and took part in the Suez operation. They returned to the Home Fleet at the end of 1956. After the 3rd DS converted to General Service commissions, **Armada** replaced **Saintes** in 1956. On 2 October 1957

St Kitts was replaced by the newly refitted *Camperdown*. A year later *Barfleur* was finally paid off and was replaced by *Saintes*, who became leader. In the spring of 1960 *Armada* paid off and the remaining two ships joined the 1st DS.

4th DS

Agincourt, Aisne, Alamein, Barrosa, Corunna, Dunkirk, Jutland, Matapan

Between November 1946 and May 1948 the eight ships of the 1943 programme were completed for service as the 4th DF in the Home Fleet. However, the flotilla was not destined to attain its full strength. The manning crisis of October 1947 left the Home Fleet with just four Battle class destroyers in service, *Agincourt*, *Aisne*, *Dunkirk* and *Jutland*. The principal casualty was *Matapan*, who, fresh from builders trials, was reduced to reserve, never joining the flotilla. By the end of 1948 the flotilla was back in full commission. However, a year later, a further reduction took place. The need for A/S escorts, together with the unsuitability of the Battle class

The 7th Destroyer Squadron in the Mediterranean in June 1958, *Jutland* (nearest), *Dunkirk* and *Trafalgar*.

(*Douglas Busby*)

for this role, brought the decision in March 1950, to pay off several Home and Mediterranean Fleet destroyers. *Dunkirk*, *Barrosa* and *Alamein* paid off into reserve and *Aisne* and *Jutland* were temporarily laid up. In 1951 the squadron was back in business. Converted to General Service Commissions, the Squadron served in the Mediterranean from December 1954 to October 1955. *Alamein* replaced *Aisne* in 1957 and a further GSC deployment to the Mediterranean took place from November 1957.

5th DF/DS

Agincourt, Cadiz, Gabbard, St James, St Kitts, Solebay, Sluys

The second flotilla, of ships completed in 1946, was kept in the Home Fleet as the 5th DF. Led by *Solebay*, the ships served in the Home Fleet until 1953. The advent of the Daring class spelt the demise of the 5th DF/DS and all six ships went into reserve after the Coronation Review in 1953. Only *St Kitts* and *Solebay* were to see further RN service. *Agincourt* recommissioned at Portsmouth in May 1962 and served in Home and Mediterranean waters as a member of the 5th DS (as well as periods with both the 23rd and 27th Escort Squadrons).

7th DS

Aisne, Jutland, Trafalgar

Trafalgar re-entered service in May 1958 and became leader of the newly formed 7th DS, joining *Dunkirk* and *Jutland*. She spent the next six years rotating between Home and Mediterranean Fleets - serving on the latter station as the last 1942 Battle class in service. *Jutland* went back into reserve in the spring of 1961. *Dunkirk* completed a further two year commission, being in the Mediterranean from April 1962 - April 1963. She paid off in May 1963, the last unconverted 1943 Battle in service.

8th DS

Barrosa

Barrosa proceeded to the Far East on completion of her conversion at Devonport in April 1962. She joined the 8th DS (later the 24th Escort Squadron). Apart from two spells at home (July 1966 - August 1967 and July - December 1968) *Barrosa* spent her whole career as a Radar Picket, with the Far East Fleet.

END OF THE LINE - THE AXEMAN COMETH

It is a sad fact that of the 26 Battle class destroyers built, not one has survived. With the exception of the Pakistani *Khaibar* (ex-*Cadiz*), which was sunk during the Indo-Pakistan war, all were to end their days at the shipbreaker's yards.

Name	Date	Fate
Agincourt	27.10.74	Arrived Sunderland to be broken up.
Aisne	27.6.70	Arrived Inverkeithing to be broken up.
Alamein	1.12.64	Arrived Blyth to be broken up.
Armada	18.12.65	Arrived Inverkeithing to be broken up.
Barfleur	29.9.66	Arrived Dalmuir to be broken up.
Barrosa	1.12.78	Arrived Blyth to be broken up.
Cadiz	1.2.57	Recommissioned as **PNS Khaibar** for Pakistani Navy.
Camperdown	27.9.70	Arrived Faslane to be broken up.
Corunna	11.9.75	Arrived Blyth, from Sunderland, to be broken up.
Dunkirk	22.11.65	Arrived Faslane to be broken up.
Finisterre	12.6.67	Arrived Dalmuir to be broken up
Gabbard	27.1.57	Transferred to Pakistani Navy as **PNS Badr**.
Gravelines	22.3.61	Arrived Rosyth to be broken up.
Hogue	7.3.62	Scrapped at Singapore following collision with cruiser **Mysore**.
Jutland	14.5.65	Arrived Blyth to be broken up.
Lagos	1.6.67	Towed from Chatham to be broken up at McLellan, Bo'ness.
Matapan	11.8.79	Arrived Blyth to be broken up.
St James	19.3.61	Arrived Newport to be broken up
St Kitts	19.2.62	Arrived Sunderland to be broken up.
Saintes	1.9.72	Arrived at Cairn Ryan for breaking up.
Sluys	26.1.67	Transferred to Iran as **IIS Artemiz** (later **Damavand**)
Solebay	11.8.67	Arrived Troon to be broken up.
Trafalgar	7.70	Arrived Dalmuir to be broken up.
Vigo	6.12.64	Arrived Faslane to be broken up.
Anzac	30.12.75	Towed from Sydney for scrapping at Hong Kong.
Tobruk	10.4.72	Towed from Sydney for scrapping in Japan.
Badr	1990	Used as a target for missiles and gunfire before the wreck was broken up in Pakistan.
Khaibar	04.12.71	Sunk in action in the Indo-Pakistan war.
Artemiz (*Damavand*)	1996	Reportedly broken up in Iran.

(T. Ferrers-Walker Collection)

Three of a kind - **Finisterre**, **Barfleur** and **Camperdown** (above) are laid up on the River Tamar at Devonport, while sister ship **Lagos** (below) awaits her fate at Portsmouth in 1964.

(Mike Lennon)

(T. Ferrers-Walker Collection)

HMS Jutland *(above) awaits the call to the breakers, while* **HMAS Anzac** *(below) awaits a similar call at Sydney, Australia.*

(T. Ferrers-Walker Collection)

(Ken Harrow)

HMS Barrosa (above) is seen under tow on her final journey to the scrapyard at Blyth, while **Solebay** (below) languishes alongside at Troon, sharing the jetty with surplus steam locomotives.

(T. Ferrers-Walker Collection)

D70

(Maritime Photo Library)

*With her masts already gone, **Aisne** (above) is broken up at Inverkeithing. The once gleaming **Finisterre** (below) sits among the scrap metal of previous "victims" at Dalmuir.*

(T. Ferrers-Walker Collection)

Sitting on the still waters of the Clyde in the winter of 1964, **Vigo** *is gradually pulled apart.*   *(T. Ferrers-Walker Collection)*

BIBLIOGRAPHY

Books

Conways All the World's Fighting Ships 1947-1995, 2nd Revised edition. Conway Maritime Press, 1995.

Janes Fighting Ships, Janes, 1942-1990

Royal Navy Destroyers since 1945, Leo Marriott, Ian Allan, 1989

Newspapers and magazines

Periscope (The Chatham Dockyard internal newspaper 1960-1981)

Navy News

Ships Monthly

Sea Breezes

Warship World

Archives

Royal Naval Museum, Portsmouth

Royal Navy Submarine Museum

Chatham Historic Dockyard

Plymouth City Archives

Portsmouth City Archives

Public Records Office, Kew

ACKNOWLEDGEMENTS

The scale of the research for this project meant that I had to rely on the collective knowledge of a great many people. Sadly I cannot mention everyone by name but special thanks to the 4th Destroyer Squadron Association, *HMS Solebay* Association, *HMS Cadiz* Association, The Imperial War Museum, the Public Records Office and the Central Library staff at Plymouth and Portsmouth and the ever helpful staff at the Royal Naval Museum Portsmouth.

I would like to thank the following for contributing information, memories and photographs. In particular Terry Parker, Secretary of the 4th Destroyer Squadron Association for allowing me access to their archive of images and personal recollections, Adrian Vicary whose Maritime Photo Library was a rich source of Battle-class photographs and Vic Jeffrey for his help with images of the Royal Australian Navy Battles.

Jim Ashby, Ashford; Alan Ashworth, Otley; Martin Bailey, Stoke-on-Trent; Francis Bate, Plymouth; M. Bayman, London; Martin Bird, Rowlands Castle; E.P. Booker, Southsea; John Brewer, Bristol; George Brown, Louth; D.J. Busby, Chatham; Steve Bush, Plymouth; Bill Campbell, Belfast; B. Davies, Rochester; Alan Duke, Plymouth; Martin Feather, Launceston; Don Foxell, Havant; John Gilmour, Dalry; Tony Hall, Midhurst; R.G.J. Herbert, Bristol; A. Irlam, Manchester; Ray Lambert, Waterlooville; D.J. Macaulay; Duncan Mackenzie, Southampton; Keith Miller, Plymouth; David Moore, Portsmouth; Ken Mowatt; Cliff Pantrey, Okehampton; I.M. Parker, Gosport; J.E. Sansom, Helston; Dave Scoble, Saltash; Peter Soutar, Portsmouth; P.J. Tarrant, Epsom; I.E. Taylor, Ilfracombe; Derek Thorne, Fareham; P. Waite, Whitby; Ben Warlow, London: Tom Watson, Carlisle; Jim Welford; Captain A.F.C. Wemyss, OBE, RN, Aylesbury; Bungy Williams, Plymouth; Harold Wood, Coventry; George Yeomans, Haverfordwest and many many more. Thank you to everyone who assisted in the research and preparation of this book.